Shop Tails

Shop Tails
*The Animals Who Help Us
Make Things Work*

Nancy R. Hiller

Published by Lost Art Press LLC in 2021
837 Willard St., Covington, KY 41011, USA
Web: http://lostartpress.com

Title: Shop Tails: The Animals Who Help Us Make Things Work
Author: Nancy R. Hiller
Publisher: Christopher Schwarz
Editor: Kara Gebhart Uhl
Copy Editor: Megan Fitzpatrick
Distribution: John Hoffman

Copyright © 2021 by Nancy R. Hiller. All rights reserved.

ISBN: 978-1-954697-04-1

First printing.

ALL RIGHTS RESERVED
No part of this book may be reproduced in any form or by any electronic or mechanical means including information storage and retrieval systems without permission in writing from the publisher; except by a reviewer, who may quote brief passages in a review.

This work is largely a memoir and relates events and conversations based on the author's memory, in addition to conversations with family and friends. Some names and identifying details have been changed to protect the privacy of individuals.

This book was printed and bound in the United States.
Signature Book Printing, Inc.
http://signature-book.com

Table of Contents

Acknowledgments   **vii**

1: What Are Dogs For? 1
2: What Is Anyone For? 29
3: Sidney and Phoebe 61
4: Binky 69
5: David 87
6: Oscar 97
7: Shadow, the Turkey Vulture 127
8: Daisy June and Her Great Adventures 131
9: Wilhelm Von Wundt, the Dog Who Saved My Life ... 149
10: Lizzie, Part One 177
11: Winnie 193
12: Louis, the Mayor of Louisville 221
13: Lucy, As Told by Herself 235
14: Alfie and the Cat Whisperer 239
15: Warring Parties 243
16: Joey Walker Kangaroo Tail 259
17: Pedro 275
18: Missing in Action 289
19: Harley and the Goat 315
20: Henry 319
21: The Cattle Dog and the Pigs 321

Bibliography   **351**

Acknowledgments

THE WRITING of acknowledgments is always a daunting task, at least for me. There are so many people to thank. You want to thank each one by name, and in a meaningful way, even as you know you'll almost certainly (if unintentionally) leave important people out. I hope that I have gone some way toward acknowledging others' contributions to this book in the text and illustrations themselves. Still, a few specifics are in order, primarily with respect to my publisher, Lost Art Press.

This book has been made possible thanks to the trust placed in me by Christopher Schwarz, Megan Fitzpatrick and Kara Gebhart Uhl. I had been writing these stories sporadically over some 15 years when I pitched the idea of this book to Chris by email in December 2020. Along with a brief description, I sent him three or four of the shorter chapters – heartwarming stories that are easy to read. At that point I had no idea the book would develop into a more complex project in which the stories of animals would become opportunities to explore some of the more challenging ways in which our relationships with companion animals of the non-human variety, and sometimes wild animals, too, can reflect our relationships with parents, children and partners while also teaching us to be more patient and understanding. Sometimes these relationships compel us to make hard decisions.

This is not the kind of book one would typically expect from a publisher that specializes in hand-tool woodworking. That said, the current list of publications by Lost Art Press has grown to encompass works that go well beyond the realm of tool usage, wood science and construction techniques. This is a book written by someone who has made her livelihood primarily through woodworking since the age of 21; it includes accounts of furniture and cabinetry jobs, as well as writing collaborations with editors and other colleagues, and is illustrated with pictures of completed work. But most of all, it is about how we make, and make sense of, our lives, which are projects in their own right – projects in which, for many of us, woodworking plays a central part.

I make no claim to provide an example to others. I have made my share of poor decisions, many of them prompted by unresolved emotional wounds or social norms and expectations (or in some cases, the absence of such expectations). In many cases I have shared the thinking that led to those decisions, along with their fallout. I have excised details that might cause embarrassment to others while providing a forthright account.

I have never seen woodworking as a field divorced from the totality of life. It's a means to furnish homes and workplaces, whether our own or those of others. Embedded in our daily experience (whether of cooking, sleeping, eating, gathering strawberries or paddling on rivers and lakes), the pieces we carve, turn or build serve as tools in their own right, as well as shape how we see the world. As with any set of skills that take years to acquire, woodworking is also a way to learn what we're capable of, to restore our spirits and learn new things. To my mind, our reasons for doing this work and the relationships we form along the way are no less important and illuminating than the finished pieces.

This last point in particular, I believe, makes "Shop Tails" a good fit for the list at Lost Art Press, a publishing business I admire precisely because its partners' and associates' understanding of books about woodworking extends beyond the basic business of sharing information on the usual subjects. From its inception, Lost Art Press has also offered fresh perspectives on work- and life-ways that many no longer deem relevant to our time. My introduction to Lost Art Press came through James Ferrell, a student in the second class I taught at Kelly Mehler's School of Woodworking circa 2007 who has become a friend. Jim sent me a link to the PDF of one of Chris Schwarz's first self-published books. I couldn't get the link to work (no doubt due to operator error), but I subscribed to the Lost Art Press blog. What really grabbed my attention was news, via that blog, of the 2014 publication of "L'Art Du

Menuisier: Book of Plates," an imposing tome with nearly 400 drawings by 18th-century French craftsman and author André-Jacob Roubo, painstakingly reproduced to the highest standards, then clothbound and printed on heavy paper with an introduction by Donald Williams, senior furniture conservator at the Smithsonian Institution. In addition to these impressive specifications, Lost Art Press had produced the book entirely in the United States – and after the Great Recession of 2008 devastated so much of the publishing industry. How could I not be smitten by the audacity of such a project, in addition to its handsome and illuminating product?

The more I learned about Lost Art Press, the greater grew my appreciation, along with my desire to support the business as a customer. Here was a niche publisher of beautifully made books that refused to sell through distributors that maximize their own profits by diminishing the perceived value of (and actual compensation for) work done by others – a publisher that made a point of supporting authors, editors, illustrators, photographers, printing companies and more who do good work, and paying them fairly. I am honored to be associated with a company whose operating principles include fairness to all (which often extends to generosity), respect for good work and a joyful, inspiring dedication to the bookmaker's art. The storefront on Willard Street has become a center of creative ventures that enrich the lives of many and offer an example of what work and business can be when people collaborate with discipline, respect and hard work.

Now back to acknowledgments of the more recognizable kind.

In addition to her copy edits, Kara offered suggestions that have made the book far better than it would otherwise have been, not least because her nuanced reading revealed some buried themes that deserved elaboration. As always, I am grateful for Megan Fitzpatrick's sharp-eyed copy editing and comments on content. And I appreciate everyone's readiness to expedite the publication of this book in view of my unpredictable health situation.

These acknowledgments would be incomplete if I did not mention the countless friends, family members and readers (not only those I have come to know through my work for Lost Art Press, but *Fine Wood-*

working, Fine Homebuilding, Old-House Interiors, Old-House Journal and other publications, in addition to woodworking schools where I have had the honor of teaching) who have buoyed my spirits through their support, whether in the form of contributions to the fundraiser organized by Megan Fitzpatrick following my diagnosis of pancreatic cancer or through notes of encouragement, many of them packed in boxes with handmade tools and other treasures that Mark and I have worn, admired, read, eaten, drunk, listened to and in some cases come to use on a daily basis. Your generosity has helped me see this project through – not because the writing has been hard (to the contrary, it has been joy-filled work, as well as therapeutic), but in view of my customary self-doubt, which in this case largely centers on the question of whether Lost Art Press readers really want to hear about my fondness for Spotted Dick and treacle tart, the tortuous thought processes that resulted in my decision to proceed with chemotherapy, or how I peed in my pants at the age of 13.

Finally, I wish to thank Karen Vaughan Clark for her shining spirit and example; my oncologist, Dr. Karuna Koneru, for treating me as a person, not a walking diagnosis; the nurses at Bloomington Hospital, for their kindness and humor, in addition to their medical care; my teachers at Queens College in London; the Religious Studies Department at Indiana University-Bloomington, several faculty members of which have played central parts in shaping how I see and think; my birth family – Herb, Mary Lee, Magda, Wyatt, and now Maggie's partner, Eric; and my husband, Mark Longacre, who has been a loving champion and helpmeet throughout my medical adventures to date. And of course, all of the animals in this book, as well as others you will not find here, who have brought delight, comfort and occasional heartache, and who have been among my best teachers.

To those who have gone before.

1: What Are Dogs For?

"BUT HERBERT," my grandma interjected, "What are dogs for?"

To anyone not acquainted with my grandmother, the question will sound eccentric, but those who knew her will recognize the plain-spoken curiosity about a practice most Americans take for granted as integral to her M.O.

To get a sense of why her question made such an impression on my father that it has become a beloved bit of family lore, you had to hear her speak the words. An emigrant from Poland who'd come to America on an ocean liner as the bride of a businessman, Grandma Stepha had assimilated only partially the customs of her adopted land. She'd had hired help with keeping house and raising her two sons; she'd given driver's ed a pass, as a result of which she spent more time than many of her peers on public buses; and she had always retained her thick Polish accent, which gave her interest in our dogs' purpose a comedic quality. When Stepha asked the question, its childlike oddness gained the kind of respectability that comes with rolling Rs and forceful inflection. "*Hedt-bedt*," she pronounced the name of her second-born son. "What *arrrrrdt* dogs *forrrdt*?"

The memory, so rich in existential import, comes to me this morning, December 26, 2020, as I contemplate how life will change in 48 hours when my husband, Mark, will drop me off at the hospital for a first infusion of Folfirinox, a sequence of drugs given over the course of about six hours followed by continuing infusion through a portable pump for two more days. I have always dreaded the thought of chemotherapy based on accounts I've read and heard – lived nightmares of nausea, baldness, exhaustion.

Grandma Stepha with my cousin Mitchell and my father, Herb. Miami Beach, mid-1960s. Grandma Stepha never had a "casual Friday."

When I think about what I'm used to getting done in a day, I feel stunned by the contrast with my recent production, which helps me understand my current perspective as that of someone about to jump off a cliff. Since March, when the state of Indiana went into a modified lockdown in response to the COVID-19 pandemic, life has been anything

WHAT ARE DOGS FOR?

John Dehner and I worked with Mark to install the cabinets and this set of hanging shelves with integrated lighting for the kitchen of Jenny and Ben Robinson, summer 2020.

but normal. Mark, a general contractor who specializes in remodeling and additions, spends a lot of time inside his customers' houses. At the start of the year he had two employees and a collection of regular subs with whom he interacted closely every day. One morning in March, before dawn, he asked me to sit down and talk. "I'm really not sure how to go forward," he began – which is to say, how to proceed in order to ensure his workers' and customers' safety, as well as his (and our) own. Although our state and local government classified construction as an

The Robinson kitchen sink area, completed. Cabinets are white oak with conversion varnish, counters are soapstone and tile is from Crossville Tile's "Penpal" series.

essential service, we both knew that neither his work nor mine was genuinely essential to the common good – nowhere near on par with that of nurses and doctors, or postal carriers, or those who work in grocery stores. We take our part in public health seriously; we didn't want to help spread the virus by being around people any more than necessary.

I had orders for a variety of work, so I switched from building a set of kitchen cabinets to drawing and writing and told my clients I'd be back on their jobs as soon as that made sense. Mark's situation was more complex; he let his newer employee go (and sent him extra money to help him keep going until his unemployment pay came through) but kept working with his longtime sidekick, John, for much of the summer and fall. John had been a friend for decades and had worked with Mark for several years. They wore masks and asked clients to do the same. Whenever possible, they asked to be left alone in the house until the end of each day.

As winter approached and we learned that I had cancer, we reassessed. We were concerned by the prospect of working inside homes occupied by clients who were themselves working remotely. Once I started chemotherapy, my immune system would be seriously compromised. My doctor told me to stay out of stores and ideally go nowhere other than to medical appointments. But even if I worked solely on writing, design jobs and commissions in the shop, the two of us would still face multiple points of potential exposure to the virus. John's wife teaches science in a high school; the school system compelled her to make all of her classes available online for students who switched to remote learning, in addition to teaching in person – an enormous amount of extra work for a dedicated teacher who already got up around 4:30 a.m. to prepare for classes, and spent much of her time off grading and developing new teaching materials. Her exposure increased John's risk. Add into the mix their older son's work as a nurse in the ICU of the local hospital, where more and more patients were being treated for COVID. Mark concluded that between these and other factors, along with the time he would spend taking me to medical appointments after which I would need a driver, he'd be better off shutting his business down for a couple of months and focusing on bookkeeping, annual reports and estimates

The cabinet I made in pippy (also known as burly) white oak with shop-made walnut-and-maple beading and hardware in walnut, based on Gimson's original 1919 design for a sideboard for Guy de Gruchy in "Ernest Gimson: Arts & Crafts Designer and Architect."

for new jobs, instead. Mark told John he'd have to let him go, too.¹ Fortunately, John found work right away with Mark's former employee, Aaron, who had gone out on his own.²

I was used to days filled with work. A typical day might start with an hour-long interview for a blog post, taking notes on my computer and saving them for whenever I had time to write up a draft. Then the truck from Frank Miller could show up with lumber for my next job, after which I'd work in the shop until lunch. I might throw a load of laundry in the washing machine at lunchtime, then book flights to Boston to give a talk at a conference, followed by several more hours in the shop. In the evening I might meet a prospective client at her home to discuss ideas for a project, get some photos to illustrate an article, then stop by the store for cream or cilantro on the way home.

The work I got done in 2020 was a fraction of my normal output. In February, after a new year's flurry of activity to prepare for the 33rd National Arts & Crafts Conference at The Omni Grove Park Inn just outside of Asheville, North Carolina, I built a Gimson-inspired cabinet in solid pippy oak, with doors and a drawer, maple-and-walnut beading and wooden hardware, then drove a truck full of furniture to Asheville, where I unloaded it all with hired help and set up my booth. I worked the show by myself, went out with Patricia Poore and her crew from *Old-House Journal* on a couple of evenings, then packed up for the drive home.

Over the spring and summer I made a pair of Voysey chairs for clients in Chicago and a dining-room cabinet inspired by a mid-century Finn

---

[1] It's easy to condemn an employer for letting an employee go in such circumstances, but this was no abdication of responsibility on Mark's part, nor over-reliance on the state. For as long as he has had employees, Mark has paid state and federal unemployment taxes. The thousands of dollars in unemployment insurance Mark has paid into this system of shared risk are meant to ensure income for employees who have lost their jobs in just this kind of circumstance.

[2] Some readers may think we were overreacting due to fear, a judgment that maddens me because it is so far from the truth. We were acting out of a sense of responsibility to ourselves and others, including our clients. Prudent responsibility based on concern for the greater good is the very opposite of fear.

Sit up straight. Some of the chairs I built in 2020 based on C.F.A. Voysey's 1908 design. White oak with rush seats woven by Cathryn Peters, The Wicker Woman©.

I designed this cabinet for the dining room of my clients' ranch-style house with style, affordability and pandemic protocols in mind. It combines storage for a variety of dining room staples with space for cleaning equipment, shoes and kids' art supplies, inspired by a classic Finn Juhl sideboard and a kitchen designed by Tage Frid.

The wall of built-in cabinetry, with bases in black walnut and upper sections in Baltic birch painted white, stores books, sheet music, scores and CDs in the home of Anke Birkenmaier and Roman Ivanovitch.

Made to match. The pantry insert I built for a home in the forest takes cues from the existing kitchen cabinetry, with red oak and shop-made pulls with inlay. The drawers are sized to hold a variety of pantry staples. Above are two "door" sections with pull-out trays. The top compartment hides a microwave behind doors.

Juhl classic that I painted in colors similar to those used by Tage Frid in a 1963 kitchen built to his design. There was a bathroom vanity, then a bed, for another client's century-old bungalow. Mark, John and I finished the modernist kitchen we'd started in spring; then I built a pantry insert to match the original kitchen in a home in the woods. Later in the year came a wall of storage cabinetry and shelving in walnut and painted Baltic birch plywood, followed by a cherry entry cabinet with doors, drawers and salvaged hardware for a 1920s house. There were other, smaller jobs along the way, and one big project: bringing my book "Kitchen Think" to a close.

As the pandemic increased in scope and thousands of deaths grew to hundreds of thousands, our lives, at least, slowed down even more. Ordinarily we made myriad quick trips to the lumberyard and stores and sometimes ate out. I traveled for work, Mark traveled for pleasure. We spent a lot of time with friends. No more. There were days when I allowed myself the luxury of reading for hours. I read for work. I read for fun. I read as I hadn't in decades, long stretches immersed in Richard Powers's "The Overstory," Ann Patchett's "State of Wonder" or Trevor Noah's "Born A Crime." I subscribed to the recipe newsletter from *The Washington Post* and made the occasional dinner that wasn't just salad. I made my first Bakewell tart and we enjoyed it on a Sunday morning with coffee on the back deck, appreciating as never before the beauties of early summer and recognizing our good fortune at living in a place surrounded by picturesque hayfields and forest, where we can go for walks and not have to worry about being packed into a building with lots of other people.

Then came my diagnosis of pancreatic cancer. It came with a phone call on our seventh wedding anniversary, November 15th. Existentially, our lives were turned upside-down. I had grown up in a culture so terrified by cancer that people spoke of it in hushed tones; for most of my youth, paternalism was still so rife among doctors that many only revealed a cancer diagnosis to relatives, not to patients themselves. In an effort to inform the general public about conditions that might be symptoms of cancer, there were public service ads on TV; one opened with "Dead tired?" and proceeded to describe the symptoms of leukemia. When I was little, my mother's mother, Esse, always stressed the importance of drying between my toes. She told me once that damp feet make an ideal breeding ground for athlete's foot (or worse, trench foot), but I made a point of drying between my toes just in case doing so might also help me avoid cancer.

My primary care doctor, Mary D. Mahern, called with the news. It was early afternoon on a Sunday. We had been going slightly out of our minds with worry since the previous Thursday, when I'd had a CT scan. I was thankful that my doctor had not only taken a chunk of her Sunday to share the news directly, but had also called colleagues in an effort to get the best possible referrals.

The news was stunning. Something I had always feared. And undeniable.

I called my mother and sister, who devised a plan to tell Dad the news together.

The diagnosis sent us into an altered reality in which we had to build new ground beneath our feet. That process began with gathering information. First came an endoscopic ultrasound of the area indicated by the CT scan, with a sample of cells to biopsy obtained through fine-needle aspiration. There was my first meeting with the pancreatic cancer specialist in Indianapolis, then a second endoscopic ultrasound and biopsy to confirm the diagnosis after the first tissue sample showed no cancerous cells. Daunting questions loomed. But at the level of every day, nothing had changed – I had to continue building, installing and writing.

After months of disruption and already-lowered productivity due to the pandemic, I now faced the decision whether to pursue chemotherapy or forgo it. Pancreatic cancer had killed my grandmother Esse at the age of 77. A client of mine died from pancreatic cancer, as did one of my professors around 1990 – he was in the classroom through the end of the semester, then gone forever. I knew it as a disease that can take people in months.

At my first meeting with the specialist in Indianapolis I asked the usual post-diagnosis question: How long have I got? A stupid question, I understand in retrospect, but I had to think about the other people in my life who depend on me being around. Mark had already lost too many family members and friends – and at the time of my diagnosis, his mother, JoAnne, was dying of cancer. This dear man did not deserve another loss. And how could I leave my sister, now that we'd grown closer than ever in our six decades together? I thought of how bereft I would feel, were she to die first. And work? Was I really at the end of making and writing? The specialist's answer: four to six months, maybe a couple of years at the outside.

I still had plenty of professional obligations. I was in the middle of building that wall of solid wood and painted Baltic birch storage cabinetry; even when I finished building, I would have to deliver the work and complete the installation – not a simple task, as the whole thing had to be scribed to fit the walls and floor. I had three kitchen design jobs in the works for people in and out of town, writing commitments for *Fine Woodworking* and an estimate to do for a slab-top kitchen table. There was also a proposal to write for a built-in bookcase to go in a 1920s Dutch Colonial Revival house. All par for the course, but every task felt far heavier now. Add the usual complement of bookkeeping, shop maintenance and putting out fires sparked by the state department of revenue's new-and-improved platform for filing and remitting taxes, and you'll appreciate that when the doctor threw out "four to six months – maybe two years" as my likely survival time, I went into full-on processing mode.

I am not afraid of death, and I am well aware of my good fortune in having made what I consider a good life. So many people I have known died younger; millions of people I don't know die at earlier ages every year. For me to die at 61 or 62 would be no tragedy, however sorry I might be to have my life end abruptly, leaving loved ones behind. If it came to it, I would make my peace with shortened time.

"Four to six months," I found, was the specialist's estimate if I forwent chemo. It seemed ludicrous, given that I felt fine, aside from the vague abdominal discomfort I'd had for more than a year, which had grown worse of late. When he'd first walked into the room to meet me he'd mentioned that most of his patients were in far worse shape; in view of my hale condition he said he was going to call me "the lumberjack." And I was so sick that I was likely to die in months?

The usual course of treatment for my condition involves chemotherapy to shrink the tumor, then targeted radiation followed by surgical resecting or complete removal of the pancreas. In my case, the tumor was pressing on and constricting some adjacent major blood vessels. In the short term, surgery, the only recognized cure for pancreatic cancer, was out of the question. There was no telling whether it would become an option.

I asked the other obvious questions and we settled on a plan to start chemo as soon as possible. Only 40 to 50 percent of pancreatic tumors respond to chemo, the oncologist told me, and there are only two chemotherapy protocols. Those odds called for serious weighing of factors, among them likely costs. But when I asked about these costs, he said no one would give me an estimate. (I now know that the hospital does give estimates of charges on request, though actual charges may be dramatically lower, depending on insurance coverage and other factors.) A slew of searches online revealed that with adenoma of the pancreas a small percentage of people live three years post-diagnosis; a soberingly low 9 percent of patients with pancreatic cancer survive for five years after diagnosis, though for those whose cancer has not metastasized, it's more like one in three. For many, my specialist's estimate of four to six months, and maybe two years, holds true. Add to that what I read about the side effects of chemotherapy, most of it already known to me from general reading, and I had a serious decision to make. If I doubled my time but half that time was a nightmare of nausea, neuropathy, crippling diarrhea and exhaustion, as I learned it could be from patient forums at websites such as that run by the American Cancer Society, what was the point? What if I resolved to go ahead, sign up for the side effects, put in the days, weeks, months of time (instead of working, gardening and anything else on which I might otherwise spend those days) and the treatment proved ineffective? Too many people with pancreatic cancer experience that heartbreak. And again, speaking as someone who is self-employed and married to a self-employed spouse, how much was the treatment likely to cost? I went back and forth between yes and no more times than I care to admit. Friends who'd been through chemo

Anissa Kapsales with her dog, Bongo.

described their experiences. I reminded myself that chemotherapy, like so many other medical interventions, has improved vastly over the last few decades, thanks to research and clinical trials.

But what really aided my decision were the messages of encouragement from friends, relatives and readers – especially Anissa Kapsales, my longtime editor at *Fine Woodworking*. At a time when it felt unrealistic to imagine surviving even a year, Anissa said she was hoping for "much, much more." She had been through her own experience of cancer several years earlier – and with two young children to care for. "[D]o not rule out the possibility of anything," she wrote at the outset of this adventure. "I am a firm believer in believing anything can happen until it is beyond a shadow of a doubt that it can't. And even then I'm a closet optimist…. So you may be looking to buy as much quality time as you can get, but I'm putting out into the universe for much more than that.

"All I can offer you is that I felt the same way. My dread on starting chemo was intense. So intense. My dread at getting the port was the same. None of it was as bad as I thought it would be. I swear. I wouldn't just say that. The first chemo is the hardest. But you wrap your head around it. You gradually settle into the idea of it, the pace of it, the work of it. Part of me wishes you were going to be in an infusion room with other people going through the same thing. I thought I'd hate that, but it was comforting. And there was a comradery to that…. Get yourself to the first chemo. It won't be as awful as you think. Does it get harder as you go in terms of the exhaustion, yes. Do this, Nancy. And if you change your mind and don't I'm on board with that, too. But I think you're making the right choice to do it…."[3]

---

[3] I never know what people may think about what I now call my friendship with Anissa. As with so many friends I have made through woodworking and writing, some of them in influential positions, I consider it important to note that I did not become friends with Anissa, Patricia Poore, Megan Fitzpatrick, Chris Schwarz, Laura Mays, Nick Offerman, or anyone else as a means to furthering my own opportunities. These people came (or in Anissa's case, were sent) to me, having seen and read my work, which has found its way to print because I have submitted proposals, then followed up, and because I'm stubborn. I persevere – at least, to quote Anissa, "until it

Some friends pointed out that the oft-cited statistics related to pancreatic cancer were averages; what I needed was information about the outliers. What had those people done that had helped them live longer? Aside from thinking about myself, I thought about others; while there was no guarantee that I would be one of those who pushed the far end of survivability were I to go ahead with chemotherapy and other potential interventions, the more people who do opt for treatment and beat the current discouraging statistics, the more hopeful things become for those who come after us.

On December 23, I had a surgical procedure to implant a port just below my right clavicle, a means to access a vein via a catheter to make it easier to take blood for lab tests and administer infusions of chemo by IV. The procedure was fascinating. I was awake the whole time. I had never been conscious when wheeled into surgery, but there was the table – stainless steel, and long enough for the tallest basketball player. There was local anesthetic and a dose of propofol, low enough that I remained aware of the surgeon and nurses but felt nothing, at least until the strange pushing and tugging to situate the device beneath my skin. I find it impossible not to feel wonder at the technical achievements of contemporary medicine. After the procedure, I was bruised and sore. The small dressings on the pair of incisions felt like shopping bags full of canned goods hanging from my skin, but even so, the actual pain was low enough not to require anything more potent than over-the-counter acetaminophen.[4]

Even after getting the port I reserved the option to cancel chemo at the last minute. I have never enjoyed interactions with the Medical Industrial Complex; I dislike being viewed as a patient, a word derived from the Latin verb for suffering, in the sense of bearing something, or having things done to one,[5] instead of being an agent, one who does

---

is beyond a shadow of a doubt" that I am beating my head against a brick wall. Then I invest my energies in other areas where I seem likely to be more effective.

[4] After several weeks, the swelling around the sutures disappeared, leaving what resembles a grayish but primarily flesh-colored egg yolk just above my right breast.

[5] "Suffering" in turn comes from *subferre*, to carry something from below, like Atlas

the doing. It's increasingly common for hospitals to emphasize the value they place on having patients engaged as partners in our own health care, but as I write from my vantage point as a deeply engaged patient four months in, I'm aware that patients have to keep an eye out for instances of intra-institutional miscommunication, as well as be ready to pivot when insurance companies deny coverage for drugs and services that doctors prescribe, despite those doctors' and their nurses' appeals. As my friend Marianne told me at the start of this adventure, keeping track of appointments, querying charges that are obviously in error (such as one for $15,000 that should have been around $1,850) and prescription refills can take hours at a time. When online patient portal forms malfunction, emails to addresses on the hospital's own website go unanswered and you end up on hold nearly every time you call, trapped in a repeating loop of corporate advertisements and jingles, the claim to value patient engagement rings a little hollow. Patients really do have to pay attention and advocate on our own behalf.[6]

On December 27, the day before my first infusion, I reminded myself again how easy it is to miss a valuable opportunity. In graduate school I'd decided to take French classes because French was one of the foreign languages required by my degree. I either had to take two semesters of basic French with Mademoiselle Julie, a whip-smart doctoral student with a short blond bob and bright red lipstick, or do my best to test out of the requirement. As much as I appreciated Mlle. Julie that first semester, I preferred the idea of swapping French, which I had already studied for two years in high school, for something of more substantive relevance to my studies. I signed up for the test, though my hopes were modest, especially after a fellow student from Canada who was fluent in French told me that her score had been too low to pass.

The morning of the test arrived, with icy gales and several inches of snow. I decided not to bother. I was sure to fail, so why invest the time? I called my boyfriend, Flynn. He insisted I take the exam. You'll never

holding up the celestial spheres.

[6] Thanks to Charles Russo for arranging a meeting at which I could share appreciative and critical feedback about my experiences with IU Health, an organization that takes patient experiences seriously and is working to improve them.

know, he pointed out, unless you take it. I suited up and trudged the mile-and-a-half to campus.

That exam was among the most exasperating experiences of my life. So many questions, with far too little time to read and consider which answer to pick from the multiple choices. I had been trained to read exam questions carefully and think them through before responding. "READ THE QUESTION!" Ava Hunting-Badcocke, headmistress at my middle school crammer, had always exhorted. With this exam, such care was impossible. Convinced I was going to fail anyway, I decided to guess. I literally filled in boxes at random. I was furious by the time it was over – allowing so little time that most students will have to guess at answers on a multiple-choice exam is no test of knowledge.

When the results came in, I learned I'd passed. In fact, the chair of the department sent a note to say my score was one of the highest ever. Absolute madness, that the course of one's graduate studies should be so affected by a test that bore no relationship to what one actually knew or understood. But Flynn was right: Even though my triumph was groundless, I was glad I'd made the effort. Instead of another semester translating passages of "Les Misérables," I could take a class on political theory based on readings of Mill and Rousseau. And now, with chemo, I would go for it, if only to find out whether I could tolerate the treatment.

My client and now friend Judith Brown painted this portrait of our cattle dog mix, Joey, in acrylics and delivered it just in time for Christmas Day in 2020, an exceptionally thoughtful gift at a challenging time.

My family has always lived with animals. When my sister and I were little, our home was a mid-century ranch in a suburb of Miami, Florida. Close to the bay, with the thinnest layer of topsoil formed over millennia across the peninsula's coral base, the area was home to jellyfish that floated through canals and bluish land crabs that popped up unpredictably out of the sandy soil. The crabs were outlandish, with snapping claws and eyes on stalks; they were also shockingly fast at scrambling away. We only saw one at a time, so we thought he was the only one there. (It was easier for our mom to give him a gender, any gender, in the early 1960s, before the introduction of the gender-neutral "they.") He could have been frightening, so our mother made him lovable by calling him Looney the Land Crab, which gave him the familiarity of a cartoon character.

The truly terrifying animals at our early home were the grasshoppers. I'd be walking through the yard when one would shoot out of a shrub straight at my face. These weren't the delicate grasshoppers we have in Indiana, barely a couple of inches long; to my 6-year-old self they appeared more like a 6-inch submarine sandwich, with hard, fat bodies and no sense of direction. They'd hit me like a bullet, sending me into a panic.

We also had ants, lots of them. Neighborhood kids would come over to visit in the front yard, and when we spotted a cluster of ants in the driveway we eagerly stomped them to death. The first time our mom caught us in this pointless killing spree she suggested we think about how the ants might feel about being deprived of their lives for no reason other than our entertainment. "How would you feel if you came back in another life as an ant?" she asked. I didn't need the perspective of rebirth as a member of a different species; all it took was my mother's encouragement to extend my empathy to these animals who, unlike dogs or cats, were not warm or cuddly, but had their own purpose, relationships and agenda. While I can't speak for my neighborhood friends, I never stomped on ants again. To this day I have trouble killing any kind of bug and kill ticks with an apology.

I can't recall a time when I have not trusted animals of the non-human variety more than those of our own species. Dogs, in particular, are especially attuned to their human familiars in all sorts of ways. Our dog, Joey, knows when it is 5 o'clock, time for his dinner. At first, he learned to associate dinnertime with the opening music for NPR's "All Things Considered," but these days he doesn't even need that prompt. When Mark sits down in the evening with a beer and I join him with a cup of vegetable broth or tomato juice, Joey insists on getting his own "cocktail," a rawhide or teeth-cleaning chew (not that I'm convinced they actually clean his teeth, but he loves them); he paws at my leg until I get up, then herds me toward the laundry room cabinet where we keep his treats.

Sure, dogs can be naughty. Joey feels no shame in telling Mark he hasn't had his dinner while surreptitiously licking the remnants of that very dinner from his lips. Most dogs who live in domestic situations become as manipulative as we allow them to be. Guilty as charged! They train us, every bit as well as take our cues. Still, unlike most cats I have known, dogs at least acknowledge us as beings who live for more than simply to serve them.

Animals who grow close to us sense our feelings. Their curiosity often extends to care, even if some may dismiss this as anthropomorphizing. (This will be the last time I acknowledge anthropomorphizing in this book.) Dogs will howl with weeping people, sniff concernedly at a wound, keep vigil at our bedside. Cats (well, some of them) will snuggle into laps when we are ill. Horses are exquisitely sensitive to prompts from those they know well – a glance, a shift in seating position, the slightest bit of tension transferred to bit from rein.

Animals can also be potent teachers and exemplars. Years ago, when I was a member of our county's historic preservation board, I did my time in the organization's booth at the county fair. I had never been to an agricultural fair, mainly because I grew up in suburbs and cities and had never lived on a farm or kept livestock of any kind. My sister and I knew nothing about the origin of the food on our plates. Although our mother cooked delicious meals with meat as the main course when we were little – my favorites were ground beef cooked with onions, and arroz con pollo (rice with chicken, cooked Cuban-style) – I'd first questioned my consumption of meat while enjoying a tongue sandwich in a basement restaurant called The Buttery at my maternal grandparents' hotel in Miami Beach. (The basement also qualified as a fallout shelter in case of nuclear assault.) I was probably 6 or 7, and in an ecstasy inspired by the combination of caraway-rye bread, with its leathery crust and chewy interior, salty meat and yellow mustard, when it occurred to me to ask about the sandwich's name.

"I know this is called a tongue sandwich, but why? It isn't made from a tongue, is it?"

My grandma said it was. I dropped the sandwich in horror. How could anyone want to eat another animal's tongue – especially one as distastefully large as that of a bull or cow?[7]

I had never been a fan of steak; an unabashed slab of muscle laced with fat was just too graphic. I'd chew and chew but sometimes couldn't stand to swallow, even if the meat was perfectly tender. I was painfully aware that I was chewing someone else's body part. One time I ended up in tears at the dinner table as my father insisted I swallow a mouthful of steak or go to my room without dinner. I couldn't do it, so I spat it out on a napkin and left the table hungry.

But the real turning point was one night when my mother had cooked lamb chops. Those were a favorite – until, inspired again by a budding interest in words, it occurred to me to ask whether lamb chops were made from lambs. Who would see a lamb in spring, gamboling on a tufty hillside, and think "I want to eat that animal"? (In fact, Mark and our friend Jenni both said just this while we hiked through Welsh farm fields in spring two years ago, though I still don't get it.) I could no longer stomach the idea of eating lamb. Eventually the same went for another of my favorites, spare ribs.

I wasn't yet opposed in principle to eating meat, but I could only bring myself to eat meat that was unrecognizable, which is to say

---

[7] My perspective on meat consumption has changed markedly since I was a child. I'm now aware that there are strong arguments for the responsible raising and consumption of animals, and if you're going to eat an animal, surely it's better to eat as much of its body as you can, so there's minimal waste. But I can no longer stomach the idea, let alone the flesh.

ground. That, too, came to an end when our parents invited some hippies from the local park to come and stay at our house in the late 1960s. Stay they did, some for years, and they brought with them all kinds of counsel on how we should be living. Meat would be replaced with vegetable proteins such as beans and tofu. I missed hamburgers, fries and milkshakes for a while, but eventually meat became something I could no longer think of as food, at least for myself.[8]

As I found my way to our organization's booth at the county fair, I was dismayed by the conditions in which so many of the animals were being kept. Many of us have nostalgic fantasies of contented sheep, cows and turkeys grazing or pecking in fields of hay, the kind of scene you'll find at historic farmsteads. That green and pleasant vision is not the reality of most contemporary agricultural fairs, or farms. Fairs are held in mid-summer; in this case, the highs were in the 90s, with humidity typical for south-central Indiana. The animals were clearly stressed by the heat and crowds, not to mention the move to a temporary location. Ducks and chickens panted, some resting their heads pathetically on the wires of their enclosures. They seemed miserable and exhausted. Cattle, too, were panting heavily; some, who had been kept in air-conditioned barns to encourage the luxuriant growth of their coats, were seriously endangered by the heat and humidity; one calf raised this way had died the previous year. Dismiss me if you must (though I'll remind you of those Biblical exhortations to care for the least among us), but my heart was heavy with fellow feeling for these beings who were clearly in distress.[9]

[8] Yes, we feed our dog and cat meat. Mark, too, eats meat. I am not judgmental about meat consumption. I just wish that animals were raised and slaughtered in ways that are humane, and ecologically – as well as economically – sustainable.

[9] I've heard the rationalizations, that bringing animals to county and state fairs is for a good cause, you're raising kids with practical skills etc. (I cannot call them justifications, because I'm not convinced that the practices are justified.) But the suffering of many animals at fairs is intense; you need only allow yourself to feel the kind of empathy that most of us feel for our family members and friends. Suffering is part of life, but to train yourself to not see or feel it on the grounds that animals (or members of any group of human beings not like you, or me, or your doctor or teacher) "don't

Dinner? Ewe! Lamb and ewe, Wales, 2019. (Photo: Mark Longacre)

My maternal grandparents, Esse and Artie, on their sailboat.

Then I saw the pigs. Pigs – forever mocked for being fat, dirty imbeciles who live to eat and roll in mud and are valued as little more than bacon on the hoof. These creatures stood out as the only non-human animals who had made peace with their predicament. Confined in a large pen, most of them napped, breathing heavily, but to all appearances perfectly content. *I want to be like them*, I thought. Every one of us faces challenging circumstances at times. Sometimes the prospect of plodding forth feels all but impossible. While Western culture celebrates the power to shape circumstances to our desires, others recognize that there is value in facing seemingly unbearable situations with grace.

suffer the same way as we do" is a willful blindness that often legitimates cruelty.

2: What Is Anyone For?

A FEW weeks into our new reality, I discovered that far more work awaited me on the existential front. I needed a goal, something that mattered to me so much that I could view chemo as a necessary means to achieving it: this book. At least if I completed this book, I could die knowing that I had commemorated some of my animal friends, who have been my companions, shared their warmth on chilly nights and taught me important lessons about what arguably is (and is not) important when it comes to living a good life. However horrible the experience of chemo might turn out to be, I would do my best to focus on that goal.

The Saturday before I started chemo, I wrote to Chris Schwarz to ask if he'd consider publishing "Shop Tails," on which I had been working sporadically for years. I sent three of the chapters as examples. Before the weekend was over, he'd had Kara Gebhart Uhl send over a contract. Beyond this short-term goal, everything I read about improving my prospects for survival stressed the importance of knowing what I wanted to live for. Big-picture. Never mind what dogs might be for; what was I for?

I was shocked to find I had no answer. The prospect of merely living another day has never struck me as enough. I've always needed to feel productive, to get things done, to make a difference for others. But these reasons for being are relatively abstract, not the stuff that fills a soul (or at least, mine) with vital purpose and motivation.

I let the question sit as Mark and I installed one job, then another. Although Mark has his own business, completely independent of mine, in view of the pandemic we'd decided it would be safest for us to be each other's helper instead of relying on anyone else.

For weeks, I had the distinct sense that a large chunk of my being was churning away, processing the potential implications of my diagnosis and wondering how it would change my body and our lives; it felt like part of me had become one of those walls of CPUs circa 1985. At times I felt like I was in jail, with nowhere to go. I'd made up my mind – in theory – to go forward with treatment. That didn't stop me from reconsidering, based on new information coming at me from all sides. Every option came with multiple downsides. But I had decisions to make, and fast.

The choices were clear. On the one hand, I could opt against standard medical treatment and do my best to enjoy whatever good time I might have left. Subjecting a strong, otherwise-healthy body to the carpet-bomb assault of chemotherapy struck me as a kind of crime. After reading the literature provided by the hospital pharmacy about how to keep others safe from exposure to remnants of drugs in my urine, saliva and other excretions – keep pets out of the bathroom; close the toilet lid before you flush, then flush again; be scrupulous about removing all traces of bodily fluids from toilets and other surfaces – it occurred to me that such toxic substances must surely leave residues in sewers and septic systems. I didn't want to harm our local amphibians or the animals they depend on for food. I didn't want to harm anyone. (And the concern about traces of chemotherapy drugs remains, as they are increasingly found in municipal and rural water supplies.[1])

On the other hand, as I heard from more people with friends and family members who have lived with pancreatic cancer for three years, five years or longer, and learned more about the part that nutrition, exercise and environmental factors can play in managing cancer, I felt heartened.

Friends and family members called, wrote, sent food and flowers, lion's mane mushrooms and medicinal herbs. Readers sent messages of

---

[1] I leave this ethical quandary unaddressed. To point out that thousands of other people go through chemotherapy, in light of which my knowledge that the remnants from my body may remain dangerous after going through our septic system are a minute fraction of what's out there, making no appreciable difference, is, as my former professor Richard B. Miller would say, not an ethical argument. It's merely a rationalization. To address the staggering amount of pollution in our air, water and land demands municipal, national and global collaboration, in addition to individual action.

encouragement and appreciation for my work. At the risk of sounding like a character in a Lifetime channel drama, I had never felt so loved. Then Megan Fitzpatrick told me that some Lost Art Press readers were asking how they could help; would there be a fundraiser? She asked whether I would be on board with a GoFundMe campaign that she said she'd be happy to organize. I gave her generous offer careful thought. On the one hand, it's outrageous that so many in America have to ask friends for help to cover the potentially crippling costs associated with cancer treatment and other types of medical care lest we lose our homes and pretty much everything else. Having lived in England for 16 years, I've experienced the realities of a nationalized healthcare system. No system is without its drawbacks, but I would take nationalized health care any day over the administration-heavy, bottom-line-focused system we currently have in the U.S. – and today, ours is more benign in some respects than it was 10 years ago, at least in terms of eligibility for health insurance; in the recent past, a pre-existing condition such as cancer could have made it impossible to buy health care coverage, leaving many to die from cancer or other, preventable causes.[2]

Asking for help is not one of my strengths. I was not going to ask for financial help at a time when so many millions of my fellow Americans were in financial straits, having lost their livelihoods, and sometimes their homes, due to the pandemic. But in this case, I realized, I would not be asking for help; it sounded like people wanted to give help, regardless of my old-school pride. So I said yes. And thanks to Megan and many others, readers, colleagues and friends contributed some $65,000 in less than 24 hours. That's more than my annual personal gross income, ever.[3] I was overwhelmed by the outpouring of generosity. I didn't want to be, or even appear, greedy. So I asked her to stop the campaign.[4]

---

[2] I personally knew one woman in her 40s, a strong, independent woman with three grown sons, who was afraid to call for an ambulance, certain that she could not afford the charges. She died as a result.

[3] I am of course talking about personal income, not gross business revenue.

[4] I was aware that between the charges for my medical procedures to diagnose and

My sister, Maggie, sent us this ridiculous cap for our young cat, Tony, knowing that it would make us laugh.

WHAT IS ANYONE FOR?

The first chemo treatment was on December 28. Between the blood test first thing, then the wait for the results, followed by the infusions of pre-medications that mitigate side effects and the cocktail of Folfirinox drugs, it took the entire day. That evening, Mark and I went for a short walk up the hill, as I familiarized myself with the weirdness of having a catheter from a pump dispensing 5 milliliters per hour of Fluorouracil through a needle in my chest propped up by an Eiffel-Tower-level exercise in architectural bandaging.[5]

The side effects started the following morning. I sat down in Mark's grandpa's recliner, a bit of mid-20th-century steel engineering that I compare to a military Humvee, and stayed there the whole day. My head was pounding, between effects from the chemo drugs and my cold-turkey withdrawal from the four to five cups of strong coffee I was accustomed to drinking. (I know – excessive.) My abdomen hurt, I was nauseated, I felt utterly exhausted and I had the overpowering sense of being shut in a steel cage that was too small for me. I got up only to use the bathroom, and I relied on Mark for everything, calling out weakly "Would you make me a cup of chamomile tea?" from upstairs. The second day was even worse. With my head in my hands, I told Mark I did not think I was up for more chemotherapy. Especially in view of the odds against its likely effectiveness, this misery did not feel worth it.

It was at this low point that I connected with Karen Vaughan Clark,

---

start treating my cancer in 2020, combined with those for 2021, the medical expenses are likely to exceed the total amount raised. As we now understand (thanks to my cousin Gail Hiller-Lee, an insurance industry professional), Mark and I have to cover approximately $24,000 per year of "out-of-pocket expenses," including deductibles, for the most affordable H.S.A.-linked self-employed persons' coverage. We bought our policy through the Marketplace; it costs us each $849 per month, information I offer to apprise others of this dimension of the reality of self-employment as a furniture maker and general contractor, respectively, though I recognize that our situation is quite different from that of many others.

[5] As it turns out, nurses and others have nicknames for many chemo drugs. Fluorouracil is known as "5-FU" – perfectly apt, considering that it causes serious burns when applied topically to the skin and does a number on the lining of your gut if you're not careful. "Irinotecan," another drug in my protocol, is "I ran to the can," in view of its most well-known side effect, which I have been fortunate to avoid so far.

an oncology nurse who had herself been diagnosed with pancreatic cancer a few months earlier. Karen had cared for a mutual friend's partner, who had died of the disease; she and the friend, Eric, had stayed in touch, united by that shared experience. The first time we spoke, she told me about the excellent response she'd had to her own treatment, a combination of conventional chemotherapy and integrative protocols such as exercise, a diet based on whole foods and exceptionally low in carbohydrates, and infusions of mistletoe, which is widely used by cancer patients in northern Europe to stimulate the immune response and minimize chemo's side effects. That day, she said, she'd baked a cake for a friend, gone grocery shopping and run the equivalent of three miles on a mini trampoline to benefit her lymph system. The very idea of having so much energy was beguiling to me – I hadn't done anything besides sit for almost two days, and the basic act of standing up from the chair took so much effort that I could only dream of feeling that good and being so productive again. Karen's optimism and suggestions for my own care were a gift that came at the perfect time. I suddenly felt hope.

The next day I woke up feeling marginally better. When you've felt so ghastly, marginally better feels like the first sunny day in spring, when masses of daffodils burst into bloom. Every subsequent day brought improvement so dramatic that I decided the misery would be worthwhile, if the treatment resulted in days when I felt far better than I had in the couple of years preceding my diagnosis. And I was elated to discover that, as Anissa had experienced, the side effects from my first chemo were by far the worst. When I asked a pharmacist why the first round had been so awful, considering that my subsequent side effects have been so mild, she mentioned that the first infusion, at least with this protocol, results in the greatest cell die-off. Yuck. But I was going to continue the chemo.

To see this project through, I told Mark, I would need to make getting well my top priority. It would be my most important job for the foreseeable future – not an easy thing for someone who has based her sense of worth on her work, but so many others had thrown their support behind me that doing my best to survive this disease had come to

WHAT IS ANYONE FOR?

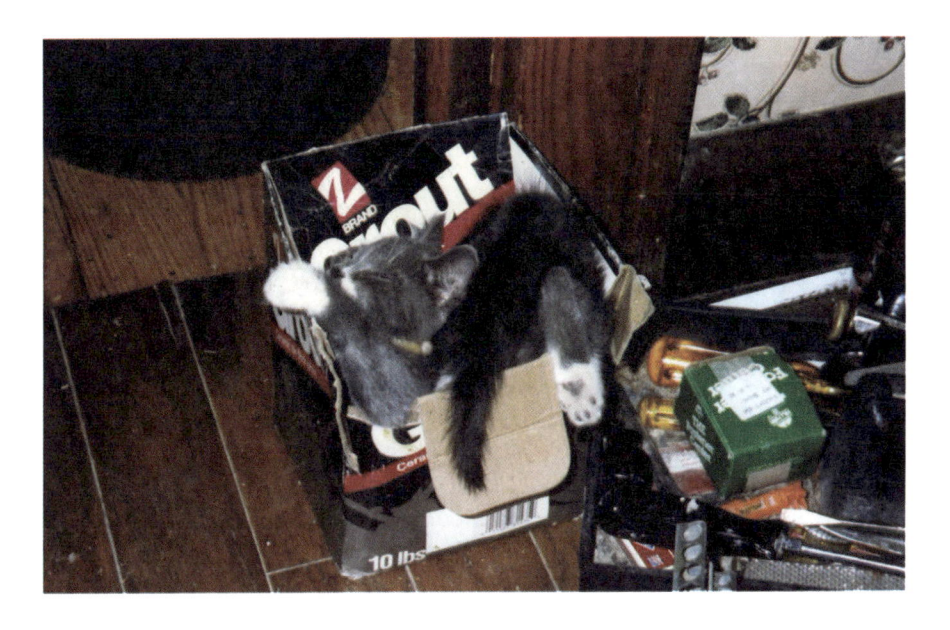

Dido, a kitten I adopted in the late 1990s from a litter of strays at a salvage yard, napping in a box of grout.

feel like a team effort. I'm a lot bolder when working on behalf of others in addition to myself.

I continued to run up against the crucial big-picture question that so many books and articles told me I had to answer: What was I living for? What gave me joy? I still had no satisfactory response. Looking back over my life while fitting doors and discussing next steps with my oncologist from the top of a ladder as I painted cubbies for sheet music and CDs, I realized that I had rarely been motivated by a vision or a dream. I could recall few well-defined goals or desires. Sure, I had a basic three-fold vision: Do good work, make a home, have a happy partnership. But this was just an outline that would take a lot of filling-in. Why was I so vague about what I wanted?

In part, I realized, it was because I was raised not to want, but to be grateful for what already was. I worked at being happy, whatever situation I faced, and went from one situation to another without any real plan. When my mother told 8-year-old me that wanting things would make me unhappy, she was probably not referring to the important stuff, but to the latest toys we saw advertised on TV. But you can't really predict what a kid will do with the Buddha's First and Second Noble Truths, which, in a nutshell, see all life as suffering, and suffering as a product of selfish desire. I don't recall any discussion about the need to envision my future, let alone plan my studies around my need to earn a living. Sometimes I was happy. Sometimes I was miserable. But eventually something would change and things got better. Only in my 30s, when I was reading Socrates, Plato and Aristotle in graduate school, did it dawn on me that desire can be among the most powerful motivations for good; what matters are the nature of that desire and its goal.

In place of motivation by well-founded desire, I had spent my life in search of validation that I didn't get at home. Growing up, it seemed my sister and I were constantly being urged to be other than we were: Hold in your stomach, don't slouch, don't whine, get off your backside and do your chores – much of it the typical, benign work of training Baby Boomers for adulthood. The critical messages far outweighed any expressions of approbation.

My sense of never doing or being enough was only worsened by the father figures introduced to our household in the aftermath of our parents' split. When I was 14, our mother's boyfriend, George, told me I had a naturally down-turned mouth and should make an effort to smile, lest my face put others off. He said I was getting fat (I wasn't) and should go on a diet, so I ran with that and developed an eating disorder. He told me I knew nothing – true, relatively speaking, but how does angrily hurling "You know nothing!" at a teenager really help matters? (Answer: It doesn't. There are more precise and effective ways to make the point about youthful over-confidence versus lack of life experience.) His general demeanor was that of a smug, entitled guy who had put his degree from Oxford to profitable use by getting a job in law or finance in London and resented the intrusion of his girlfriend's teenage daughters on what would otherwise have been his uninterrupted "me time." I recognized his bitterness as evidence of his own unhappiness, but his words had lasting effects.

So when this arrogant man who arrived at our doorstep a few times a week, only to be ushered into a comfortable chair and handed a drink to enjoy while he read the evening paper, promised me 5 pounds for every A I got in my O-Level exams, I happily stuck it to him. I'd already experienced the satisfaction of earning good grades in middle school and realized I had the power to view my teachers less as unreasonably demanding authority figures than as partners in my education; I would do my best for them, as well as myself, not least because at the slightest imposition of real discipline, most of my fellow students complained. It had to be tough, being a teacher.

I lived by my As and A-pluses, my 10s-out-of-10. With every one, I felt better about myself and hoped that my teachers felt better about themselves, too. I worked hard to get into the University of Cambridge, only to discover, once accepted, that I had no idea why I was really there, even though I loved the day-to-day life of a scholar. What mattered most to me, I'm embarrassed to say, is that I got in – and with an honorary scholarship. No one could ever again call me lame-brained, even though my stepfather would do his best to prove my intellectual inferiority to his own sophistication in argument and repeatedly called me "useless" to my face. The same went for university after I returned to the States. I was determined to graduate Phi Beta Kappa, as my mother had. And I did. But again, in grad school, I was struck by the realization that I really had no idea why I was there, beyond my awareness that I enjoyed learning, having my mind lit on fire by new perspectives, and proving my ability to excel. In the end I did not want the life of a professional academic. And the most oft-cited alternatives for those with a doctorate in ethics, which I had planned to pursue, were nothing I wanted, either; I had no interest in being an ethics advisor to some big corporation, a job that too often means circumventing profit-diminishing foundational moral stances through arguments on behalf of ethical exceptions.

What I wanted, for 50 years, was to prove that people were wrong about me, to exceed their low expectations. When people mentally

No ducks and bunnies. Edwardian Hallstand, circa 2002. Curly white oak with locally quarried limestone counters. (Photo: Spectrum Creative Group.)

translated my work as a furniture maker to "She makes 'furniture' out of pallets or fruit crates and decorates her work with cut-outs of ducks and bunnies – you know, because that's what women like," I would show them my take on an Edwardian hallstand with a perfectly fitted door and drawer and a cornice of compound bevels. Anyone who assumed that, as a tradesperson, I would be less intellectually curious and articulate than someone who works in an office (any kind of office would do; this is a matter of longstanding prejudice against "manual" and "blue-collar" workers) would have to square that assumption with a growing body of published essays and books in which I brought my academic training in Classical languages, history and ethics to bear on the social and economic significance of commonplace things such as kitchen furnishings. I did my best to illustrate the ways in which a house, typically thought of as "property," could fulfill many of the roles we usually associate with a human partner. In response to the critics who might deride my ways of putting cabinets together, I would point out that there really are as many ways to build a cabinet as there are cabinetmakers, not to mention that the cabinets I build, however simple their construction, are far stronger than most that are commercially made.

Throughout all of this, I now saw, I had moved forward in reaction to others. I was dangerously dependent on outside forces, people who expressed their opposition, no less than their approval. It suddenly felt deeply exhausting. I let my awareness of that exhaustion sink in. Whatever might happen with the course of my cancer, I was not going back to my old ways of living.

To be fair, those other-influenced decisions always reflected something of me – a love of houses, gardens and animals; an intellectual fascination with the endless ways in which people make meaning out of the seemingly random circumstances into which we are born; a desire to make myself a home. But viewing the span of my working life as a whole, I was staggered by a deep, yet vague sense that I had always been running away. What was I running away from – the person I was not, but was too often taken to be? This, and my unending need to prove that others' low opinions of me were wrong, were reactions to unhappy

Tony in one of the architectural wall cabinets I made for a Fine Woodworking *article.*

stimuli, not the stuff that gets a person through cancer treatment. Take these away, and what was I living for?

As I pondered this question, I realized I had to start with the first big wound I could remember, because it, above all, seemed likely to have set me on this course of reacting to circumstances and looking to others for my sense of self-worth. I had to write a letter to my parents – not write it, then recycle it, or keep it in a box, as "Dear Abby" might recommend. I had to send them my words, which meant allowing myself to be more vulnerable in relation to them than I had been willing to be for many years.

Shortly before the procedure to implant my port, I spent three hours writing a two-page letter to my parents. I printed it out and reworked it over the next few days. As I continued to absorb what it meant, to me, that I had developed pancreatic cancer, I found myself focusing on one particular event: my last visit with my mother's mother, Esse, when she herself had been in the hospital being treated for pancreatic cancer.

It was the last time she and I saw each other. I was in my early 20s; I'd flown over from England and was sitting with her in her hospital room, on one of those vinyl-upholstered metal chairs. At one point in our conversation she became angrier than I had ever seen her; she was talking about my parents splitting up years before, and how their actions had hurt everyone in the family. Her anger was specifically aimed at my dad; she said she was furious at him and would never forgive him for abandoning his responsibilities. It felt as though she was shooting a poisoned arrow at my father, and I couldn't stand it. I wanted to protect him from that anger. It felt dangerous. So I made an intentional decision to absorb her anger into the center of my own body. I will never forget that decision to take a figurative bullet for my father. I knew it might hurt me. I hoped it wouldn't turn into a physical illness. But at least my dad would be safe.

Over the years I came to understand that my grandmother's anger really could not have been meant for my dad alone. It rightly applied to both of my parents, but I understood that at that moment she needed to focus on my father. It was he who had told my mother, when my sister was 9, and I 11, that she had to leave. I hadn't known anything about it until I got up the next morning and went to the bottom of the stairs by the kitchen to call for her, as I did every morning. "Mom!" I called. No answer. I called again, impatient. After a few minutes my father came down to the landing and said, "Your mother is gone." That was it. No emotion, no explanation.

To a kid of 11, this translated as, "Your mother has died." She hadn't died, I'm happy to say; she had simply left, though I had no idea of this at the time. Years later, she told me she'd felt she had no alternative. No alternative to leaving her children, without researching other possible responses, such as asking our father or her parents for help and getting a job? No alternative to escaping from the responsibilities that she, as an adult, had undertaken? Reflecting on the lack of open, adult discussion in that and subsequent situations eroded my respect for both of my parents in their capacity as parents. For my sister and me, the stakes were far higher than either of them had bothered to consider.

After I had spent the day crying over the loss of our mother, she came home that evening to say goodbye. I remember her apologizing to me and telling me she'd had to leave the night before. I wanted to go with her; she was planning to drive west, camping in her VW bus, which she'd outfitted with storage compartments and a cool makeshift bed. She considered my idea; we even took off together that night. I was elated at the prospect of roughing it on the road with my fearless mother. After driving a while, she pulled over someplace where we planned to sleep. But as we settled in, she decided – no doubt wisely – that I would be better off at home, so she turned around and took me back.

She was obviously sorry to have caused us so much distress. But when she tried to console me, something in me switched off. I was not going to be consoled by the same person who had helped cause the damage. "I'm fine," I said, resolved not to cry any more. Whatever she may really have been feeling, I sensed something like pity, and I was not going to be an object of pity. I would not be seen as a victim. I may only have been 11, but I spent most of my time with people who were 10 years older: the hippies who lived with us. On a winter night in the late 1960s, our parents had invited some young people who were planning to camp out at a local park to join us in the warmth of our home. A few

WHAT IS ANYONE FOR? 43

When the hippies moved in, a couple of them suggested that they turn our backyard swimming pool into a pond, just visible through this tangle of foliage. Out went the chlorine and in came the aquatic plants, such as the lotus and papyrus visible here surrounded by banana trees. They also populated the pond with several species of freshwater fish, including some that ate the debris created by others, as well as dead plant parts. To oxygenate the water, they constructed a small pump-circulated waterfall out of coral.

of them ended up moving in, at least in a manner of speaking – they lived in a variety of small structures they built with our parents' encouragement in our backyard. I identified with them, not with kids my own age. I considered myself a proto-adult. I had no time for babies, and I was determined not to be one.

While my experience doesn't begin to compare to that of a child raised in a household where family members go to bed hungry, or a parent is verbally or physically abusive, let alone to the experiences of children living as refugees, the sense of betrayal and the child-logical implication that my sister and I just weren't that important to our parents, that being there for us was somehow optional, went deep. Several months later, when my sister and I were at boarding school in England, I would often start crying without any provocation, especially in woodworking class. I don't know why tears came so easily in the shop, but I suspect it's for the same reason that, as an adult, I find shop work conducive to reflection. It wasn't the usual kind of crying; there were no sounds. My eyes were simply leaking tears. I couldn't articulate what was wrong when friends or the woodworking teacher asked. As far as I was concerned, nothing was wrong. I was just crying. Crying was natural. Get over it. Stop paying attention to me. I'm not a victim.

I never wanted to be a parent because I felt sure I was not up to the responsibility. But my recognition of the enormity of that responsibility did not absolve my parents of the responsibilities they took on by having children, even if thinking something along these lines was one of the mental contortions I engaged in as an adult, trying to understand and excuse what might have led them to behave as they did. For decades I told myself to remember that they were relatively young at the time, around 30. It was the '60s; they had surrounded themselves with younger people who'd shown them that life could be, *should* be, about so much more than success as defined by middle-class American norms. Instead of revolving around buying the latest "best" thing and worrying endlessly about how you measure up against others, a good life should be rooted in growing, building and making. The avocado trees planted by the original owner of our home were a bountiful source of food, as were the kumquats and loquats, tamarinds, citrus and carambolas. My mother was already a great cook, but thanks to the hippies, we had now learned about homemade bread, pizza and ice cream. These people stressed the importance of authenticity – living according to your highest values, enjoying the basic activities of every day and doing, instead of consuming. On the other hand, this vision of a life worth living was delivered through a haze of euphoria-inducing and psychedelic substances that seemed to gloss over some common, decent values, mainly on the grounds that they were conventional, products of a culture the hippies taught me to dismiss for being "straight" (or in today's parlance, Dictated by The Man). Our family unit became a casualty of this collision between the expectations, behaviors and habits of mind that had shaped my parents over the course of their upbringing and this new understanding of what might constitute a well-lived life.

***

I wrote my letter because doing so felt like a prerequisite to whatever healing I might be capable of. I noted that it would be reasonable for my parents to ask why I had never brought up the event with my dying grandmother. I had known the answer to that for decades: At a fundamental level, I didn't trust either of my parents as *parents*; to put myself in a position of vulnerability with them did not feel safe. On the other hand, I have long appreciated my parents as people. My mother's mechanical aptitude still in many respects exceeds my own; as a user of hand and power tools, she was a great example for a girl who would grow up to be a woodworker. She is an accomplished gardener and cook. As an adult, she studied sculpture and printmaking and excelled at both. She and my father have a kind of intelligence that finds connections between things that are seemingly unrelated; their example in seeing those connections has taught me to do the same. When I was learning to write essays in middle school, my mother sat with me for hours, teaching me how to engage a topic. She taught me how to plant seeds and weed flower beds, how to prep and paint a room, how to hang wallpaper. Most valuable of all, she taught my sister and me to value the lessons of hardship, to choose the teacher with strict rules and high standards over the one concerned with being "nice."

My mother also possesses a powerful will that has been an important example in the face of frightening situations. When I was about 13, she dreamed she'd developed lung cancer; the dream was so vivid that she quit smoking, cold turkey. Several years later she was diagnosed with a medical condition that, while not life-threatening, warranted attention. Her doctor recommended surgery, but based on what she had learned over the years from books about holistic health care, she

My mother, Mary Lee, at London's Portobello Road Market, where we bought our fresh produce every week.

WHAT IS ANYONE FOR?

London street, circa 1972. Left to right: Magda, Nancy, Mary Lee and a woman pushing a pram, as Brits back then called strollers or baby carriages.

decided to try a fast. She ate no food for a month, while continuing her work around the house, shopping and cooking for her then-husband (my stepfather) and their animals, and turned her condition around, if temporarily. She also raised us to be self-critical, which is a gift. She insisted we help with housekeeping jobs and taught us how to perform them; from the time my sister was 12 and I 14, we had an alternating weekly schedule for vacuuming the flat (most of which had wall-to-wall carpet), washing the dishes, cleaning the kitchen and bathrooms, and doing our laundry. She taught me to bake bread using "The Tassajara Bread Book" as a guide. We also shared the grocery shopping with her, which meant taking the bus to the Portobello Road Market for fruits and vegetables each Saturday, followed by take-out vegetarian gyros from a place called Louis Kebab. Sometimes we walked home from the market instead of taking the bus. The bags of produce were so heavy that by the time we reached our front door we thought our arms might come out of their shoulder sockets. It was solid training in doing what's necessary, with no whining.

  My father has a brilliant intellect and an insatiable love of reading, music and learning that continues in his 90s. I admired his resilience in coming up with affordable ways to live after my mother and stepfather came back to the States and took over our family home, as he and my grandparents had agreed. They had supported us after our parents' split, and I will always be grateful to them for my high-school education. He bartered his services in public relations for extended stays at one or another of the inns owned by his clients. I was amazed by his skill at making a comfortable place to cook, work and sleep, all in the space of a bedroom and bath. In the '70s he pioneered a type of travel that we now know as ecotourism, which would immerse tourists in the culture, history and natural features of the place they were visiting, instead of feeding and entertaining them in essentially the same ways they could have enjoyed in Climax, Georgia, or Topeka, Kansas, but with a view of palm trees and a bottomless mojito in hand. He continued this work and taught its principles at the college level, riding his bicycle 20 miles each way to and from campus after hikes in auto insurance rates made it unaffordable for him to drive a car. Then he turned this real-world experience in alternative transportation into years of work as an advocate of cycling and trails. He has always encouraged our interest in art and design, with gifts of educational books such as "What To Listen For in Music," "The Art Pack" and a Plexiglas box made by a sculptor who had filled it with cubes of different wood species, each with its name inscribed for educational purposes – a gift which by purchasing he was supporting an artist friend. For my 14th birthday he gave me the two-volume set of "The Concise Oxford English Dictionary on Historical Principles," and another time, the four-volume set of Churchill's "History of the English Speaking Peoples."[6]

  He also brought us up (at least, in our early childhood) with a healthy mix of discipline and fun. When we were little, we would go into our

---

[6] Plexiglas is called Perspex in the U.K.

parents' bedroom in the morning while they were getting dressed. Every so often our dad, in an undershirt and boxers, his long socks held up by the kind of garters men used to wear in the 20th century's middle years, would say, "Look at this!" whereupon he'd unwrap a piece of candy; instead of eating the candy, he would eat the paper wrapper. We were terribly impressed, even as we understood that we should not follow his example. When Maggie and I got into an argument in the car (a near-daily occurrence), he would wait for a pause, then jump in and finish both sides of the argument for us in falsetto. Once, when I was complaining about religious dogma, he pointed out that one of the great things about religions is that they encourage an attitude of reverence, which is generally in all-too-short supply. His determination to do good work amid constraints, many of them unintentionally self-imposed, has been among my life's most valuable lessons.

For decades I secretly hoped that I would die before my parents, because I couldn't bear to imagine the pain of losing either one. So this is not some angry adult-child diatribe.

After being told repeatedly by her own mother, "Those children didn't ask to be born," a statement with implications that took me years to grasp, our mother resumed the job of being a parent in London in 1971, with her parents' financial help. But even then, she often showed her loyalty to our stepfather over us and told us regularly, in words and other ways, that we didn't "need" this or that, whether "this" was having her attend a high school event or graduation, or "that" was a heartfelt affirmation of our worth. Like the conventional celebrations my parents had come to regard as "Hallmark holidays" – occasions for big corporations to make a killing on chocolate, cards and generic "gifts." They seemed to regard these small acts of recognition as empty gestures that might lead us to imagine we were more important than we were – or as my friend Marianne put it, speaking from her own experience, might "swell our heads." It's not lost on me that I learned to seek evidence of my self-worth through academic and professional accomplishments.

After writing my letter I worked on it sporadically over the next three days. Then I sent a copy to each of my parents separately, even though they live together. I didn't want one of them to read it before the other, or to keep it from the other lest the content prove upsetting. I sent the letters via the postal service because email seemed too blunt. I worried my letter might upset my parents, but I told myself to stop worrying about them. I hadn't written in anger. I wasn't intending to distress them. I simply had to confront a wound I had compartmentalized and been unwilling to acknowledge to them for 50 years.

My father's reply to the letter arrived via email during my first chemo infusion. He spoke about his own childhood in a home where he had been born a disappointment and felt little love; his mother had desperately wanted a daughter, not a second son. He was raised to fit prevailing standards of success, with no regard for what might be of interest to him – to jump through conventional hoops without questioning or even *understanding* their significance. No wonder he had come to see so much of what passed for The Good Life as hollow. He acknowledged that he had abandoned my mother, sister and me – if not in terms of affection, at least when it came to our financial care. Instead, he did his best to support himself with work on behalf of others. He made valiant, if quixotic, efforts to persuade the tourist industry to treat people fairly and with respect in the Caribbean islands where his former job had taken him; he helped found a farmers' market in the area of Miami known as Coconut Grove, to support small-scale farmers and community members who valued fresh, locally grown produce; he helped organize Miami's now-longstanding Goombay Festival, a celebration of Bahamian-American culture; he advocated for public transportation and bicycling; and more. My story about our grandmother's anger had come as no surprise to him. He'd long been aware of that anger.

After years of seeing my mother as the one who had abandoned us, I now saw our family history as far more complex. I was impressed and grateful that my mother and her parents had never tried to turn us against our father; in fact, they had made many opportunities for us to spend time with him, a powerful example of magnanimous, loving behavior. My mother said she would reply, but when we spoke by phone I told her to do so only if she wanted to. My letter was more about me bustIng through old scar tissue than eliciting a response.

WHAT IS ANYONE FOR?

Our mother often took us to see our grandparents at their hotel on Miami Beach, where we swam in the ocean or pool. I never really understood the attraction of a day at the pool; it was too hot, and the sun was blinding. The changing rooms, called cabanas (in the background here), had floor drains and smelled of urine, salt water and chlorine. "Having fun" was a slightly foreign phenomenon to me, though my sister seemed to be much better at it than I was.

I read my dad's reply that morning, and again that evening. It left me filled with a torrent of appreciation for the functional adults my sister and I had become, largely through years of acknowledging, analyzing and learning from our own mistakes, as well as those of our parents, which the two of us have been discussing with each other for years. I felt newly and astonishingly empowered.

In an instant – and this is no exaggeration – the life I had made appeared in a new light. There was my house, cobbled together on a genuinely slender budget over the first few years I lived there, in the chaos of a building site, while doing my best to run a business. When orders dropped off precipitously with the Great Recession, I'd moved in with Mark and rented my house to others, which allowed me to continue covering the mortgage payments and so, keep my shop. For years I missed my house. I'd put so much work into it while living in the midst of tools and construction materials. (Who else sleeps with a cordless drill on the floor next to the bed and a pile of hickory floorboards on the mattress beside her? I'm sure I'm not alone.) I viewed the experience as a creative adventure. To expedite the completion of the interior, I'd finished the house to lower standards than those I adhere to when working for clients. But even so, the place was filled with details I loved – a pair of fresh green sconces from Rejuvenation in the bathroom, with hand-painted decoration on their glass shades; built-in bookshelves in the attic; a salvaged leaded-glass window and a 15-lite glazed door to let light pass from one room with windows to another, without windows of its own; salvaged plumbing fixtures; cypress cabinets in the kitchen. While living with Mark at his house and renting my place to others, I'd missed my home the way a scholar abroad on sabbatical misses her dog; every visit to change out a leaking toilet fill valve or pour a line of boric acid powder across a threshold to deter ants was a kind of communion. In a comprehensive process of scaling down and simplifying our lives, we sold Mark's place and moved to mine – now ours – in 2016. I've loved seeing how Mark has made this place his home, with neatly tilled beds of herbs and vegetables in the summer, a garage/workshop/reading room for his use and new beds of flowers, including one for native transplants such as goldenseal and bluebells on the edge of the woods.

There was my work. So many kitchens, each one different from the others, and the freestanding and built-in pieces that now furnished my clients' homes, as well as our own. There was my writing, with its opportunities to reflect on the mind-blowing ways in which making and things-that-are-made both express and shape those who build, buy and use them. As a young person, I had never imagined I would run my

WHAT IS ANYONE FOR?

Each winter Mark starts seeds indoors under lights, then plants them in the garden.

own business. But between my interests, skills and the demands imposed by circumstances I'd encountered, many of my own inadvertent creation, I had ended up running what has mostly been a one-woman business, grateful for all sorts of help from others: my serial life partners; Daniel O'Grady, who worked with me for a couple of years and has become a real friend; my family, who have hired me on several occasions when I was short of paying work; my clients, many of whom have also become friends.

There's my garden, significantly reduced in scale since its inception, when excitement led me to establish beds all over the acre, only to discover that there were not enough hours in the day to maintain them. My now-smaller garden remains a source of satisfaction and pleasure as

I prune and weed, transplanting a daylily here and introducing a cardinal flower there, constantly editing the view with bare hands in the soil, then recording it in photos to enjoy in winter.

There are our family members and our circle of friends, both close and far away. And our dog, Joey, who has become a dear companion, the emotional distance between us in his early years long since replaced by tenderness and mutual concern.

There's my marriage to a man who really understands who I am and loves me for it. How many decades had I spent beating my head against the proverbial brick wall in an effort to "make" other relationships "work?" Mark is the eldest of four siblings. He grew up in Elkhart, a once-thriving industrial city in northern Indiana known for manufacturing recreational vehicles and brass musical instruments. Mark's parents, Jack and JoAnne, raised their children with solid Midwestern

WHAT IS ANYONE FOR?

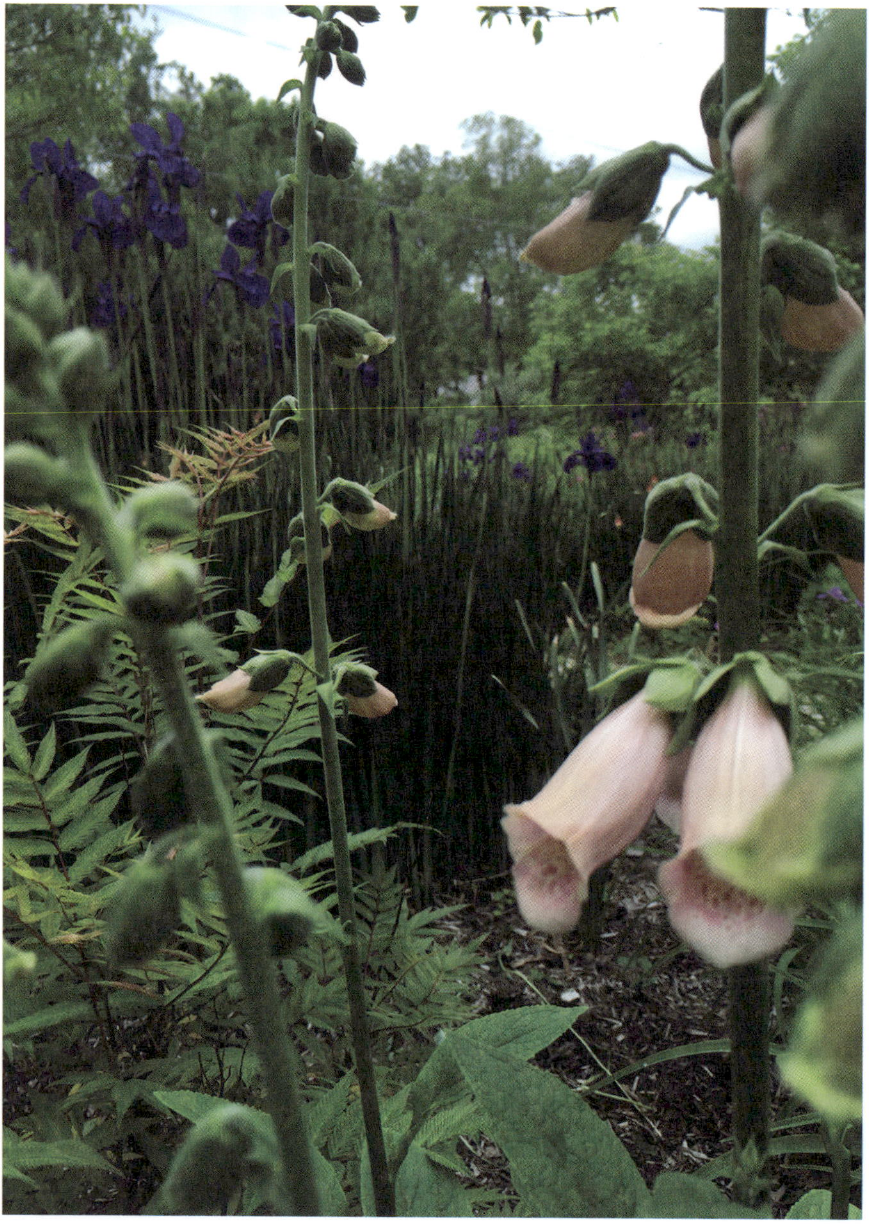

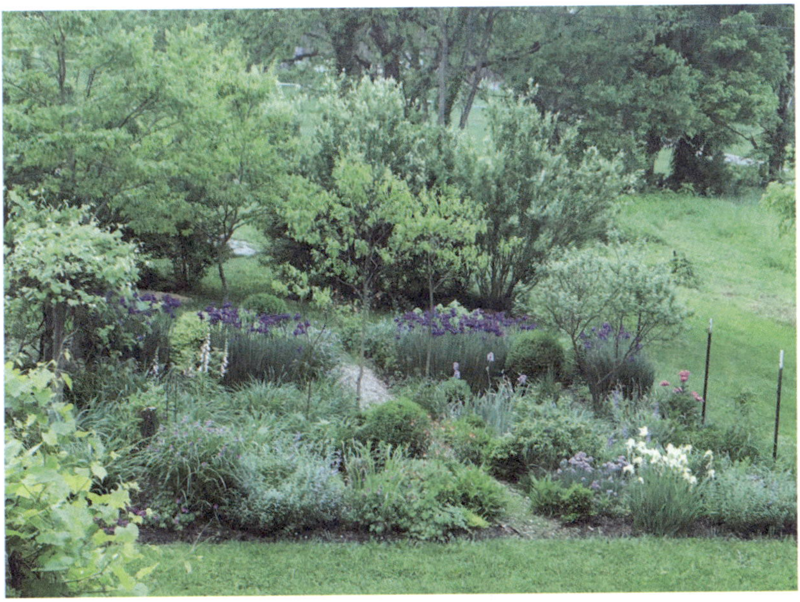

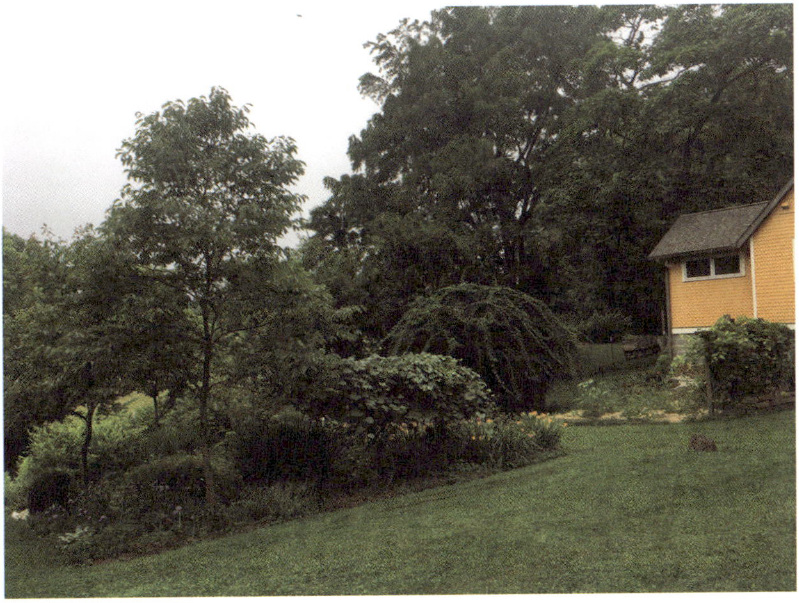

Toad and prince. Mark loves snakes and amphibians.

values: Take responsibility for your actions, be kind and helpful, beware of superficial trends. Early on, Mark became fascinated by the natural world; in high school he worked as an interpreter at the Woodlawn Nature Center and set up a chemistry lab in the family's third-floor attic, which he and his brother Gregg used as their bedroom. He read widely – books about birds, trees, Native Americans and medicinal plants. After experiencing the monotony of factory work, he started his college education with a commute to Indiana University-South Bend in an old VW station wagon with a passive, engine-fed heating system so inadequate that in winter he had to throw a blanket over his legs to keep them from going numb. He later transferred to the campus of Indiana University-Bloomington, where he completed a bachelor's in anthropology, then got into carpentry through his longstanding interest in building a house of his own, inspired by "Shelter," *Whole Earth Catalog* and related publications.

Mark has always struck me as a hybrid of the hippies of my late childhood and a wholesome Midwestern guy. Devoid of pretension, he has a healthy ego and doesn't take himself too seriously. His influences include Thoreau, Tolstoy, Gandhi, Wendell Berry, Gary Snyder, Mary Oliver and Ram Dass. And to all of this he added the eye-opening example of patient, responsible, devoted parenting of Jonas, his son. I have known few people more willing to listen, to understand others without judgment, to empathize even when under fire. I have watched Mark work through crises of his own, as well as his friends'. He is a rock.

To savor this jewel of a life that I had patched together as a salve while fleeing old wounds and trying to prove myself to others, and use my abilities for greater good – *this* was reason to live.

3: Sidney and Phoebe (1966-1973)

FOR AS long as I can remember, my sister and I wanted a dog. Well, I wanted a dog. My sister, Maggie, wanted a horse. But when you're a kid in a middle-class family with limited disposable income, a dog makes for easier negotiation.

We lived in a ranch house in suburban South Miami and attended Pinecrest Elementary School, where I was once banished to the hallway for excessive giggling. It was the mid-1960s. Our dad went to the office of the public relations firm where he worked. Our mother ran the house, ferried us back and forth to school in the station wagon until we were old enough to ride there on our bikes, sewed us matching outfits from tissue-paper patterns, remodeled one room after another in our home and hosted stylish cocktail parties for our father's business friends. Aside from our mother's construction and repair projects, it was the typical gender-based division of labor in middle-class households at the time.

When we began agitating for a dog, our mother told us we would be the ones in charge of feeding it.

"Can't it just eat grass?" I asked.

"No," she said. "You'll have to open a can of dog food every afternoon and put it in a bowl." Opening a can once a day seemed manageable, so we agreed.

Our parents brought home a medium-size mutt with floppy ears and black and brown spots. He arrived with a name, Sidney Warga, given by his former family; my father knew Sidney's "dad" through his work with the Time-Life Bureau in Miami.[1]

---

[1] The bureau did different work in the '60s than its current website suggests.

Sidney (right) and Phoebe in their prime.

I thought of Sidney as my dog but quickly realized that he really just tolerated me, the way a bemused 9-year-old boy tolerates a 7-year-old girl his parents' friends brought to dinner – which is to say he patiently acknowledged my existence while occupied by his own agenda.

He'd sit for me on command or lie on his back and let me rub his tummy. But the people he really wanted to impress were our parents, because they were the ones with the power to make important stuff happen, like opening boxes of biscuits or the back door.

Having a dog was a lot less satisfying than I had imagined, but I still thought of Sidney as mine and felt we had a mystical affinity. And for all my disappointment at finding I was less central to his daily life than I would have preferred, I grew to appreciate that living with a dog was less about being joined at the hip, or having him do

Our family with a crew member who posed for pictures on one of the ships owned by the company for which my father worked in the mid-1960s. We went on several cruises. I did not enjoy them at all, though I found the places we visited fascinating, among them small communities in the mountains of Jamaica and a remote village in Haiti where villagers cooked on open fires and pooped communally on a designated log. Maggie always found ways to have fun, between buying candy from vending machines and gambling (small-time, with nickels and quarters) in the casino.

Our mother in the garden at our primary school.

what I wanted, and more about giving him the space to be who he was, while savoring the affection he was able to show me. I could not make him conform to my will, beyond performing a few tricks in exchange for a treat. He was his own person.

    I decided to think of myself as a dog, or at least model myself on Sidney. Dogs knew what was important to them and went after it. They were open and honest. They didn't waste time on petty jealousies or slights (though they certainly defended their position when challenged). They didn't try to fool people (except on those occasions when they had

SIDNEY AND PHOEBE (1966-1973)

Our mother sewed many of our clothes from tissue-paper patterns.

a chance to tell one of their people that the other had not yet fed them, even though that was untrue). Their communication was direct, their points clear. *Oh, the sun! I love its warmth and brightness. It makes my eyelids heavy. I'm just going to lie down right here and take a nap.*

THAT IS MY BONE. STAY AWAY FROM IT OR I'LL GIVE YOU WHAT-FOR.

I REALLY NEED TO GO OUT!

Without speaking a single word, Sidney taught me a lot about what matters to a dog, or at least what mattered to him. Dinner was the focal point of his days; he divided the rest of his time between checking all the important spots in the yard and marking them with his scent, napping, and warning the postal delivery people (and, for a brief but magical few weeks, the Krispy Kreme donut delivery drivers) not to overstep their bounds. He occasionally brought me gifts; the most impressive was a crusty, flattened frog he carried into my room and buried under my pillow while I was at school. I was elated. Never mind that the road-killed frog was gross and unhygienic, it was proof that this animated, independent spirit who belonged to another world with different interests, goals and priorities recognized that he and I really did share a special bond. I let Sidney be who he was, and he honored me with a present. That was how it worked.

Maggie decided she wanted a dog of her own. When we were at the park one day, a family was giving away puppies. They were black, with soft ears and short, smooth coats. Maggie chose a female; she or our father named the dog Phoebe.

Sidney and Phoebe ran loose outside. Phoebe, in particular, liked to chase cars; before long, her tail had been hit and broken and had to be docked. When I was 8 and Maggie was 6, we moved to an old house on the outskirts of Coconut Grove. They ran loose there, too, though we did our best to keep them inside the fence by compulsively latching the front gate. Miraculously, considering that we lived directly on a busy commuter route, no one was killed by a car.

Our parents made sure the dogs got their regular vaccinations, but neither one was fixed. As a result, they had a few litters of puppies, all of which we gave away. Other than the puppies, who were cute – and unlike their parents, willing to play with us – my main memory of living with those dogs centers on the anguished cry of our mother, heard at least once a month: "SOMEONE POOPED ON THE RUG!" which was followed by lugging the rug outside to hose it off, then the smell of Lysol pervading the house.

I missed Sidney after our mother took us to live in England just before my 12th birthday, but there was so much else to occupy my attention that I didn't have much time to dwell on the loss. There was a whole new version of English to learn – potato chips were crisps, French fries were chips, the trunk and hood of the car were the boot and bonnet. Not only was the vocabulary different; the pronunciations were, too. Instead of "zee," they pronounced the name of the letter Z "zed."

Wayne was one of the puppies born to Sidney and Phoebe.

They didn't drink milk, as we had at home, but hot tea with milk in it, or cold orange "squash," a sugary, artificially flavored soft drink.

One evening when I was 13 or 14, my father called my mom. He'd continued to live in the house on the outskirts of Coconut Grove, where Sidney and Phoebe had moved with us when I was 8. Transatlantic calls cost a fortune in the early '70s; there was no internet or email. Letters took a good week to arrive from the States, but they were our primary way to communicate with family across the globe. A phone call indicated something urgent. I was in the bedroom of the tiny flat in London where I lived with my mother after I left boarding school. I could tell from her reaction that the news was bad, and probably something as upsetting for our dad as it was likely to be for us.

"Is it Phoebe?" I cried, ready to lament her loss.

No. It was Sidney. He had died of kidney failure.

Impossible. How could the world continue to exist when I would never see Sidney again, never rub his tummy, scratch his neck or fit my chin against the curve between his snout and his forehead and give him a kiss? The thought of Phoebe dying was bad enough, but Sidney? Looking back with the perspective of another 50-odd years, I appreciate that Sidney's death ruptured one of our family's remaining bonds, leaving our father and Phoebe the lone survivors in our former home – at least, aside from the hippies who still lived there.

It was the card we had been dealt, so I did my best to honor Sidney with happy memories and concentrate on schoolwork, chores at home and trips to the ice rink with my friend Tina, followed by soft-serve cones from an ice cream truck in the park.

4: Binky (1971-1972)

THERE'S NOTHING like climbing into an old truck, settling down on the cracked vinyl upholstery and buckling yourself in with a good steel-on-steel *thunk* – even more so when there's a thin steering wheel, acres of dashboard and a bracing aromatic blend of shoe polish, pipe tobacco and leather, perhaps with a hint of fresh newspaper or wood-finish sample thrown in. In contrast with these nostalgic scents, my truck, even after years of mellowing, had a bitter stench that ensured I would never forget its backstory. I called my truck The Mousemobile.

Before I'd even paid off the loan, a pregnant mouse had made a nest somewhere under the hood and given birth to her offspring inside the labyrinth of hoses that made up the ventilation system. How the mice lost their lives is open to dispute. That they lost their lives is, however, undeniable, as was the resulting smell that filled the cab – a choking, acrid putrescence. When I first discovered it, I turned the truck off and got right back out. I was scheduled to teach a class at Kelly Mehler's School of Woodworking in Kentucky (now The Woodworking School at Pine Croft) in a couple of weeks and could not imagine surviving a four-hour drive, even with the windows wide open.

I took the truck to a radiator repair shop whose employees cleared out the remnants of the nest and sent me off with a heads-up that even if the smell abated, it would probably always be there. And so it was. With time, the smell gained the kind of familiarity that makes even once-unpleasant sensations feel like home. I came to appreciate that I couldn't climb into that truck without thinking about my friend Cathy's pet mouse, Binky, at boarding school in England, when Cathy and I were 12.

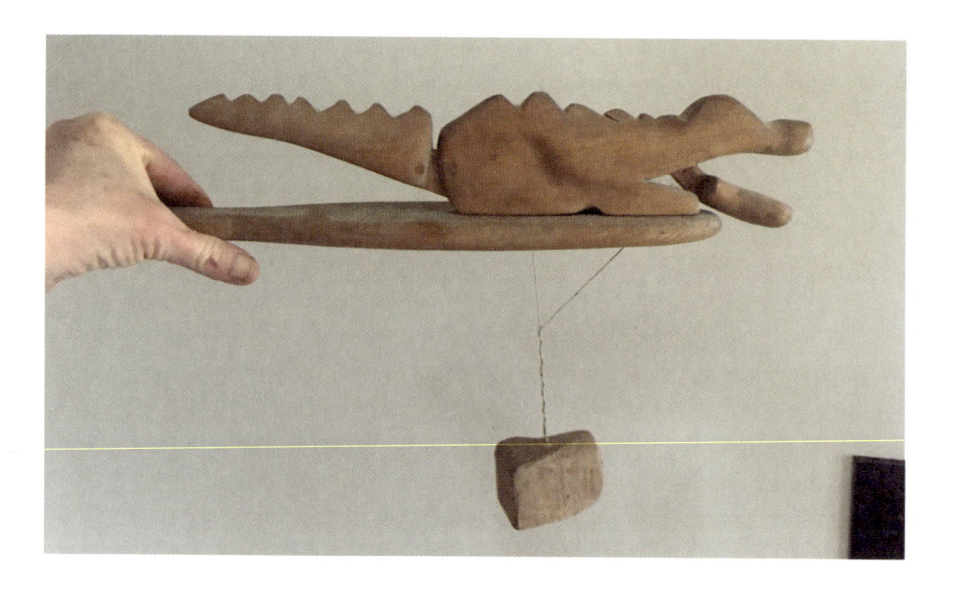

Not so fine woodworking. One of the projects in woodworking class at boarding school was to make a mechanical toy with working parts. I made an alligator (which looks more like a dog in some respects; I was 12). The wooden weight, which is attached to the jaw and tail by a string, makes the mouth snap and the tail go up and down when you move the toy back and forth.

In the early autumn of 1971, my mother sent Maggie and me to boarding school so she could begin to rebuild her life in London after splitting up with our dad. One of my fellow students was a Canadian girl, Cathy, who had a pet mouse. We became best friends based on our mutual recognition that, being from North America, we were outsiders, rougher around the edges than most of our fellow students. I was in awe of Cathy's abilities as a gymnast and her embrace of outdoor adventures.

Pets were not allowed at this school, so keeping Binky a secret presented challenges. At night Cathy put him in a small wire cage beneath her bed, where she fed him bits of rusk with peanut butter or bread crusts soggy with Heinz Sandwich Spread that she'd pocketed at teatime. But most of the time she carried him around in her coat pocket, pulling him out occasionally to kiss his nose or make a classmate shriek. Considering that this is all I remember about Binky, it's striking that he made an impression deep enough for the smell of my truck almost half a century later to summon him back.

On top of the usual academic subjects, our school required all students to take classes in woodworking and sewing. No mother should have to hem her grown son's trousers, and really, what good is a woman who can't turn a fallen limb into a matching salad bowl and tongs, given a sturdy workbench and a few carving tools? Most of the potholders and pencil bags I made in sewing class disappeared decades ago, but the projects from woodworking have stuck around. My parents still use the cheese board I carved from a block of apple wood, and a wooden alligator toy sits on my bookcase in front of volumes by Kant, Mumford and Hesse.

Those of us from out of town boarded at Brimstone Hostel, a smaller and slightly shabby version of the grand English houses made familiar to most Americans by Masterpiece Theatre. It was a sprawling structure of brick and stone with a steep roof and lots of gables, set amid rolled lawns fringed with ancient yews, oaks and beeches that had survived the cutting of the Ashdown Forest.

The house's layout was a perfect architectural expression of 19th-century British class structure, with a sharp divide between spaces for servants and well-appointed rooms for the owners' family. The kitchen, scullery, laundry, mudroom and larder were clustered at one end; these spaces were connected by a cramped, winding staircase to the house's top floor, where servants had originally slept. The public rooms, with their high ceilings, quartersawn oak floors and paneled walls, were at the opposite end. There, a wide staircase led from the spacious entry hall – ideal for holiday parties, when the kitchen staff filled tables with platters of marzipan-covered Christmas cake and mincemeat pies – up to the first floor, as it would be called in Britain (the second floor, in the States), which had several bedrooms that had once belonged to family and guests.

By the time we came along, the basis of Brimstone's interior organization had been switched from class to gender. It's one thing for boys to knit Shetland gloves and girls to cut spatula blanks on a band saw, but when you're running a school, teenage pregnancy's not good for business. The first-floor bedrooms were now dormitories for boys, with the hostel managers' rooms sufficiently close to detect any sign of nocturnal escape. The girls' dormitories were in the former servants' quarters on the top floor, accessible only by the dogleg stairs in back. Although I accepted this as just the way things were, I sensed an appropriateness to this banishment of girls from the comfort of spaces meant for family and guests; it paralleled much of what I was learning about gender relations in the early 1970s, when women were still widely seen as less valuable than men. Even several years later, when I had my first job at a cabinetmaker's shop at the age of 21, the occasional stranger would upbraid me for having "taken work away from a man" who might otherwise have been able to support himself and a family. (On what I earned, though? Not likely.) Many women still worked in the home or in service and secretarial jobs, the kind of positions that ads for shorthand courses encouraged urban bus riders to consider "exciting." There was a time when the interior of many a London bus featured posters reading "if u cn rd ths u cn train wth us and gt a grt jb!" *Well*, I thought without a shred of sarcasm as I rode those buses a few years later, *If nothing else works out, I can always take a shorthand course and get a job!* But overall, my take on our banishment to the Siberian ranges of the grand old house was that we were trustworthy and tough, while the boys were inclined to behavior that warranted closer oversight. This isn't an easy gender-biased jibe; some of the boys even bragged about how fun it was to do stuff that they themselves recognized as stupid and obnoxious.

Our floor had five bedrooms – four for students and one for Miss Mingeley, cousin of one of the hostel managers. An important part of her job was to keep watch over third-floor activities, particularly at night. There were two bathrooms on our floor, both of them above the servants' workrooms. One, a half-bath with a toilet and wall-hung basin, offered the only private place to use the loo. A large room adjacent to this was a full bath fit for an institution, with a row of basins and two or three toilet stalls with plenty of space above and below their doors to ensure full-volume transmission of every sound produced by your body.

Bath time at Brimstone Hostel. There was no shower, at least on the girls' floor.

The centerpiece of the room was a deep tub large enough for two. We were limited to one or two baths a week, shared with a fellow student according to a roster posted on the door. Bathing on other days involved a washcloth at a basin. I always wished I could have relayed word of this schedule to the woman who babysat my sister and me one night when we were little; when she announced it was bath time, I told her I wasn't dirty. "Do you want people to think you're a moron?" was her response. I had no idea what a moron was, but I was pretty sure I shouldn't care if people considered me one based on my disinclination to take a bath I didn't need. (Today I would respond with something about the role in health played by the human microbiome.)

The school made little impression on me academically, but what my time there lacked in scholastic rigor it made up for through an aesthetic awakening. It was my first introduction to nature, seasons and historic architecture. There were hazelnut trees and beetroot growing in the gardens, wild berries and potatoes on the walk to school.

For some time before my mother, Maggie and I moved to England, I'd been living with my dad and several families of hippies who built small structures around our half-acre yard. My sister had gone to live with our grandparents. I was no longer attending school; my father told the authorities I was being home-schooled, though that instruction had fizzled to nothing after a few weeks. My education consisted of learning life skills, philosophy and the fine points of pot culture from the people who shared our home, all on my own time, and reading books from the shelves in the dining room, among them a 20-volume set of the "World Book Encyclopedia" that our parents had bought as an investment in our education. By the age of 10 I was done with childhood. I figured I might as well bypass what was left of it, as well as the pointless confusion and weirdness of the middle-school years, and go straight to adulthood, if only in my own mind.

After this lack of boundaries during my family's hippie era, the tightly scheduled, orderly universe of the hostel, with its lists of clothing and other supplies we had to bring from home – "2 pairs black plimsolls [lightweight sneakers, in the States], 1 school cap or beret, 1 mackintosh, 2 flannels (with hanging loops)" – was healing balm.

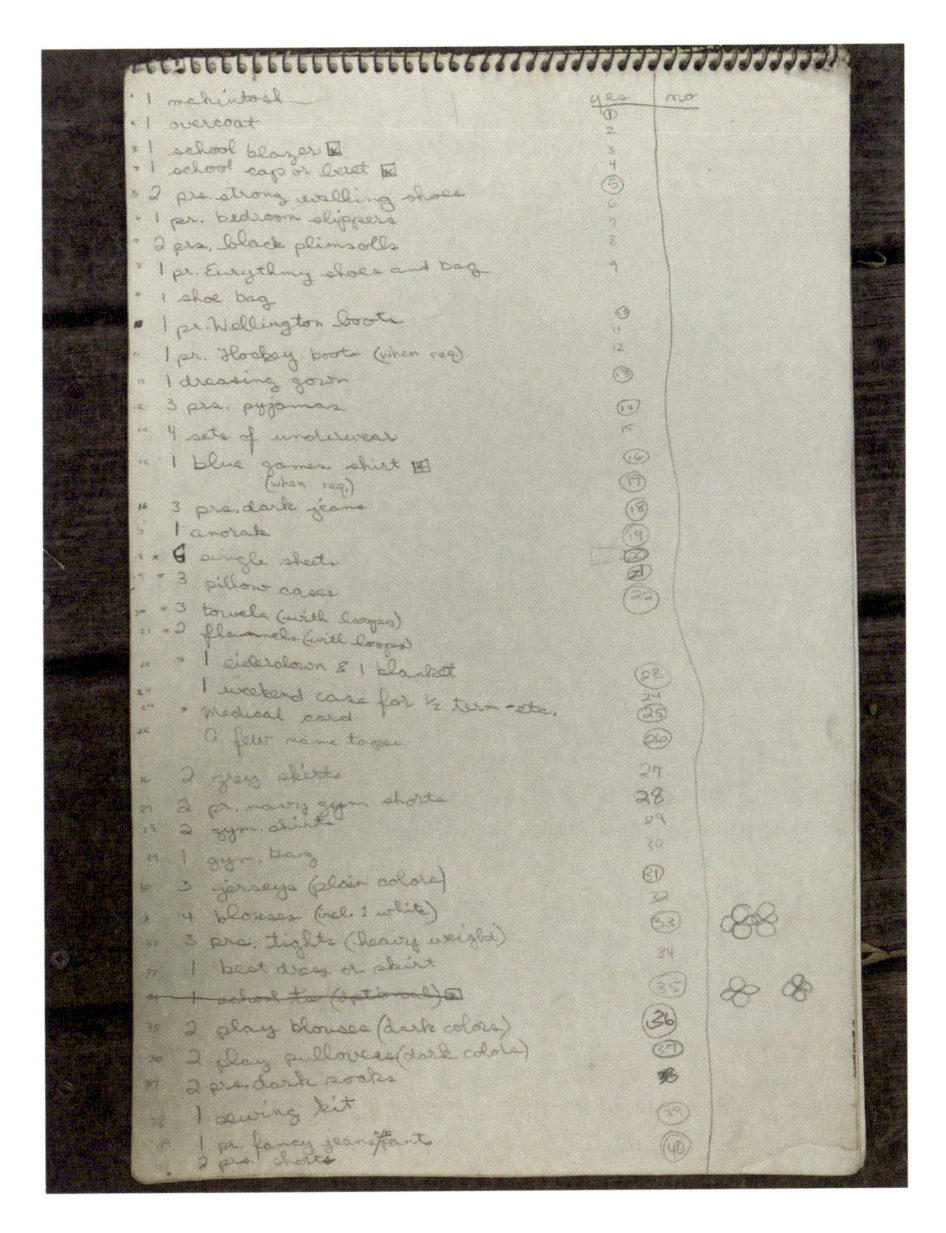

The list of clothes and linens we had to bring to boarding school in 1971.

The summer before we departed for East Grinstead on the analog-era train, with its perilous operable windows and pokey wool-upholstered horsehair seats, we had to go shopping with our mother to buy the 40 items on that list. Our mother hand-sewed cloth name tags onto everything, per instructions. One of the former servants' workrooms had been turned into a cloakroom for outdoor wear, with cubbies to store our shoes and rows of racks for coats. Each evening we brushed the mud off our shoes and polished them before putting them away. We also had daily chores – specific tasks such as washing the melamine dishes and silverware in scalding soapy water after teatime, then drying them with a towel; running soaked laundry through an old-fashioned mangle (a wringer, in the States) and hanging it to dry on long racks suspended from the ceiling; scrubbing the bathrooms; sweeping, then waxing, the dining room floor.

A married couple, Mr. and Mrs. Wallop, were in charge of running the hostel. Originally from Yorkshire, they had a dialect's-worth of colorful pronunciations and sayings. On weekday mornings, Mr. Wallop, pipe hanging from one side of his mouth, scared us awake by flipping on the lights and shouting "Wakey wakey, all the bodies!" Cling to your hot-water bottle a few seconds longer and he'd tear the blanket right off your bed. Only after everyone was standing did he move on to the next room. Once you were out from under the covers, you knew better than to delay getting dressed; the room was that close to freezing.

We stumbled downstairs to breakfast in the dining hall. The doorway from the main foyer opened onto a raised wood-floored expanse with a large fireplace, in front of which the staff arranged long tables to serve meals. For breakfast there were industrial canteens of tea; you filled your melamine mug, then served yourself cereal from a trough of Weetabix, Force flakes or raw rolled oats. Long wooden refectory tables held bowls of brown sugar and jugs of fresh milk from nearby farms; sometimes in winter, when farmers fed their cows turnips or swede (rutabaga, in the States), the milk was stomach-turning sour, but the Wallops encouraged us to see it as a lesson in the importance of seasonality and *terroir*. Every table also had trays of rusks (cubes of stale bread dried in the oven until their outsides were crisp but their insides were

The road from Brimstone Hostel to the A22 when I visited with my friend Bronwen in 2017 had changed little over the previous four decades.

still chewy) and jars of butter, peanut butter, chocolate spread, Heinz Sandwich Spread and jam.

Straight after loading our dishes into restaurant-size bins, we grabbed our satchels and left for morning classes. The school was a mile-and-a-half from the hostel. We walked there in all weather, and that journey, which we made four times a day – over to school after breakfast, then back to the hostel for lunch, the cycle repeated each afternoon – is one of my favorite memories. The route began on the back edge of the property, where a path led through a gate. Beyond a grassy stretch lay a narrow trail through the woods called the Snake Path. Thick ferns flourished in the canopied shade, becoming a sea of glowing green by midsummer. By late autumn the ferns dried to bracken, only to vanish and be reborn in tightly furled fiddleheads of chartreuse the following spring.

The Snake Path delivered us onto a lane that wound through a residential area on the outskirts of the nearest village, Forest Row. People heated their homes with coal-burning stoves that filled the street with a pungent smoke I grew to love. The road was barely paved; bits of loose gravel made it easy to slip and fall. It's still the same, a half-century later.

At the edge of the A22 highway we clambered up a steep bank and waited for a break in the two lanes of traffic speeding by. On the other side of the highway, the path wound through another small woods adjacent to a Bramley apple orchard with enormous, sour fruit. After school I often climbed the fence and picked a fallen apple out of the clumpy grass to eat on the way home.

After the orchard came the final stage of the journey, the cow path, a raised walkway of rough concrete through acres of pasture dotted with clusters of cows chewing their cud. It was there, one day when Cathy and I were making our way to school, that I stopped to admire the view. "Look at those clouds," I said dreamily. "It's a mackerel sky."

"You're simple," she replied. She rolled her eyes and reached into her coat pocket to give Binky a pat on the head. Apparently I couldn't even compete with a secret mouse.

Ask me to name a single main course at dinner (lunch, in the States) and I come up blank; the only one I recall is neck o' mutton stew, a foul-smelling, grease-speckled dish ladled from a vat. As a vegetarian, I was not obliged to eat it. I lived for pudding (dessert). After the Jell-O we'd grown up with – to be fair, our mom also made a mean crème brûlée – the puddings at Brimstone were a wonder. Most were served warm, with Bird's Custard, a pale-yellow sauce made by thickening sweetened milk with cornstarch colored and flavored to evoke memories of real custard made with eggs. (Real custard makes Bird's seem more like wallpaper paste.) There were warm puddings of rice and semolina served with jam, a rich steamed pudding with currants called Spotted Dick, chocolate pudding with chocolate sauce, and buttery crumbles of all kinds – apple and blackberry, apricot, rhubarb, gooseberry ("gooze-bree"). Best of all was the intense salty-caramel of treacle tart, a crust filled with golden syrup and breadcrumbs, again, served warm with custard.

Every mealtime Mrs. Wallop sat at the head of the longest table, a mountainous plate of food before her and Mr. Wallop at her side. She was a large woman – tall, and nearly as big around. Every day, no matter the season, she wore a thin cotton dress in a cottagey print topped with a cardi. Her feet strained the seams of her Oxfords, and beige support hose encased her calves. The butt of merciless jokes whispered behind her back, she insisted her size was due to a hormonal imbalance. "It's me glands," she'd say to anyone who dared ask. "I've seen docta afta docta, but there's nowt they c'n do about it."

Much of the fruit for crumbles came from industrial-size tins with gorgeous labels reproduced from original paintings of berries or plums. Such was the world of product label art before computer-aided design. But at least some of our fresh produce came from the cottage garden just outside the mudroom door. The garden, too, was a work of art, all neat rows of lettuce, herbs and onions with tidy borders. A kind older gentleman named Mr. Seeds (he was probably no older than 40 – in other words, ancient) looked after the garden. He lived in a tiny dwelling of just three rooms at the far end of the radish row. Mr. Seeds also doubled as a music teacher; many of us took recorder lessons in his front room, and some of us moved on to the cello. A cello may not be an animal, but I felt the cello ~~on which I scratched out ear-splitting~~

~~tunes~~ was almost alive; I held it between my legs, my body wrapped around it so the resonance filled my being. After the cacophony of recorders in the hands of first-year students, the cello's steady, whole-body vibration had a healing effect, bringing my emotions into a kind of harmony with the sights, smells and sounds of nature all around. I became a fan of Sir Edward Elgar and Ralph Vaughan Williams.

Saturday mornings were meant for more chores, a whole morning's-worth this time, unlike on weekdays. In autumn, I often signed up to rake the lawn. There was an international nuclear standoff going on around that time, and I convinced myself through some magical obsessive-compulsive thinking that as long as I got every single leaf off the section of lawn beneath the chestnut trees where we played conkers,[1] all would be well. I raked for a couple of hours, pulling the leaves into big piles, then loading them into a wheelbarrow and carting them away. But leaves kept twirling down; the breeze, too, posed a serious threat to world peace. With single-minded obsession, I raked until there was only the occasional leaf on the grass. I hung around another hour, removing every one by hand, then decided it was probably safe to stop. My plan worked. There was no nuclear attack.

After chores we collected whatever spending money our parents had sent us and walked down to the village to buy a quarter-pound of treats at the sweet shop. It was an old-fashioned sweet shop, the kind of place you could find all over England in the early '70s. Along one wall were shelves, filled floor-to-ceiling with commercial-size tins and jars of every sweet you could imagine, including Victory Vs and pear drops. The former, flavored with chloroform, had been a national favorite since the Second World War; the latter were flavored with something reminiscent of lacquer thinner and dyed the natural pear colors of neon pink and screaming yellow.

Once we'd stocked up, we were free the rest of the day. Cathy and I hiked for miles through the forest and over the downs. In winter, we'd hop down into brooks and wade in our Wellies, imagining ourselves explorers.

---

[1] Conkers is the name of a game played with chestnuts threaded onto a piece of string. A pair of players would knock their respective chestnuts together – hence, "conkers" – until one of the nuts broke open.

The old wooden doors, trim and furniture in our dorms were lovely enough to record in my sketch book.

The shelf-like banks were home to tiny creatures that scurried into holes away from our gaze. In the burbling water we'd spot the occasional fish or drowned plimsoll, and in summer we sometimes went skinny-dipping in a hidden pond, following our dip with a secret picnic of crusty bread and cheddar. Anything went, as long as we were back by 5.

Other students shared my best friend's view of me as a simpleton and taunted me by refusing to share an object they had fetishized, The Black Book. Getting your period qualified you to see The Black Book, which one of the girls had spirited out of her parents' bedroom. It was small, and she kept it wrapped in a white cloth, like a sacred artifact. "Why can't I see the book?" I'd ask, over and over.

"Because you haven't got your period yet," they'd answer, rolling their eyes because the reason should have been obvious.

"But everyone else gets to see it," I'd object. This went on for weeks, until at last I'd worn the owner down.

"OK then, here you go." She unwrapped it carefully, insisting on keeping it in her hands – no one was going to take away her prize. She flipped to a page and I saw a naked man on his knees having sex doggy-style with an equally naked woman. There was no expression on either face. It was like, "OK, take the picture. We're just doing this for the money." The photos were all in black and white. She turned to another page; this time the man and woman were theoretically having oral sex, still with no expression on either face. After years of photo shoots with Anissa Kapsales for *Fine Woodworking*, it occurs to me that the models' lack of expression may have had nothing to do with the gig being done for money. Instead, it may have been comparable to a multi-day photo shoot: First thing in the morning on Day Two your editor asks you to take off your clothes and put on the ones you wore the day before, so readers will focus on the important information, not the changes in clothing. Similarly, I suppose you might not want to distract "readers" of The Black Book from the really important information about sexual positions by having them show any sign of pleasure, interest or affection. Either way, I found the book a letdown – pretty weird and boring stuff.

My sister, Maggie, and her two best friends, Susie and Karen, were constantly playing pranks and getting in trouble. One day when I walked into their dormitory room, Karen and Maggie, barely able to contain their excitement, whispered "Come here!" From under her bed Maggie pulled a large pillowcase stuffed like the midsection of a pregnant sheep. "Look what we got!" she exclaimed. The pillowcase was full of candy.

"Where did you get that?" I asked.

"We stole it from the golf course sweet shop!" Karen said. I was mortified on their behalf. Not long after this, the owner of the sweet shop on the golf course banned all students at the hostel from his establishment.

Susie, middle sister to Anne and their baby brother, Jonathan, always struck me as exuberantly alive, with warm blonde hair, skin like Jersey cream and an athletic build. Her parents ran a dairy farm, which seemed appropriate – what better representative could a dairy farm have than someone of Susie's wholesome good looks?

Susie, Karen and Maggie got up to all sorts of naughtiness. They'd sneak down the back stairs to the pantry for what they called a midnight feast, pulling blocks of raw jelly (pre-reconstituted English gelatin) molded like a thick bar of chocolate out of the carton and savoring its chewy sweetness in the tiny space lit by a single bare bulb. Once, they braced themselves at the top of the servants' stairs with a fire extinguisher and sprayed anyone foolish enough to come up.

Not surprisingly, the invisible shield between boys' and girls' quarters was less than 100 percent impermeable, and Jonathan (Susie's younger brother) developed a habit of sneaking upstairs on a regular basis for a bedtime cuddle with Jane, whose dormitory room I shared. Most nights they cooed ridiculously at each other, seemingly oblivious to the rest of us, but one night I overheard him bragging about having stolen a neighbor's bike. Imagine waking up to find your bike gone. Awful. I had to tell someone who could return the neighbor's bike.

I chose Miss Mingeley, the most approachable of the authority figures. I found her striding up a darkened hallway in a mauve cardigan and gray wool skirt, just enough skin visible above her knee-high socks to reveal a few dark hairs.

"Miss Mingeley?" I whispered. "I need to tell you something serious. You must promise not to tell *anyone* who gave you this information."

"Fair enough," she barked with an impatient look. She was a woman of few words.

"Come in here," I whispered, leading her into a nearby broom closet. I could only share my secret in complete privacy and darkness. Without turning on the light, I closed the door. "I overheard Jonathan telling someone that he stole a bicycle from one of the neighbors."

"Well, thank you for informing me, Nancy," she said. "You've done the right thing."

"Remember, don't tell *anyone* you heard it from me," I pleaded as she left. I waited in the darkened broom closet a few minutes longer to make sure no passing student would spot the two of us together. I prayed that Jonathan would never find out who'd told on him.

The next day was like all the others until teatime. "Miss Mingeley has passed on an important bit of news," read Mrs. Wallop from her prepared notes. "Nancy Hiller has informed us that Jonathan stole a bicycle from one of our neighbors."

That was the beginning of the end of my time at boarding school. I was devastated by the betrayal and no longer trusted anyone, thief or authority figure. Even though Jonathan made a point of telling me a few days later that he thought I had done the right thing (he even said he respected me for it), the suspicious and critical looks I now got from other students convinced me that most of my fellow students at the hostel saw me as a snitch. True, I'd told on Jonathan. But I had done so because I wanted to uphold the greater good, not improve my standing with those in charge. No one should have their bike stolen; Jonathan had to return the bike, with an apology. Reporting this crime took a lot of courage, even if I had insisted Miss Mingeley join me in the closet in the dark.

The next time I went home I collapsed, weeping, on the floor of the front room, begging my mother to let me live with her and go to school in London. Fortunately, she did; I began taking classes at Ms. Hunting-Badcocke's educational establishment at the start of 1973.

Maggie in the garden at Brimstone Hostel.

5: David (1973-1975, approximately)

"I AM not going to the park with that guinea pig," said my grandmother. This was Esse, my mother's mother, who visited us often when we lived in London, eager for any chance to spend time in a cosmopolitan city with great restaurants, museums and parks. My sister and I adored this grandma; she and our grandfather had lived less than an hour away when we were younger, so we'd spent a lot of time with them when we were kids.

Esse had grown up in a small town in New Jersey, the fifth of six children born to Lithuanian immigrants. She wanted to study art at college, but when her father said no to anything other than the practical subjects of nursing or teaching, she went straight to work instead. As young women, she and her sister, Elizabeth, ran a tea shop; after she married our grandfather, she took care of the bookkeeping at his hotels. But having seen her own artistic dreams thwarted, she had special appreciation for art and craft of all kinds and cheered on the women in her life who earned advanced degrees or other kinds of training, then went on to pursue a career.

We were always giddy at the prospect of her visits and counted down the days to her arrival. Just being in her presence was a joy – she paid attention to us and seemed to appreciate us as people, and she always smelled like her perfume, Yves Saint Laurent Rive Gauche. What's more, she had a slightly naughty sense of fun. When we approached the border crossing between Switzerland and France on the trip through Europe that delivered us to London, we had to use up our remaining Swiss francs. "Let's spend them all on chocolate!" my sister and I screamed. She was in. We pooled our coins and bought pounds of bars, Lindt and Suchard, in every flavor.

Four generations. From left to right: Esse, my mother, me (in lap) and my maternal great-grandmother, Flora Rau.

Esse had always appreciated my affinity for animals, even if she didn't exactly share it. So when, on that rare sunny day, as the fine grass at Hyde Park was greening into springtime clumps, I suggested we take my guinea pig to make our trip to the park *even better*, she would have none of it. "He'll get out of the cage and get lost, and you'll be devastated," she insisted. She was probably right, but my heart was set on taking him. *"Please!"* I begged. "It will be so much more fun if we take him. Think of how much he'll enjoy the grass and the sun. He's inside all the time."

"You can take him and go without me, or go without him," she said. And that was that.

DAVID (1973-1975, APPROXIMATELY)

***

After I left boarding school, my mother and I lived in a tiny flat my grandparents had bought when we arrived in London. The building had a resident caretaker, Millie. She and her husband, Jim, lived in the basement; their living room had a window overlooking the brick-paved mews at the back. Millie always wore a work apron over her dress. I don't know whether she and Jim had kids of their own, but she was always happy to have us visit. At Christmas we exchanged cookies and small gifts. Their flat was cold and sparely furnished, with a concrete floor covered in a 1970s version of vinyl composition tile or something equally austere.

Even when I was still at boarding school, I came home on the occasional weekend to see my mother. Sometimes she met me at Victoria Station and we rode the bus to Marble Arch; she'd bring her latest project from art school to show me on the ride. One time it was a hand-size carving of a twin apple seed carved in wood. I was fascinated by her description of the processes involved. The apple seed was perfect – deliciously smooth, a pleasure to hold and stroke. It took me a while to realize that it also doubled as a very good likeness of a pair of testicles. Another favorite among my mother's works was a series of winter trees she made in wire, each an unmistakable model of the species it represented. I was amazed by her skill at observing natural forms, then giving them 3D expression.

But on this particular winter day I was coming home from Victoria Station by myself. I had to pee when I got off the train, but I didn't want to spend the penny to go to the station loo. I decided to wait until I got home. I got on the bus and sat down, crossing my legs more tightly as the drive went on. When I got off at our stop, I slung my satchel over my shoulder and ran to our front steps, which led up to a locked door with a small foyer beyond. I pressed the buzzer, hoping that Millie would come upstairs to the ground floor and let me in. No answer. I tried again. Still no response. Things were getting desperate. My mother was still at art school. I sat down on the stone railing, hoping I could make it until someone showed up. But after about five minutes my body said *Enough!* and I felt a swelling warmth envelop my backside, soaking through my duffle coat. What was I going to say to whoever came to let me in? I was 13, not a baby who wet her pants. When Millie unlocked the door, I was ready with a story. "I went to the loo at the station, and the strangest thing happened! When I pulled the chain" – toilets in those days had a cistern hung high on the wall to ensure that no turd or diaper-size sanitary napkin would be left behind – "it leaked all over my back." She didn't say a word.

***

My mother and I got David at a pet store. I have no idea where there would have been a pet store that sold guinea pigs in that part of West London – perhaps on the Edgeware Road, home to a wide variety of establishments in the early '70s, from the hole-in-the-wall luggage store where we bought our boarding school trunks to sandwich shops like the branch of the ABC Bakery where, later, at the age of 16, I would have a summer job. In that role I was grunt to the head prep cook, Hilda, a dour middle-aged lady who wore a hairnet and shouted orders. "After you boil them eggs put the pot in the basin and let the cold water run over it for 10 minutes, then peel and slice them," or "Cut open one o' them rolls and cover it with margarine. Don't skimp on the marge; the customers love it. Lay out three leaves of lettuce, then the eggs on top and finish it up with three bits o' tomahto." I walked to the bakery at dawn, varying my route through leafy streets of terraced houses built around gated parks with elaborate iron fences, but at work there was no time for such niceties. There was little love lost between Hilda and the Egyptians who owned the store, to whom she referred as "Ali and that lot," pronouncing his name "Alley." She did her job with a heavy chip on her shoulder, resentful of "them foreigners" who were turning her hometown into a sophisticated international city.

But buy David we did, along with a small cage, food bowl and water bottle with a small metal tube for him to sip at. We lined the bottom with paper and sawdust and were ready for action. He was

DAVID (1973-1975, APPROXIMATELY)

David was a friend, even though our relationship was different from those I had with dogs and cats.

small enough to hold in my hands and had a sleek black coat. He was also very loud. As we soon learned, volume was his superpower. His "SQUEAK! SQUEAK!" was just below the level where it might have broken glass, and grew in its insistence as his frustration mounted. *FEED ME! NOW! OR SO HELP ME GOD, I WILL MAKE YOUR LIFE HELL.*

I adored him. I'd take him out of his cage and just hold him against my chest, peppering him with kisses and stroking his fur. He rewarded me with nuzzles and soft sounds, sometimes falling asleep in my arms. He was like a small teddy bear brought to life – someone warm and interactive I could care for. Other girls had dolls with fashionable wardrobes and lifestyle accessories designed to train them in the ways of consumption: Ride a bike in your work clothes? Perish the thought. Bicycle riding meant dressing in pink or aqua spandex. Going out to dinner after school? Don't even think about dining out in your day clothes; going out required dressing up. Some of my schoolmates had an outfit for every conceivable activity (though I'm pretty sure none had a fashion-conscious outfit for cleaning other people's flats, one of my vacation jobs starting at the age of 15). In place of dolls with extensive wardrobes, I had a miniature pig who pooped in my lap. David was the ideal companion for a girl of 13 who was a loner and lived with her mother in a tiny urban *pied-a-terre*. He was also my muse; I loved to draw him.

Sometimes after school I went downstairs and knocked on Millie's door, David and his little cage in hand. She and Jim were tickled by him. "'E's ever so sweet!" she'd say in her East End accent.

One day she told us Jim had cancer – "cansa," she pronounced it. I can't remember what kind it was, but she decided it was time to buy Jim a guinea pig of his own as a companion. Theirs was a female with long hair. They adored her.

Not long after, we moved to a bigger flat because my sister was going to leave boarding school and join us in London. Our tiny one-bedroom was already cramped with my mother and me; a third person would be too much. Our new place was in the basement of another terraced house, this one near Paddington Station. The multi-story house had

DAVID (1973-1975, APPROXIMATELY) 93

All Greek to me. Combine a pet guinea pig with a love of drawing and languages (preferably so-called dead ones) and you may end up with something bizarre. After a few decades I've forgotten most of the Greek, so I asked retired classics professor Betty Rose Nagle to translate. "Dr. David's house. Figure on left: 'Woe! Woe! I wanna eat! (I strongly desire to eat). Upper right figure: 'Doctor, you need to stop eating.' Lower figure: 'Doctor, come close so you can help me.'"

> have finished my ...
> Millie and Jim returned from
> their holiday in Hastings. They
> brought a stick of pink rock for
> Maggie and I and a cute cloth with
> little cat designs on it for Mom. Jim
> was extremely disappointed to see
> that Arthur was pregnant and his
> first thought was to the purpose of a
> new name. First came Josephine,
> then Anita and Annabella, then the
> sensational Anna. So now we have
> Anna and they have Anne! Theirs
> is due to have babies any day now.
> Monday

Arthur becomes Anne. Entry in my diary on June 24, 1973.

originally belonged to a wealthy family; the basement had been their servants' quarters. Just as we had on the top floor at boarding school, we felt right at home. A property developer had redone all the houses on the street, turning each story into a self-contained apartment. Ours had a set of spindly metal steps from the parking area down to our front door. By the door there was a small tiled patio open to the sky where my mother planted wisteria, hoping it would grow up the railing and reward us with blooms.

Our kitchen window, which saw many a jam-packed party once my mother began seeing the man who would eventually become our stepfather, looked out on the wisteria-decked stairs; you had to crane your neck to see a bit of sky above the plane trees across the parking lot where our mother kept the Citroën 2CV that she bought shortly after we moved to this apartment.[1] The building had been constructed around an open space at the center, which gave us natural light and a view of white-painted brick walls from the living room and both bedrooms. One perk of being in the basement was that we had a patio we could reach through a door in the hallway between the front and back of the house, a decent place for David to go outside, even if there wasn't any grass.

I kept his cage in that hallway, by the patio door. It was the perfect spot to amplify his squeaking. Shortly after we moved there we got him a companion, a long-haired guinea pig we called Anna. They even mated and had a pair of babies, but the babies died right away.

I can't remember when David died. Anna went first, which I thought was sad for David, but I didn't care as much about her. Then one day David was just lying on the floor of his cage, gone.

Such a strange and dear person he'd been – so unlike a dog, let alone a member of our own species. He ate. He slept. He rooted around in the sawdust we bought for his cage. What a sterile life he had, bred in captivity, deprived of opportunities to forage and feed, to mate in the wild and go about the other kinds of business that mattered to a guinea pig. It took a while to get used to the quiet.

---

[1] Plane trees are known as sycamores in the States.

6: Oscar (1980-1993)

WHENEVER SOMEONE at Farmstead Furniture asked what type of dog Oscar was, my boss replied "a Hearthrugger." He was a large black dog with wavy hair that gave his lanky frame the appearance of at least 50 percent more than his highest-ever weight of 45 pounds. Spread out on the floor, he bore a striking resemblance to a sumptuous long-haired animal skin rug, the kind that lends a primal edge to a crackling log fire, leaving you all the cozier for knowing that you are not on a patch of frozen ground beneath the stars.

I was able to take Oscar with me to work at Farmstead because at 27, I had finally earned my driver's license. I bought a used Ford Escort van through a classified ad in the local newspaper. For years, I had resisted the pressure to learn how to drive, daunted by a vehicle's potential to kill. Many of my school friends in London had learned to drive at 17, an age when I wondered why I should learn to drive when public transportation was so readily available, not to mention that there was no way I'd be able to afford a car in the foreseeable future. Instead, I decided to let circumstances dictate when it was my time to learn to drive, and even considered going my entire life without driving a car, as Grandma Stepha had.

My resistance to driving lasted well after I left London. When I was 19, my boyfriend, Patrick, and I moved to the burg of Friday Bridge in Cambridgeshire, where my mother and stepfather had bought an old schoolhouse that came with an attached cottage, the former schoolmaster's home. We moved into the simple brick cottage – two rooms upstairs, two rooms downstairs – and my stepfather built a small addition for a kitchen and bathroom. I got a job at a metal-casting factory that

We sometimes dressed Alistair in our clothes. He was exceptionally obliging.

summer and rode my bike to work. After signing up for City & Guilds furniture-making classes at the community college in Wisbech, four miles away, I rode my bike to and from school in all weather. I did the same at my first cabinetmaking job, when I went to work for Raymond Green shortly after my City & Guilds training.

When I started work at Farmstead in 1986, a few years after that first cabinetmaking job, Oscar and I were living in a row house in Cambridge with three strangers. Two of my fellow tenants, Mel and Paul, quickly became friends. By this time Patrick and I had married, then divorced.

Each day I rode my bike to the train station, put it in the baggage car and rattled along until we reached the country station closest to the workshop, then retrieved the bike and rode the rest of the way. Anyone who lived in England in the mid-1980s will know that back then, sunny days were few and far between. No matter the season, most days were chilly, beneath an overcast sky – character-forming, and it certainly made the occasional sunny day all the more worthy of wonder. Riding a 10-speed bicycle through the dark in lashing December rain only to wait on the wind-swept platform for the train back to Cambridge did nothing to bolster my spirits. It was finally time to learn how to drive.

I inquired with a driving school and found a teacher who would cram the instruction into a single week. Now I just had to arrange for time off from work. My bosses wouldn't give me a week off but agreed to let me take driving lessons for half of each weekday, so that's what I did. I'd heard stories about the difficulty of passing the driving test on the first try. I really needed to get this thing done, so I took every chance to practice. And it wasn't as though I had to force myself; I found I loved the process of driving, the way I could turn my will to go from A to B into action through a gear stick, steering wheel and pedals. (Nearly all English vehicles back then came with manual transmission.) The car became an extension of my body. To my relief, I passed the test on the first try.

Now I could take Oscar with me to work instead of leaving him in my room at home. A few years old and safely beyond the destructiveness of puppyhood, Oscar was well-behaved. He stayed by my bench most of the day while I worked, leaving briefly at lunchtime to hunt for dropped bits of ham sandwich or breadcrumbs off a fellow worker's Scotch egg.

He was the best kind of dog – affectionate, loyal, attentive. He loved to chase a ball but was equally glad to take off across a Fenland field in pursuit of a jet from the nearby Royal Air Force base. As a pup he'd been endlessly curious. He loved to snuggle and play. When thwarted, his need for attention occasionally turned to damage, as when he pulled the copy of Ernest Joyce's "The Technique of Furniture Making" that I had borrowed from the Isle of Ely College library off the bookcase at home and tore its 495 pages into a paper puzzle, wolfing down a chunk of the spine and chewing the top right inch and a half of the clothbound cover. Aside from making me pay for a replacement copy, the people at the library wanted me to return the original. I persuaded them to let me keep it and spent hours piecing the pages back together with cellotape that has since turned yellow-brown.

Oscar and I were together for 13 years. Then I let him go in a moment I will always regret. What follows is his story.

***

In the summer of 1980, several years before I worked at Farmstead, I was close to completing my coursework in furniture making, when our neighbor's red setter, Sherry, gave birth to a litter of pups. My mother's bearded collie, Alistair, was the father; he'd escaped from the backyard of their house in Friday Bridge and run across the road when Sherry was in heat. Alistair wasn't alone in wandering the 'hood; a compact, light-brown, smooth-coated dog named Sniffer was quite the lad and likely had many a litter to his name. But there was little doubt these had come from Alistair – the doghouse was squirming with red and black puppies, not a brown or smooth-haired one among them.

We hadn't had a dog since Sidney and Phoebe. Now that I was an adult and nearly finished with my training, I longed for a dog of my own. I felt a sense of obligation to our neighbor, given that my mother's

Mel Larsen in front of the house we shared on Vinery Road in Cambridge around 1986.

Esse with Alistair in the living room of the old schoolhouse in Friday Bridge, where my mother and stepfather lived. In the background at right is a wooden sculpture of my mother's; at the left is one of her wire trees.

dog was responsible for the pups. They spilled out in a clambering mass, falling over each other to meet the visitor. A few moments later, a tiny black face with intense brown eyes and a rumpled moustache poked out, peering around to assess conditions. That was my dog: the loner, the shy boy, the cautious one. I reached inside the opening and pulled him out the rest of the way.

Oscar loved to run. Unfortunately, I did not know how to train him. I had an ordinary collar and lead, not the kind that would have discouraged a dog from pulling; he would lean so hard into our path that I could scarcely contain him. It was exasperating. I yanked his leash angrily, too ignorant to know how ineffective (not to mention dangerous) my correction might be.

Patrick and I were married in 1981. By then, we were both working for my first cabinetmaking boss, Raymond Green, building kitchens in a frigid old horse-stable-turned-workshop. A couple of years later, we moved to the industrial town of Reading. By then I was ready for a change – not just a new location, but a new line of work. Although I'd learned a lot from Raymond about the business of cabinetmaking, as well as new techniques, I felt emotionally and physically beaten down by my two-plus years of professional woodworking. The work had become depressingly monotonous and repetitive. I wanted to make a living in a more social setting, ideally an office.

At first we stayed with Patrick's mother at her council flat in Bracknell, on Reading's outskirts. She doted on Oscar and spoiled him like a grandson. She always had a box of Good Boy Choc Drops on hand, and after a few tries, loved to take him out for walks. He slept in the guest room with us and stayed home with her while we looked for work.

I'd answered an ad for a clerk position in the travel office at the students' union of Reading University. What clinched the hire was my happy guess at the capital of Yugoslavia, as it was then known: Belgrade. I could not believe my luck in getting the job; I would be working in an office with several women, all of us under 35. The office was not in a freezing barn, but a comfortable building. The position involved selling tickets to professors who were going on book tours around the United States and agricultural students flying home to Dakar or Denpasar. Those were the days of hand-written airline tickets on paper and bookings made over the phone. There was a lot to learn, and I found all of it a welcome challenge.

My mother's mother, Esse, had always said she wanted to help me buy a house and make a home. Reading looked and felt like home, so one day I made a very expensive transatlantic collect call from a pay phone and asked if she would help us buy a row house about a mile-and-a-half from the office where I worked. A basic two-up, two-down with a tiny kitchen and bath in a lean-to addition at the back, the house was one away from the precipice at the end of Edgehill Street, which was aptly named. The neighborhood was still decidedly working class, so it was affordable, even to people like us who made close to minimum wage. I comforted myself with the observation that the house at the end would go over the hill before ours did. Esse was ill with pancreatic cancer at the time, so my grandfather flew over by himself to look at the house, gave us the down payment (around £5,000) and co-signed for the loan. I was ecstatic and have never stopped being grateful for that help.

Each morning I got up early and took Oscar for a long walk, then had breakfast and walked to work. Sometimes I took him with me. My co-workers loved him, and Bronwen, especially, always made a fuss over him. Oscar couldn't get enough. A few years later Patrick and I moved to the old cathedral town of Saffron Walden in Essex, where our marriage fell apart. There, Gregor, a classmate during our training as furniture makers, took over from Bronwen as Oscar's favorite friend. He took Oscar for walks to Audley End Park and sneaked him the odd treat from the fish and chip shop. Gregor would occasionally drive over in his jeep and pick us up. One day he parked the jeep in front of the house where Patrick and I had lived and Oscar refused to get out. He sat there, eyes forward, as if to say *You can't make me get out. There has been too much disruption of late, and I'm staying put. I'm going wherever you go.*

I moved back to the States in the summer of 1987. My sister had moved back several years before, and my mother and stepfather had followed; they were living in the house where we'd lived with our

With his black leather nose and beautiful eyes, Oscar reminded me of the puppies that often appeared on boxes of chocolates in England in the early 1980s.

father before our family split up. It would make an ideal place to land and make a plan.

I'd visited New England the previous winter. I knew I wanted to be in the Northeast – if I had to leave England, it would be for a part of North America that looked and felt as close to England as I could find. I'd rented a car on that trip and first explored the Hudson Valley, then gone as far as western Massachusetts, where, after a long expanse of no towns, I came upon what appeared to be a semi-abandoned industrial town, North Adams, which had had a thriving mill industry thanks to its location on the Hoosic River but now seemed more like a beautiful mirage full of 19th-century houses with turrets, fretwork and other elaborate architectural details. I might not have a particular place in mind, not to mention a job, but New England would be my general destination.

I sold some of my possessions, gave a lot of others away, then had the rest shipped with a moving company, to be held at the Port of New York until I had a place to live. My friend Edward was going to America with me.

After putting Oscar in the officially mandated crate, I said goodbye at Heathrow, praying he would survive the eight-hour flight in the hold.

At Miami International Airport, Edward and I went through baggage claim and customs. I spotted Oscar across the hall. No sooner had he glimpsed me than he let out a heartbreaking, groggy howl, still under the influence of the sedative he'd had for the ride. But the most rewarding reunion came when my mother picked us up and took us home. She and my stepfather still had Alistair, Oscar's father; they'd brought him when they moved from England. When the two dogs saw each other for the first time in years, they sniffed each other tentatively. Then, all of a sudden, there was a frenzy of perked-up ears and wagging tails. It was enough to bring tears to my eyes.

I bought a used two-door Ford Escort car, and after several days, Edward and I set off with Oscar on the drive north. We stayed in motels that allowed dogs, and finally stopped in South Hadley, just outside of Amherst, Massachusetts, where I signed a lease for a one-bedroom apartment on the second floor of a house. Edward

OSCAR (1980-1993)

My mother with her German shepherd, Zak, and Oscar.

found a job in Worcester and moved there. I applied for office jobs but was turned down for every one. While looking through job ads in a local paper I came across one for furniture makers at a business in Vermont. By this time I'd had my fill of rejection; perhaps I should give my own trade another chance, instead of trying to fit my square peg into another round hole. I called. The people seemed genuinely nice. We set up a meeting.

I drove up with Oscar for a visit. The company had arranged for me to stay at a bed-and-breakfast. Before the interview I was so nervous

Kent and Oscar on a hike we took with a couple of friends up Mount Abraham in Vermont. I tore the ligaments in one of my knees after slipping on ice as we went back down; as a result I had to work in the shop on crutches for a couple of weeks. I didn't have surgery to repair the tear because I had no medical insurance and couldn't afford it, let alone time off work. The knee healed and has worked fine, if not perfectly, in the 34 years since.

that I bought a package of cookies and ate the entire box, diverting a few from my mouth to Oscar's. It was comforting to have an ally on this journey away from a home that was not yet home.

I took the job gratefully when they offered. Oscar and I moved to Montpelier, Vermont, the closest sizable town to the shop, where I rented a small apartment in a depressing house with stained shag carpet and fake wood paneling on the walls. Oscar and I were together. We would make it work.

Again, I got up early each morning and walked Oscar before driving to the shop. I'd never had to leave him alone for so long, but he was fine as long as I took him out right away when I got home. On one of our walks I noticed a For Rent sign in the window of a turn-of-the-century Queen Anne up the road; it was a one-bedroom apartment on the top floor, reached by an exterior staircase. Just inside the door was another staircase up to what would be my apartment. The place was charming, with lots of original architectural details: a tiny room inside the turret, which was all windows; a large bedroom; a light-filled kitchen and bath. The description said "No Pets," but I brought Oscar to the meeting and asked whether the landlady might consider making an exception. He jumped out of the car with a wag and sat obediently at her feet, gazing into her eyes. "*This* dog..." she said, "*this* dog can stay." I bailed on the funky apartment up the road and let the landlord keep my deposit. It was worth it to live in a place that felt more like home.

Here, too, I took Oscar for a walk each morning in the dark before work. Winter came, and along with it, feet of snow. We had never seen such snow or felt such cold; going out first thing in the morning with the temperature at minus 20 literally took your breath away.

I saw my landlady one afternoon a few months in and asked whether the tenant downstairs had complained about Oscar on days when he was alone. Had he barked at postal workers? Howled in loneliness? "Not at all," she replied. "The only sound they've heard has been Oscar dropping a ball."

Shortly after I went to work at the company in Vermont, I met another new hire, Kent. We were the first to arrive in the morning, and before long we were seeing each other outside of work. Kent and Oscar loved each other right away. Kent took us hiking every weekend up mountains, or to searingly blue lakes. We'd take a picnic lunch and share it with Oscar, who ran up and down the trail, covering at least twice our ground. Kent had moved to Vermont from Missoula, Montana, where he'd done his furniture training at the (now-defunct) Primrose Center for Fine Woodworking and Design. The move had not been entirely to his liking. The people in Vermont were less friendly, he said, and there were so many more of them. "I used to be able to pick my nose while driving my truck without passing anoth-

Oscar loved to wade or chase balls and sticks in the shallow, clear-flowing streams on the outskirts of Missoula.

er car," he'd complain in jest. He also resented the locals who called him a "flatlander"; little did they know he'd come from the land of real mountains. But what rankled him most was the nature of the work. He'd answered an ad in *Fine Woodworking*, only to find himself building furniture with biscuits and screws in place of the hand-cut joinery he'd learned in his training. Granted, the visible parts of each piece were made with striking architectural veneers and hand-rubbed finishes, but for Kent the work remained a disappointment. The business owners had not misled him; he just hadn't fully understood what his daily reality at work was going to be.

   Kent was ready to leave after several months. I didn't want to lose him, though I was happy enough in Vermont and in the job. It was the first woodworking job where I worked with like-minded people. The days were long – we started at 7 a.m. and quit at 5 p.m., with an hour for lunch. In winter it was dark when we arrived in the morning, and again when we left at night. But the people were great. The managers and owners of the business wanted their employees to be happy and fostered a good working environment with a gender-inclusive culture. The shop was in an old factory with plenty of natural light – and heat in the cold seasons. The long days were part of a plan to give everyone a three-day weekend every other week and a half-day on alternate Fridays. They gave everyone, even new hires, a Christmas bonus. Had we stayed, we would have been eligible for a growing number of benefits including health insurance and paid vacation time, none of which I had ever received in a woodworking job.

I loved living in Vermont, and Montpelier, in particular. It was a small New England town with old buildings, a thriving main street, the Winooski River and several parks. I also felt a strong affinity with the townspeople for their ban on billboards and their determination to preserve their oddball status as a state capital without an interstate highway.

At Christmas I flew to Indianapolis with Kent to meet his family. Other than Vermont, I had never been to a state without a coast on the Atlantic. Kent's parents picked us up at the airport and drove us south to their daughter's home outside Nashville, Indiana, a historic artists' colony that, over the years, had traded its history with fine arts and traditional crafts into a vanilla-candle-scented movie set of old-timey shops selling trinkets, many of them made overseas. Most of the drive south from the airport was on I-65, where semi-size billboards advertised personal injury attorneys, HVAC contractors and "gentlemen's clubs." *Thank God I don't live here*, I thought from the back seat of the car.

But it was a good visit. Meeting Kent's parents gave me new insights into his background and character. His parents lived on a large suburban lot near Indianapolis. His mother, Jill, was a prolific and skillful crafter who sewed quilts, mended clothes, painted the most covetable Pysanky (Russian-style Easter eggs) I had ever seen and tended acres of flower beds. She had grown up in Wisconsin, where her father, Calvin Stott, was the kind of forester and naturalist who appreciated the woods for more than their instrumental value to industry. Inspired by his perspective, Jill had become a passionate activist and opponent of the rampant development that was rapidly turning premium arable land into subdivisions and corporate office parks. We spent a couple of cozy days with Kent's sister and her family, cooking, hiking and eating a variety of food that ranged from raclette to jambalaya.

Kent was going to stay the whole week, but I had to get back to work; I couldn't afford to take more than the minimum time off. My flight to Burlington, the closest major airport to Montpelier, left Indianapolis in the evening; I didn't get back to my apartment until the wee hours of the following morning, which was a work day. Oscar was still at a kennel, so I went straight to bed, setting my alarm for the usual time, 5:20 a.m.

The alarm went off after what felt like 15 minutes. I flirted with the idea of going in late. It took all my resolve to get out of bed and ready for work. But punctuality was important; I could catch up on sleep that night.

By this time the snow had been on the ground for at least a couple of weeks. The area routinely got so much snow that the local authorities didn't even attempt to plow down to blacktop, then salt; they let cars pack the stuff down and added a fresh layer of sand for traction after every new fall. I was pushing it in terms of getting to work on time, so despite my hesitation even to approach the speed limit, I upped my speed to 25 mph. My two-wheel-drive car seemed to manage just fine at the higher speed. Other people were driving at the speed limit – it was probably around 40 mph – so I decided to follow their example.

Things went well until I reached a long, straight stretch. A car was heading toward me; all of a sudden I found myself unable to steer. Despite my frantic efforts, my car was on course for a head-on collision. I turned the wheel harder. The next thing I knew, I was spinning out of control.

I am going to die, I thought calmly, just before I heard a deafening CRASH.

Am I dead? I wondered. I checked my fingers on the steering wheel; I checked my toes. Miraculously, I seemed OK.

Less so was the front wall of the coffee shop-cum-grocery that had blessedly halted my trajectory. There was a big hole in the façade. I went inside sheepishly, apologizing to the woman who'd just put the coffee pot down on the counter in shock. A couple of retired patrons were taking in the unexpected entertainment.

"I'm very sorry," I stammered. She said the police were on their way. "Could I please use your phone? I need to call my foreman and tell him I'm going to be late." So much for my effort to show up on time.

In the end, the relationship won out. Kent and I decided to leave Vermont in late winter and stop to visit his parents on our way west. Our financial situations were totally different. Kent's father had worked his way up from a son of grocers in Nebraska to an executive at a major U.S. corporation. Kent made clear that he did not have to worry about money the way I did. I was in a constant balancing act to keep my bank account from slipping into the red. "You'll have to rely on me," he said. "No arguing. This will only work if you let me pay." For someone who'd kept track of every half-penny my first husband and I owed each other during our nine-year relationship, it would be uncomfortable for me to rely on Kent to cover expenses, but I would learn to do it so that we could be together.

We packed our stuff in boxes and scheduled a moving company to pick up our possessions and store them until we'd found a new home. Walking from the kitchen to the bedroom I happened to glance at a box on the landing. Oscar had jumped into it and was sitting bolt upright – *Wherever you go, I'm going with you.*

For the next few weeks we drove west, then south, and west again, through southern Illinois and Missouri, clipping the corner of Arkansas before facing the interminable length of Texas. It was my first real road trip as an adult; I'd always been too busy with work and made too little money to take off and drive across a country. Oscar traveled in the back of the truck most of the time; Kent had a window installed between the cab and the bed, so Oscar felt like he was with us. Most nights we stayed at a motel, with Oscar in our room. We hiked wherever we stopped – in Palo Duro Canyon, on the outskirts of Mesa Verde, wherever Oscar was allowed to go. We spent a few days in Albuquerque, one of our potential destinations, but decided to keep going. Then we spent a couple of days in Arizona – it was extra-cool to watch "Raising Arizona" in our room at a funky motel while eating pizza in Arizona. To me, those Southwestern states felt too parched to be home. So we kept going – up through the Four Corners of New Mexico, Colorado and Utah, then eventually to Missoula, Montana, which at least had the advantage of being familiar to Kent, thanks to his training. There we rented half of a two-story duplex in a 1920s house near the railroad tracks, and I got a job working at Mammyth Bakery, while Kent found work at a timber-framing operation about an hour's drive south of town.

Spring turned to a hot, dry summer. After I'd spent a few weeks on the earlier shift, which started at a body-clock-disrupting 4 a.m. that meant rising by 3:30, my boss, Kim, allowed me to change my duties from forming loaves of bread and overseeing their baking to making bagels and Danish, then spending the rest of my time on bookkeeping. Now I started work at 6 a.m., which felt luxurious. I still got home early enough to go for a bike ride or take Oscar for a hike in the afternoon. On Friday afternoons, we bought a sack of salted peanuts in their shells from the barrel at Worden's Grocery downtown and cracked them open while drinking beer on the front porch as Oscar busied himself with a ball. On weekends the three of us often hiked; once or twice we went camping. Oscar would chase a ball or a stick through clear-flowing mountain streams for hours.

Although I enjoyed baking, I had never aspired to do it professionally. I loved Kim, who owned the bakery and worked there every day alongside her employees. But the products of my labor were so ephemeral compared to furniture and cabinetry that I found the work increasingly less satisfying. There was plenty to love about our life in Missoula, but even after seven months it didn't feel like home.

By autumn I'd had enough. I was going to leave, whether or not Kent went with me. As it happened, while Kent loved Missoula and had a strong interest in timber framing, he didn't enjoy the long drive to and from his place of work. He suggested we move to Brown County, Indiana, near his sister's home, where we'd spent Christmas the previous year. With his father's financial help, we would start our own business

Spot the dog. Oscar in a field of lupines on a day trip to Idaho.

making custom furniture and cabinetry in a state that had no problem with obnoxious billboards and interstate highways.

We got married in jeans and sweatshirts at a public office on November 1st, then took Oscar for a walk in the woods to celebrate. We packed up our things again, rented a box truck and hooked Kent's truck up to it for towing. By the time we left Missoula, we'd picked up another family member, a stray orange tabby/tortoiseshell we named Tim, who had been hanging around Kent's workshop. We could have Oscar with us in the cab of the rented truck, but Tim was too panicked to be up front, so Kent put him in the back of his truck with food, water and a litter box. Tim spent much of the drive plastered against the door of the truck cap, his legs splayed out in terror like a Garfield the Cat magnet.

We arrived in Indiana on election night, 1988, and stayed in a motel,

After a bare-bones marriage ceremony in a public office with no guests, we took Oscar for a hike in the woods.

where we watched the results on TV in bed. The next day we drove to Kent's sister's house, where we would stay in the basement while looking for a place of our own. We put our possessions in storage.

Around Christmas we closed on a property north of Nashville, Indiana, along a road that ran parallel to a creek. Houses were built on the side of the road that rose up to hills forested with oaks, maples, hickory and beech. Across the road were farm fields. The house had been built by one of the neighbors' sons, but he and his partner had split up and put the place on the market. The one-story house was simple in design and would be fine for us. There was just enough flat ground by the road to build a shop. We hired Jim McGrayel to build it, then Kent finished the interior.

A couple of weeks after we moved in, we let Tim outside. At first he

Oscar and Tim in the ruana that was a gift from my maternal grandfather, Artie.

seemed overwhelmed – so many trees! But before long he developed a routine, dividing his days between naps and hunting mice. In chilly weather we'd find him under the woven mat at the front door, which made us laugh because he seemed to think he was invisible.

We were about 17 miles from the nearest sizable town, Bloomington, where most of our customers lived. As a college town, Bloomington had a relatively cosmopolitan population. To get commissions, we ran small display ads in the local paper, did some underwriting for the local public radio station and joined a co-op crafts gallery. We made built-ins, entertainment centers (it was the '90s) and freestanding pieces – sideboards, tables, desks and chairs.

We'd lived in Indiana for about a year when Tim's appetite decreased

While I was studying at Indiana University-Bloomington, I continued to do design work, bookkeeping and installations for our business. Kent built this sideboard in birch with ebony details, circa 1991. (Photo: Sander Studio.)

dramatically. Before long, he'd stopped eating. We took him to our vet, who diagnosed him with feline leukemia. We'd had him vaccinated, but she said the vaccine is less than 100 percent effective, an important detail neither of us had known. There was nothing she could offer, other than release. We buried him at home, with Oscar watching. Afterward, Kent and I sat down together on the couch and cried. The next thing we knew, Oscar was standing behind us, joining in with howls.[1]

[1] I said I wouldn't mention anthropomorphizing, but this is one place where I must. Did Oscar know that we were crying over the loss of Tim? I can't say. But dogs recognize howls of distress. "Sympathy" means fellow feeling, feeling pain with someone else, or multiple others. He knew we were distressed and crying, so being a good

Walnut bookcases/room dividers made by Kent circa 1991. (Photo: Sander Studio.)

We had a few friends, but none lived very close by. I was feeling desperate for intellectual stimulation. I visited the campus in Bloomington one day to ask about taking classes, then decided to sign up for one. I could take one class per semester without diverting much time away from work or breaking the bank. All it took was lecture number one in a course on religion, medicine and suffering to convince me I wanted more. I took classes in each summer session and, thanks to a scholarship, arranged to attend college full time.

Kent was adamant that I should cover the costs of college myself. I wouldn't have had it any other way; I've always been stubborn and independent. I applied for every scholarship, grant and teaching

member of the pack, he joined in.

assistantship available and entered essays in every contest. By the time I graduated in 1993, I'd paid for it all, in large part because tuition was still far more affordable than it is today. I had also kept up with the demands of our business: design work, drawing, bookkeeping and helping Kent with installations.

Living in a wooded part of Brown County made Oscar easy to care for. All we had to do was open the door, and he could take himself up the hill for a quick run, or out to the ravine to do his business. Now that we had a real home, I went into full-on domestic mode in my spare time, building new cabinets with ash faces to replace the generic dark-stained oak ones the previous homeowners had bought from a building-supply store. We tore out the "butcher-block" laminate counters and installed white laminate with a solid ash edge (again, it was the '90s). While Kent was on a hiking trip out west I pulled out the same generic oak cabinets in the dressing area just off our bedroom and replaced them with a vanity designed after the circa-1815 counter at the Shaker Museum in Old Chatham, N.Y., pictured in June Sprigg's book "Shaker Design." I painted it pale blue, added a solid maple top and plumbed in my first sink, following the page of directions that came in the box with the faucet. I made flower beds in front of the house, digging compost and manure into the hard-packed clay while Oscar rolled in the grass and occasionally trotted off to investigate a rustling at the edge of the forest.

Oscar knew he was an integral member of our family. We made him hamburgers with a celebratory candle for his birthday every year and homemade Christmas crackers with Milk Bones inside for the holidays. We took him with us on trips to visit my family in Florida. We took him hiking. On the rare occasions when I joined Kent for a paddle, we put him with us in the canoe. I loved knowing that after so many years of living in small apartments where he had been cooped up alone all day while I was at work, he finally had the perfect home.

Our marriage, though, was less happy. I quickly became so consumed by my studies that Kent felt neglected. I gave him less and less attention as I devoted every available moment to reading and writing. Instead of really listening to his complaints and talking about what might make

Oscar with birthday hamburgers, circa 1989.

him feel less lonely, I told him to stop being needy. It didn't even occur to me at the time that my obsession with excelling in my studies was fueled by a deep-seated urge to prove my own worth.

I had already decided to go on to graduate school and applied for fellowships to fund that project when we got a commission for a large armoire in hard maple. I can't recall the exact dimensions, but this thing was big – around 42 inches wide and at least 6 feet tall, with a pair of massive doors. When delivery day arrived, we removed the doors and drove it to our clients' house. "I'm so happy you're delivering it, and not a moving company," said the wife. "I know you'll take more care with the wallpaper on the stairs."

Kent took the top position, with me below. I have always found it easier to bear weight from below than to be the one on top, leaning over a massive piece of furniture while walking backwards up a flight of stairs. The staircase had a couple of steps at the bottom, then a dogleg landing before the main flight. After we'd maneuvered the beast around the turn, I repositioned myself for the long haul; to push with my shoulders, I had to bend my head sharply to the left, which immediately felt like a bad idea. "Be careful of the wallpaper!" our client reminded us. I powered through. We re-hung the doors, adjusted the piece so it was level and left with a check.

About a week later I was giving Oscar a bath, something he reluctantly allowed me to do. It was late summer, 1993; my first semester of grad school had begun. I leaned over the tub, wrapped Oscar in a towel and lifted him out. I felt a *click* in my upper back but thought nothing of it and carried on with the rest of the day.

A burning ache developed in my upper right back, between my shoulder blade and spine. Over-the-counter painkillers took off the edge, but the pain was unrelenting. One night I awoke around 2 a.m. feeling as though a stick was wedged in my esophagus. It hurt like crazy, but more troubling to me was the thought that one of my ribs might somehow have become dislodged and was poking into my throat. (I have a vivid imagination. Anything can happen within the invisible recesses of the body.) I woke Kent up and said I needed to go to the hospital. "You can drive yourself," he replied. Not wanting to argue – time seemed of the essence – I got up, dressed and headed to town. It was pitch-black out; I was driving myself to the emergency room in tears, terrified about what might have gone wrong in my body and hurt by Kent's unwillingness to go with me.

An X-ray showed no apparent injury to the ribs or spine, so the doctor prescribed a muscle relaxer and sent me home.

After my trip to the emergency room, things between Kent and me went downhill fast. We both felt neglected, hurt and angry. I started spending more time with my fellow students instead of with Kent; when I was home, I was reading or writing in the office. Sure, I did what I had to for our business and to care for Oscar. But my heart and mind were increasingly elsewhere. When Kent told me for the third time, "I hate you. I don't like you. I wish you'd leave," I rented a room in a shared house in Bloomington.

Did I really want to leave our marriage and our home? No. But I felt pushed too far – by both my own scholarly compulsion and the sense that things weren't going to get better if I stayed, considering how long we'd failed to address our problems adequately, despite some feeble tries. It takes a lot of power to break free of the pull exerted by the familiarity of home. I would have to be single-minded.

The ad for the house said "No Pets," but the existing renter was living there with her dog. She'd managed to keep Roxy a secret, concealed in her car or bedroom whenever the Realtor who managed the place stopped by. I thought I could do the same with Oscar, so I brought him to town with me one day. He was uneasy about the new location, with the new person and dog – no wonder, considering where we'd been living for the previous five years. At the age of 13, he didn't need a jarring change. I told Kent I was bringing him home.

For the next few months, I studied, wrote essays, made new friends, exercised and did my best to avoid crippling depression, which manifested itself all the same, through insomnia. "Oscar's having problems," Kent told me repeatedly. "We're going to have to do something." Specifically, he explained, he'd let Oscar out, only to have him not return. Kent had to go looking, sometimes for a long time, only to find Oscar splay-legged on the ground, unable to get up.

Every week I'd drive back home to take care of design jobs or bookkeeping, filled with resentment. Why couldn't I pursue my own interests and stay in this marriage? Why couldn't we have different interests and appreciate each other as spouses who happened to be quite different people? Wasn't that the point of a relationship, to be with someone *other than* myself? Kent was a sensitive, intelligent man, an excellent craftsman and hilarious when he wanted to be. He had high aesthetic standards and a wide range of practical skills, was a serious reader, knowledgeable woodsman and adventurous cook. The first time I met his mother, she described him as the sweetest of her three children. My parents and sister, along with Oscar, loved him.

It would take a few years for me to fathom my part in our marriage's end, and at this point I accept that we were simply not well-suited.

In the meantime, there was nowhere I wanted to be less than our home. Seeing me at the door, Oscar would lift his head hopefully. I ignored him, focused on the work at hand and eager to leave as soon as possible – not because I loved him any less than I ever had, but because my being could not handle one more ounce of emotional load.

"We have to do something." Kent couldn't bring himself to say "We have to have Oscar put to sleep," let alone "We have to find another place for you to live so Oscar can live with you." I had already decided against asking Kent for money, other than enough to cover my health insurance premiums (which were very affordable, given our youth and general good health) and the $325 a month rent for my apartment for one year. Beyond that, I lived on fellowships, teaching pay and the occasional paid furniture design work. I may have been legally entitled to half our assets, but I didn't want his money, so the possibility of moving to a new place didn't even occur to me – I could not have afforded to move again without financial help from him. He knew as well as I did that Oscar was living in the best-possible place; if he had really been worried about Oscar getting stranded in the woods, surely he could have spent 5 or 10 minutes three times a day walking him around the yard on a leash. Instead, Oscar now reverted to being "my" dog, and I would be the one on the record for calling the shots.

The next time Kent said "We have to do something," I told him I would make an appointment with the vet. The pressure was unbearable; I did not know what else to do. I shut off my heart. Years later I wondered whether that was how my mother had felt the morning she'd left us with our father at our childhood home.

Kent brought Oscar into town. We took him into the backyard of the house I was sharing. He explored the perimeter, which was marked by a fence. I brought him a saucer of milk and some biscuits. He ate them slowly, with enjoyment. He may have been a shadow of his former self, but he still had plenty of life in him. I could not believe what I was about to do. And I could not afford to question the plan. Again – I had shut down my heart; it was the only way I could break free from the pull of our marriage and home.

Mary Alice Cox had been Oscar's vet since we'd arrived in Indiana, five years before. Now we were asking her to euthanize him. "You know he still has a good quality of life, don't you?" she asked, or something like it. We did. Her disapproval, her disappointment, could not have been clearer. She did what we were there to have done.

Kent carried his body out to the truck, wrapped in a blue wool ruana my grandfather had brought for me from Peru – one of my favorite things, so it belonged with Oscar. We dug a grave along the path from our house to the shop and lowered him in.

I have never forgiven myself, and have often wished that I could go back in time. I would have made many different decisions. But I couldn't go back in time, so I would do my best not to repeat those same mistakes, with dogs or men.

7: Shadow, the Turkey Vulture (1986-1987 and Circa 1992)

AMERICA WAS a scary place in the 1980s – or so I believed, based on movies and news reports in the British media, my primary source of information about my native land during the years I lived in England. Between the muggings, shootings and rapes, it seemed you had to be constantly on your guard to stay alive in the not-so-United States. So when I flew over to scope out New England as a place to live in the winter of 1986-87, I was on suitably high alert.

I'd spent a couple of days driving around Upstate New York with Raymond, my former boss. We'd stayed in touch over the five years since I'd left his employ, and he had come to the States to research possibilities for expanding his cabinetmaking business with a base in Greenwich, Connecticut. After we said our goodbyes, I rented a car and planned to explore western Massachusetts.

The first night I stayed in Kingston, New York, where I'd rented the car. It was already late afternoon, so I decided to make it an early night and be ready to go first thing the next morning. There was a convenience store across the road, so I walked over to get a bar of chocolate, a bit of comfort in an anonymous place. A man was staring at me from across the candy aisle; I made a point of not returning his gaze as I paid and left the store, hoping he wasn't paying attention to where I went. About a half-hour later I was watching TV, a guilty motel pleasure, when there was a knock at my door. I wasn't expecting anyone – I knew no one in the area. On the other hand, it could have been a staff member at the motel, so I got up, walked over to the locked door and asked "Who is it?"

No answer. "Please go away!" I shouted. I called the front office and asked for a member of staff to make sure no one was loitering outside, then kept the light on in my room all night, worried that the stranger from the convenience store might come back. After hoping to turn in early, I barely got a wink of sleep.

The next day I drove around Upstate New York. The Hudson Valley was breathtakingly lovely, with 19th-century buildings, mountains of deciduous forest and that broad, historic river – a Thomas Cole painting brought to life. I figured I should at least consider it as an alternative place to settle. That night I stopped at an old-fashioned motor lodge, as they used to be known, balanced on the side of a hill. The wind was picking up as heavy rain began to fall. I was glad I didn't have to go back out.

I read a few pages of my book and turned off the light. Around midnight I sprang awake at the sound of someone trying to break down the door of my room with an axe. BANG! went each blow. BANG! At any moment the axe was going to break through the door. Terrified, I grabbed the phone on the bedside table and called 911.

"There's someone trying to break into my room," I whispered to the dispatcher, doing my best to keep the attacker outside from hearing my report. "They're trying to break down the door with an axe. Please come quickly." I hung up the phone and fled to the bathroom, locking the door behind me. Minutes dragged like hours. Then I heard a shout.

"Ma'am? Sheriff's department. Are you in there?"

The movies had taught me to be wary. "How do I know you're from the sheriff's department and not the person who's trying to break into my room?" I called.

I can't remember their answer, but they convinced me, so I unlocked the door. To my astonishment, the door was fine. No one had attacked it with an axe. The noise had come from the unlatched storm door slamming itself repeatedly in the wind. We hadn't had storm doors at any of the houses I'd known in England. I hadn't realized I had to lock this one shut.

The deputies now suspected they were dealing with someone under the influence of something besides adrenaline, or perhaps even suffering a psychotic episode. Either way, this 27-year-old woman probably should not be trusted to drive a car. They asked for my driver's license, hoping to get my address, but all I had was my license from England. My only legal address was across an ocean, which intensified their suspicion. They called in their report. By the time they left, I was mortified.

Several years and many miles later, I had settled in Indiana with Kent and was working at our business while taking college classes in Bloomington, 17 miles away. Kent's sister had given us her old compact car when she bought a new one; it was the car I drove to campus, as well as to meet clients. The route to town snaked through farmland and forest, climbing up long hills to trace a ridge, then dipping back down. I always drove warily because deer, squirrels and birds crossed the highway and I didn't want to hit them.

One autumn day I was rounding a sharp curve when I spotted a large bird on the opposite side of the road a few hundred yards ahead – a turkey vulture with a damaged wing. The bird was clearly in distress – flapping its wings as it tried to get aloft, in vain. A driver had apparently hit the bird, injuring it.

I couldn't just ignore the bird and continue on my way. I had to stop. Once I'd pulled over, I had no idea what to do. I had never been so close to a vulture; I had mostly seen them aloft, visions of grace as they rode the thermals in search of carrion, their wings spread wide. To have your path darkened even momentarily by that shadow is to know foreboding – *OK, who died? And where?*

I was pacing back and forth, desperate to help the poor creature but repulsed by the thought of trying to pick it up, when a young man in camo carrying a backpack stepped out of the woods. He saw me, too, and called out: Did I need help? I pointed to the vulture and said I was trying to figure out whether there was a way to get it in the car so that I could take it to the vet.

The stranger said he'd be glad to help and asked if I had a blanket or a tarp. I didn't, but I grabbed a towel I kept in the car – we'd delivered enough furniture in the rain to know better than to leave home without one. I handed it to him and asked whether I could give him a ride to town. He explained that he was on a long-distance hike but wouldn't mind skipping a few miles to help someone out. I took the stranger's pack, bending down as I put it in the car and realizing that what I was doing might imply that I valued the rescue of a bird more highly than my own life. *Huh*, I thought, hoping for the best.

Meanwhile, the young man had thrown the towel over the vulture and scooped it up. He climbed into the back seat, set the bird down next to him still covered by the towel, and pulled the door shut. I got back in and drove the last few miles. When we arrived, the young man offered to carry the vulture in and waited until we were in an exam room, then said goodbye. I thanked him for being so thoughtful. The car was unlocked, so he could get his pack while I stayed with the bird.

The vet examined the patient. "God, they're ugly, aren't they?" he remarked. If you've ever seen a turkey vulture up close, you'll know why they're compared to turkeys: their heads are bright red, with a featherless, dinosaur-like face, their skin as wrinkled as an empty scrotum – completely different from the charmingly feathered heads of most birds. But *ugly*? I've never thought of them that way; they are as God, or nature, or however you think of the source from which we come, created them. To call them ugly seemed chauvinistic. How do we look to them?

Sadly, the vet concluded the wing was too badly damaged for the vulture to survive in the wild. He asked if I would like him to euthanize the bird, then dispose of the body. I said yes, regretting that our world isn't big enough to accommodate a flightless bird that looks like a monster, yet relieved that the bird would have a quick and painless end to its distress.

The episode affected me deeply. Maybe Americans didn't deserve such a bad rap. Especially when I remembered the notes of concern from relatives in the States in the '70s and early '80s, when news coverage was filled with dire reports of Irish Republican Army bombings (long before Facebook existed, with its "mark yourself safe" notifications). Bad things happened everywhere.

8: Daisy June and Her Great Adventures (1990s)

AROUND 1991 my father decided to ride his bicycle from the central Florida town of Winter Park to Washington, D.C. The purpose of the trip: "adventure," he says today. "I was going to write about it, which I did for a weekly called *Miami Today*."

A writer and consultant about bicycling, travel and place, he had at least 20 years of experience at coming up with ideas for trips that people would pay to read about. He wrote for *The Atlantic*, *National Geographic Traveler*, *Land and People* and *Florida Trend*, among other publications, in addition to authoring related books under his own name and sometimes as a ghostwriter.

The first time I really became aware of this work was when he came to visit us in England over Christmas break around 1972. I would have been 13. He planned a family vacation with our mother that would take us from London, where she lived, to Scotland by train. (My sister and I were still at boarding school most of the time.) We would stay at a nice inn in the countryside. He was hoping to get an article about the trip published by a popular weekly publication based in London, which would help offset expenses.

My memories of that trip include interminable train rides north, then south, during which my sister and I got bored and cranky; spending the night at a bed-and-breakfast in the Lake District where my father and I consumed so much Queen of Puddings that I felt sick and needed the support of both parents to shuffle down the dark street for a breath of air; arriving at the hotel in Scotland, an imposing sandstone edifice perched on the slope of a rhododendron forest laced with gravel paths; and my father sitting on a bed surrounded by receipts for reimbursement and tax time. My most vivid memory, however, is of breakfast in the formal dining room – Mom and Dad on one side of the table, Maggie and I on the other. Pressed linens, polished silver. We placed our orders with the aproned waiter; he carried our tray of food to the table with a flourish. I don't remember what anyone else had (kippers were certainly involved), but I had a bowl of porridge. As a kid in America, I knew porridge to be cooked rolled oats served with milk, brown sugar and raisins, a special treat in South Florida's sorry excuse for winter. This porridge was something else entirely, made with steel-cut oats simmered overnight and served with butter, salt and cream.

"Thank you," I whispered to the waiter.

"YOU MUST SPEAK LOUDLY," said my father in an irritated tone I hadn't heard in years, probably since the last time he'd spanked me, and that would have been when we lived at our first house, in South Miami, before the hippies had arrived with their Good News about peace and love. I fought back tears.

"You need to speak loudly enough for the waiter to hear you," he explained. It was the first time I remember him stressing the importance of giving thanks. Years later he mentioned that his father's motto was "Beware of unappreciative people."

But back to 1991. My dad planned to make his bike trip alone, mainly on back roads, and had arranged overnight stays at a series of small inns along the way; he'd camp on the stretches without innkeeper friends. He packed his panniers with a tent, food, basic cooking supplies and a modest supply of water, expecting to top up those supplies as he passed through small towns. Of course, he also carried clothing, toiletries and tools for emergency bike repairs. I can only try to imagine how heavy this load made the bike. At almost 60, my father was in good shape because he cycled all the time. It was his main form of transportation. On the other hand, most of his cycling had been in Florida, where the highest elevation is 345 feet. His route through western Georgia and North Carolina would take him through mountains.

Kent and I were living in Indiana at the time. Never having braved a long-distance bike ride myself, I was impressed by my father's ambitious plan, as well as concerned for his safety, between the risk of dehydration, injury or heart attack in the middle of nowhere. Sixty! That was old. None of us had cell phones, so if my dad found himself in trouble, he would have to find a pay phone or ask a stranger for help. But as he pedaled northward, calling in updates every few days, my worry eased.

He'd headed north-northwest through Florida and Georgia. A couple of weeks or so in, he called from Waynesville, North Carolina, in the Maggie Valley, with news of his progress and a happy meeting on the way. It was June in the South, so once the sun had burned off the early morning chill, the days were hot. He'd overestimated how much baggage he could carry and decided to mail all but the essentials home.

The meeting had involved a dog. "She was silhouetted on a mountaintop in southwest North Carolina," he recalls. The next thing he knew, "She suddenly showed up alongside me. I had seen her at quite a distance. I was probably in the foothills. She must have had a good run to get to me. She obviously knew right away that this was somebody she wanted to meet up with and work her canine wiles on.

"The first thing she did was to roll over and say 'Rub my stomach! That will mean that I'm your friend and you're my friend and you'll adopt me.' I got all these wonderful messages from her; it was precisely part of the adventure that I didn't know I was looking for. It was very, very dear. This was utterly unexpected and I loved that I gave way to her.

"I had no hesitation," he continues, adding that he "was quick to set one term with her, one fundamental agreement: She had to keep up with me. She knew that. So she would run alongside me. Sometimes I was getting way out front of her and I would carefully look back and see her at quite some distance, running. She was determined that she wasn't going to lose sight of me. Her paws were hurting her from running on the pavement. There was a ditch with water in it, and when she was alongside me, she would leap into the ditch to cool her paws off, then come out, and I would remind her 'You've got to keep up.' I think in part the urgency was because I had some number of places where I knew I was overnighting … I was never a true camper. That was probably the only camping trip I ever made. So I had to be someplace."

Her looks suggested she was part German shepherd crossed with at least one other breed, from which she'd inherited her floppy ears. She was respectful and extremely friendly and had obviously been desperate to reunite with a human companion, though my father knew nothing of her story. "There's not a bad bone in her body," I recall him telling me all those years ago, adding that while he had little to offer her, he hoped she could keep up with him on the downhill parts of the ride. Fortunately, she always caught up.

"I remember stopping at a store and having a woman come up to us in her car," he goes on. "I told her my story, and she either had food in her car that she right away took out, or something like that. We were truly a defenseless pair; we were safely approachable by anybody! It was either there that I bought two boxes of dog food that she immediately scarfed down like Garfield the Cat, or it was after I went by the shelter, and …" here the details escape him. "Were they closed? I wound up taking her to where I was staying for the night. I told her she had to stay outside for the night, and said, 'Don't leave me,' because *I* wasn't leaving *her*. She could sleep right outside and know I was there. And so she was, the next morning."

Someone at the local shelter gave my dad the number of a man named David. "I called him and told him the story and he said he would take her."

It was a touching story with all the best characters – a friendly dog separated from her people (possibly on purpose), kind strangers who loved animals. I asked for David's number, thinking it would be lovely if we could somehow arrange for my dad to adopt the dog when he returned home, however unrealistic that might have been, considering that he was living in a studio apartment at an inn in Miami, for which he bartered consulting and marketing services.

A few days later I called David to check on the dog. I mentioned how touched I was that he had taken her in and asked whether he had found her a home. He hadn't. He wondered whether Kent and I might want to adopt her. It just wasn't realistic, I said; we already had Oscar, and between our business and my schoolwork, our time was stretched pretty thin. Much as I loved the idea of adopting the dog based on my father's story, I was not in a position to drive to southwest North Carolina to get her. I said I hoped he would find her a good home.

A week or two passed. It was a Friday evening and Kent had driven up to Indianapolis to spend a rare weekend with his parents, when our phone rang.

"Hi," said the voice. "This is David. I have your dog and am calling from a pay phone at a Hardee's just off I-65 in Columbus, Indiana."

"My" dog? I nearly dropped the handset. I didn't know what to do. It was incredible that this man had taken it upon himself to drive the 430 miles to deliver the dog with nothing more than a name, phone number and vague idea of our location. What kind of person would make such a trip without first calling the people at the other end of the drive to make sure they were willing to take the dog? And what if I hadn't answered the phone? I could have been in Indianapolis with Kent (again, this was the era of landlines), or just out to dinner with friends. Kent and I might even have been on a trip to the other side of the country! David obviously loved animals, a strong mark in his favor. But was he out of his mind? I didn't feel safe driving to meet this stranger alone, so I told him I would have to call my husband then call back.

I called Kent's parents' number. There was no answer. I called again, a couple of times. I knew I was probably annoying them but felt I had no alternative. Finally someone answered and I asked for Kent.

"We don't need another dog," he said impatiently when he came to the phone. "And we just sat down to dinner. I haven't seen my parents in a couple of months and I'm not leaving to drive down there and get that dog from a stranger."

He was angry that I would even consider taking her in. But she needed a home, and my dad had said such lovely things about her. More to the point, at that moment, I couldn't imagine not going to get her after David had driven so far to ensure she'd have a home. I had to press my case.

I no longer remember what I said, but it was a fraught discussion.

After about 15 minutes, Kent grudgingly agreed to turn around and head home, then we'd drive to Columbus together. I called David with the plan.

The atmosphere in the truck was as tense as a drawn bow, so my talk with David in the Hardee's parking lot was short and strained. But I took the dog, who David said had already eaten two hamburgers, and put her in Kent's truck for an equally silent drive home.

I couldn't understand Kent's resistance to taking her. He was a good, kind man who loved animals. Of course I understood the imposition, not to mention his parents' disappointment at seeing him leave so soon after he'd arrived. But how could anyone in good conscience do anything other than fetch the dog, if only to relieve the kind stranger of the responsibility he'd taken on himself to help another stranger (my dad) and a friendly animal who was lost – or more likely, given that no one had claimed her, abandoned? We could always find her another home if we had to.

Things between Kent and me were strained for days. But I did my best to make the visitor/new family member welcome. My dad had named her Daisy; the happy simplicity of the flower fit her trusting spirit and her openness to take on the next adventure. At some point my dad added "June," in honor of the month they'd met: Daisy June.

Oscar wanted nothing to do with her and refused even to look in her direction. I could see Daisy June was disappointed and felt terribly out of place, which only made me encourage her harder to feel at home. She trusted me, and had clearly trusted David – and before him, my dad. But she had no confidence that this new place was going to be her home. I imagined her thinking *I appreciate what these people are doing for me, but where am I? Am I going to stay here? And why won't this other dog even acknowledge me?*

Her palpable sense of being in a place where she didn't belong sent me back to a time in England shortly before I returned to the States. I'd sold my house and was piecing together what income I could from small jobs, without a shop of my own. Raymond had offered me the use of a workshop in an old industrial building in East London. It was a big space with a wooden floor, a half-bath and a crude kitchen. My friend

Edward and I were building some doors for a pair of recessed cabinets on either side of a fireplace in another friend's house. We decided to live in Raymond's shop until the job was done.

During that transitional interlude I went for lonesome rambles around the neighborhood. While searching for a cup of coffee one day I happened on an eel pie shop that was probably a century old, with a high ceiling, quarry-tile floor, marble counter and subway tile all the way around the room in a captivating shade between moss and sage green. The coffee was weak and served with milk – nothing like what most Americans call coffee. And despite the bracing historic surroundings, I couldn't really enjoy the place thanks to the smell and sight of chopped eels.

As I got up to leave, I asked the fellow at the counter whether there was anywhere nearby to take a bath. The question may strike some readers as odd, but access to baths was critical to public health in a long-impoverished part of London where most houses had originally been built without indoor "facilities." As it happened, there were public baths a few blocks away, so I walked over and paid a few coins for the blissful luxury of a half-hour in a cubicle with an ancient tub that held 75 piping-hot gallons and came with a freshly laundered towel. It was like nothing I'd ever experienced, and I felt selfishly grateful that the area had been neglected by modern property developers.

Unlike me during that bleak London limbo, Daisy had someone in her cheering section. I was doing my best to make her feel loved, despite the troubling vibes coming from Kent. But the person she really wanted to engage was Oscar, her fellow canine. She'd provoke him gently, trying to get him to play, but he was steadfast, determined that our household would not take in another dog.

Kent agreed with Oscar. Shortly after we took Daisy in, we went canoeing in a nearby lake. The boat was only big enough for us and Oscar, Kent insisted; Daisy would have to watch from the shore. I wasn't happy about her exclusion but was doing my best to keep the peace in the aftermath of the disruption I'd already brought on our household.

The farther we got from shore, the wider Daisy's eyes grew. *They're leaving! I hardly even know these people, but they're all I've got. I can't let*

With Daisy, Oscar, Teddy and Kent on someone's birthday, circa 1991.

them get away! With that, she dove into the water and paddled frantically toward our boat.

"We have to go back," I said to Kent. It wasn't fair to cause this innocent animal more distress. Another damning entry in my column. Fortunately, he agreed to go return to shore.

One day I happened to be walking past the living-room windows when I spotted Daisy chasing Oscar. He wasn't just running, but actively running *from her.* They were playing! Suddenly both dogs looked up and saw me watching. In an instant, the running stopped and they assumed a clueless expression: *We have no idea what you think you saw, but whatever it was, you didn't see it.* Despite the denial, their cover was busted. A few days later they were playing together openly.

Over the following weeks Daisy grew much more comfortable in her new home, and before long, she found a new calling. Ever since we'd lost Tim, the cat we'd brought from Missoula, I'd felt our home lacked

DAISY JUNE AND HER GREAT ADVENTURES

What is cat litter for?

a feline presence. This awareness was new to me. I'd always been a dog person. Even though we'd had a couple of cats, Olga and Humphrey, when my sister and I were teenagers in London, I hadn't really appreciated the charm of the often-aloof, self-possessed, take-it-or-leave-it attitude of most cats. But now I got it. We needed a cat, preferably another orange tabby. I called the county shelter. They had a pair of orange kittens who had been abandoned. Not yet weaned, they were tiny; their eyes were still not fully formed. In view of their vulnerable condition, the shelter staff wanted them to stay together.

"We are not getting two kittens," said Kent when I hung up the phone.

"But let's at least go and see them," I replied. "You never know; one of them might die anyway." Of course I wasn't hoping that either kitten would die; I was on the ropes, doing my best to save them.

The kitten debate went back and forth. Finally we went to the shelter and came home with the pair. I fed them with a syringe and wiped

Daisy with her kittens.

their butts, because my sister said that's what their mother would have done. They had no idea what the litter box was for, other than to play in or take a nap. The litter was fun to dig, and when they'd exhausted themselves with digging, they'd collapse in a hollow and pass out.

Daisy adopted the kittens, whom I named Teddy and Sherpa after the famous Everest explorers, because they loved to climb up mountains of laundry. Gentle and solicitous, Daisy invited them to snuggle against her, then lay perfectly still so as not to disturb them. Reclining on her side like a mother who'd just nursed her pups, she'd lift her head and give me a look that said *I'm the luckiest dog in the world to have these babies.*

Meanwhile, Kent's mind was not changed about Daisy. "She's a very nice dog and I love her," he'd say, "but I don't want her, and I never have." He called her "your father's dog."

A couple of years passed. I started grad school in 1993, then left Kent and moved into a rented house in town, the one where my housemate kept her dog, Roxy. Kent and I had Oscar euthanized that fall.

After one year in that house I had to find another place because the homeowner, a professor who'd been on sabbatical, was coming back to town. I moved into the garret apartment in an early 20th-century triplex several blocks to the west, a more affordable part of town. My apartment had one bedroom, a living room, kitchen and bath. The kitchen was the best part of the place; it was spacious, with north-facing windows and an original dark-blue linoleum floor. There was one wall of cabinets and a classic '50s fridge, though the freezer compartment was minute and had to be defrosted once a week in order to shut the fridge door. A mid-century electric range on the opposite side of the room had thick coiled burners and illuminated controls that shifted from blue to red as you cranked up the heat, like a game at a carnival.

By this point Kent and I had divorced, and he was planning to move back west. I rented a storage unit for most of my stuff, though he helped me move my workbench into my apartment kitchen. It made a fine desk. I brought Teddy to live with me in the garret; Kent kept Sherpa and took him to live in Missoula when he moved.

Meanwhile, my mother and stepfather had decided to sell the family home and drive across the country in search of a new place to settle down. They put most of their worldly goods into storage in Indianapolis (which turned out to be among the most affordable spots in the country) and set out in search of a new life, ending their trip at Joshua Tree when my stepfather became involved with another woman at a Buddhist retreat.

My mother had moved back to Miami and was living in a small rented house. She had a job at an art gallery and was doing volunteer work with Habitat for Humanity when my dad asked whether she'd consider getting back together with him and moving to an island in a Central Florida lake. He'd visited the place once when a friend was running it as a bed-and-breakfast. The property had a three-bedroom house built in the late 19th century, along with a small outbuilding, pasture for horses and a grove of citrus trees the owner's family had planted a few

With nowhere else to store my workbench during my second year of graduate school, I kept it in the kitchen of my garret apartment.

decades earlier while preparing for the end of civilization. He knew our mother loved to garden; there was plenty of room for that. On the whole, the neighbors were a pretty close-knit bunch of creative, can-do, unconventional friends. Living there would be isolated compared to what either of my parents had known, but it would be a great place for people to visit. Best of all, the house was just yards from the lake, with a postcard-perfect view of the water through a row of royal palms. You couldn't reach the island by road, but a ferry ran according to a schedule approved by the county. Most people who lived on the island had their own small motorboat for getting back and forth to the mainland.

Dad knew there was no way he could manage such a place himself. He could only make the place home with the help of a partner who possessed the tools, skills and gumption necessary to perform the endless maintenance and repairs that underlie the reality of any postcard-perfect destination: our mother. Or, as he puts it today, "As I remember, Mom and I were driving someplace together in or near Miami. I told her where I was relocating. Daisy-like, she said, 'You know, Herb. I could live together with you again.' I replied somewhat like, 'OK. Come on.'"

People see such places and imagine that living in them is a dream come true. For those wealthy enough to have others deal with the constant maintenance and repairs, it may well be; it takes Sisyphean labor to keep up a wood-framed house in a remote island location that's completely exposed to the weather in a region infamous for hurricanes. At this point my dad was in his early 60s, my mother in her late 50s; she would be in charge of the maintenance and repairs. But it was another adventure, and they agreed to go ahead.

They bought the place and moved in. That summer my mother flew to Indiana and rented a big moving truck into which we emptied the storage unit of her possessions, along with those of my stepfather. It was a long, hot, sweaty job, and several times my mother openly wished she'd brought a flamethrower.

Now that my parents had a place together, they became the stable members of our family. It was time for Daisy to go home. I would accompany her and help my mother unload the truck. With my mother driving (her name was on the truck rental paperwork), we stopped at Kent's house – our former home together – and picked up Daisy on our way south. We also had another passenger, a small black kitten I'd found mewing in a shrub at the front of the place where I was living. I couldn't take another cat; I already had Teddy, and my apartment was small. But there was plenty of space for a kitten on the island. I called him Charles Taylor after one of my favorite philosophers.

The drive south took two days. It was my first visit to the island. Despite the reservations about the place I'd had on my parents' behalf, all it took was the trip across the water on the ferry, the big moving truck on deck, for me to appreciate my parents' new dream.

***

Daisy was in her element. She had two people who genuinely wanted her. She even had her own cat in Charles Taylor, though when my mother took him to the vet she learned he had feline leukemia and had him euthanized at the vet's insistence. Daisy was particularly intrigued by the raccoons and armadillos, and she loved Dan and Lisa, my parents' closest neighbors, who also had a dog.

"Daisy became my companion in a mostly solitary life on Drayton Island," says my mother, taking up the story. "She joined the animal part of the family that then consisted of our sister cats, Edna and Freya, who had spent much of their lives with German shepherds and knew how to deal with her, and two palomino mares, Feather and Dazzle, who were far more interesting to her. Out of ignorance we allowed Daisy more freedom to roam; we, too, were pretty new to the island and hadn't yet heard the frightening tales of gator attacks on dogs. And roam she did, visiting friends and neighbors, accompanying us to holiday parties, getting to know other island animals. She fit right in," said my mother.

"As with most aspects of island life, mail was a big deal. The mail boxes were set up at the ferry landing two-and-a-half miles on a dirt road from our house. Herb and Daisy would collect the mail on days when it wasn't so dry that the dirt became sand, or too wet, when it became mud that Herb's bike couldn't handle." Just as they'd traveled

Daisy with Charles Taylor, the stray kitten I found outside the garret apartment, shortly after we arrived in Central Florida with my mother in the mid-1990s.

at the start of this story, Dad was on his bike, Daisy running alongside.

"As Daisy explored, I carried on with the chores that came with our new life," my mother said. "There was the garden, a 40-foot x 60-foot compromise that I agreed to after refusing to plow under and plant the 10-acre pasture Herb wanted me to cultivate." Let's pause here to note the disconnect between the dream of self-sufficient vegetable production and the realities of being a woman nearing 60, then in her 60s, on an island with no road to the mainland and no easy access to water. Even the much-smaller garden demanded many hours of work a week, almost all of it in scorching, humid weather. "Dealing with irrigation and weeds, bugs, plant diseases, climate, soil amendments, building raised beds (starting with wood, replaced with concrete blocks when the wood rotted), it was all part of the 'adventure.' And the produce was really pretty good, though tomatoes and carrots never made the grade.

"We soon realized that water would be a problem. The house supply came from a deep well that drew from the aquifer supplying Salt Springs, Florida. It was salt water, which corroded metal and was definitely not potable. The big project became an alternative source: a shallow well, which works pretty well until the drought years, when it dries up. What about that huge lake out there? With help from an eccentric retired ferry captain, we set up a complicated system that worked with three pumps to bring the slightly saline water from 500 feet out in the lake into the pump house, ran it through a water softener, then a whole-house reverse osmosis system. Given the number of storms in central Florida, you can imagine the maintenance.

"No," she quickly adds, with heavy irony; "you can't. Add in the salt and sand factor and you might imagine how skilled I became at replacing pumps, not to mention all the other plumbing jobs to do with the house and the sprinkler system. No plumber (or carpenter, landscaper, electrician, handyman, painter) on the mainland would come out to the island for less than a full day's pay plus the ferry fee. Herb was researching a book that involved traveling five days a week, but he doesn't do that kind of work. I learned a lot." What she learned was on top of a lifetime of hands-on repair and maintenance at each of her previous homes.

There was no store on the island, so people who lived there had to bring everything they needed across the lake from the mainland. From my parents' house, this was a 15- to 20-minute trip in each direction, depending on the weather. The same applied to disposing of trash; the nearest place to drop recyclable materials was a further two towns away. My mother, a sculptor and printmaker by training, used the outbuilding as an outdoor welding studio. To minimize the quantity of recyclable glass from the house, she began painting wine bottles and turning them into incense burners or kerosene "candles," which she sold at the local Catfish Festival.

"Daisy's low maintenance was a huge gift," my mother continues. "Vaccinations were the only reason to see the vet, and his visit could be combined with a checkup on the cats and whatever attention the horses

Daisy with my parents at the end of the dock as my mother was about to take me to the airport.

might need. I'd pick the vet up at the marina where we docked our skiff on the mainland." For many, the word "marina" will evoke visions of yachts, maybe also a toney restaurant specializing in freshly caught fish. This one was a decidedly low-key operation at the end of a sand lane, without so much as a vending machine. "The vet would do his job, then go back. No surprise that the vets and farriers enjoyed the trips on the lake, a nice break from their regular office hours."

The horses, Feather and Dazzle, had been part of the property purchase. Dazzle died while my parents lived there. "She didn't come to eat that morning," my mother says. "Neither of them did. I went to the pasture and looked for them. They were in the woods, where they slept at night. Dazzle was on the ground, dead. Feather wouldn't leave her; she couldn't stand being alone. She was so lonely, it was terrible. She cried, a haunting moan-whinny that didn't stop. I had to bring a backhoe over from the mainland. They had to dig a huge hole. Then they had to go into the woods to pick Dazzle up. The whole time they were working on that I had to hold Feather in another part of the pasture so she couldn't see what was going on. She hadn't wanted to leave the body. I had to drag her away from Dazzle. That was the saddest funeral I ever attended." My parents got Feather a new companion, Spike.

After hurricanes, the cleanup was monumental, with tree branches strewn across the yard. One storm completely destroyed the 300-foot dock and boathouse, and washed it all up on the front lawn along with 500 feet of PVC pipe and two pumps from the filtration system. It all had to be rebuilt. Just preparing for big storms entailed days of work; she'd drag her 20-foot extension ladder out of the shed and climb up the side of the house to nail sheets of plywood over the windows to keep severe winds and flying debris from crashing through them.

Daisy was a seamless part of the picture, an outstanding example of responding to adversity as an opportunity for adventure. "Mostly she was just a wonderful companion," my mother says. Daisy's best life lasted into her dotage; one day she just lay down and died. Mom buried her near the garden. Thanks to caring strangers, she found her way home. She will always be part of our family.

9: Wilhelm Von Wundt, the Dog Who Saved My Life (1995-2008)

WHAT I recall most fondly about William[1] is the sight of his round pink tummy – specifically, the look of it as he sat beside me on the seat of my truck, eyes forward, as though in charge of navigation. We spent a lot of hours together in that truck, driving back and forth to Franklin, Indiana, where Doug and Marsha, friends from grad school, had bought a house.

Doug's work was in Bloomington, where he was studying for a doctorate. Marsha worked in Indianapolis, more than 40 miles away. They'd started their marriage in a rented apartment between their places of work. When this particular house came up for sale in another town roughly midway between Bloomington and Indianapolis, they went for a look. It was a brick house built in the late 19th century – elegant windows, high ceilings, hardwood floors. What made it affordable was its sorry condition; the Realtor was marketing it as a fixer-upper, with the questionable bonus that a fellow named Max had already gone some way toward getting the job done. Unfortunately, as it turned out, Max's idea of rewiring a room or rerouting the plumbing rarely conformed to code. In fact, a few of his ingenious solutions might have cost someone their life. Need to add an electrical receptacle on the other side of the room? No worries! Just clip a length of wire up the wall and over the ceiling to where you want it, then cover it up with textured drywall mud. Doorway not high enough?

---

[1] Wilhelm von Wundt is the nickname my erstwhile employee, Daniel O'Grady, gave William.

As a puppy, William often waited for me in the mudroom on top of my shoes.

Grab a crowbar and remove that header; those bricks above aren't going anywhere – they've been there a hundred years!

Doug and Marsha hired me to remodel their downstairs bathroom, just off the kitchen. I can't remember how it looked after Max's "improvements," but based on what I recall of other rooms, it probably had fitted carpet on the floor, and maybe fake wood paneling on the walls, because that's a great way to hide crumbling plaster. At the end of Day One, which I spent gutting the room to the studs, Doug came home, took one look at me and declared "Nancy! You look like a street urchin!" I was dredged in decades' worth of coal dust.

William was still too young to be left alone all day; he needed to go out a few times, not to mention be fed. Doug and Marsha had a fenced yard and had said I was welcome to bring him to work. I would put him in the yard and go at it, checking periodically to make sure he was OK.

The job spread out over a few months. I had previously remodeled just one bathroom, for a client named Andrew. That experience had introduced me to the importance of toilets that are designed to flush. I don't mean "flush," as in "shoot a whirlpool of water from the tank into the bowl," but "remove the bowl's entire contents," which in Andrew's case had proved a challenge. My job for him taught me that the most effective flush available in the then-new age of water-efficient lavatories was the American Standard "Champion," so that's what I recommended to Doug and Marsha. After roughing in the plumbing while I had the floor open to the joists, I hung drywall on the ceiling and walls, then laid down subfloor and tile underlayment, followed by unglazed porcelain mosaic in a period-authentic pattern. I cleaned up and re-installed the original baseboard and trim, then tiled the walls, rehabbed a floor-to-ceiling storage cabinet in a corner, added the sink they'd chosen and referred my friends to an outfit that would resurface their old clawfoot tub, which I fitted with a reproduction shower curtain rod and riser.

William enjoyed the commute, which took a bit over an hour. He watched the scenery go by and barked at the occasional herd of cows. We started on the highway north of Bloomington, then took a two-lane road that snaked through the countryside. My favorite landmark on the drive was the Jesus Barn. Against the blood-red backdrop of one side, a local church youth group had used black to depict a silhouette of Jesus on the cross. Everyone who drove the road knew the barn. It's gone now, but memorialized on the internet; it even has a documentary film with a Facebook page. The red and black side included a message that felt damning: "HE DIED FOR YOU." Doug and Marsha called that the Scary Jesus. The other side was blue, with a triumphant Jesus waving a sword, in white. That was the Nice Jesus, though off the top of my head I don't recall anything in the Bible about Jesus literally advocating the use of weapons. Along the way were other fun spots such as the tiny settlements of Bud and Cope. For much of the route we passed through farm fields; even when you knew the crops were genetically modified, the pastoral scenery was easy on the eyes.

The bathroom, after. (Photo: Spectrum Creative Group.)

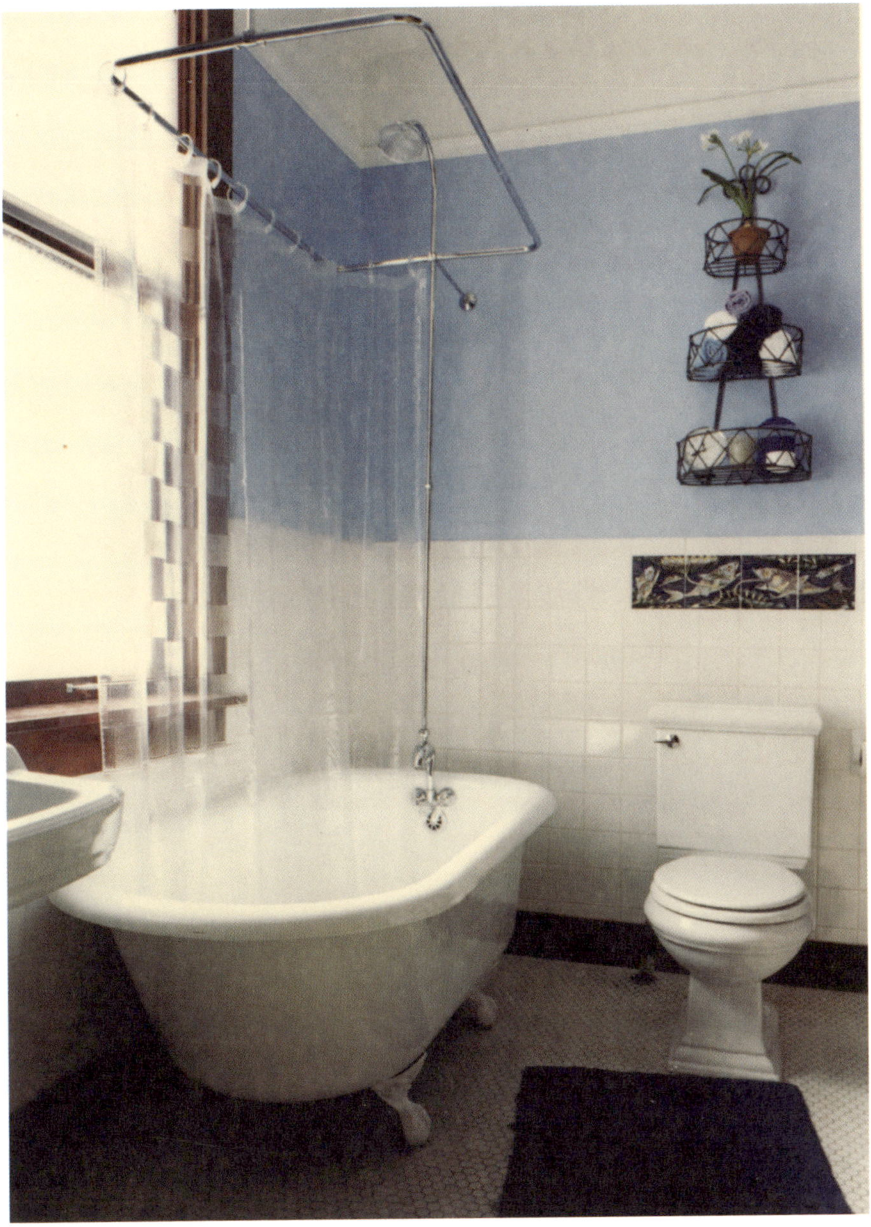

My bungalow in town was built in 1925 and was home to the Pope family until I bought it 70 years later.

Flynn and Teddy, 1995.

Sometimes on the way home I stopped at a fast-food drive-through and got William a hamburger as a special treat. He'd wolf it down, then settle in against my leg for a nap.

The previous year, 1995, I had moved into my 70-year-old bungalow in Bloomington with my boyfriend, Flynn, a professor of microbiology who specialized in a particular bacterium, *Shewanella putrefaciens*. He was researching its potential to consume PCBs and render them harmless. PCBs were a dangerous source of ground-level pollution in the Bloomington area after years of use in the manufacture of capacitors at the local Westinghouse factory.

I was looking for a job but having a devil of a time finding one. Being a cabinetmaker in her mid-30s with degrees in religious studies pretty much guaranteed that most small-town employers would place your application in the circular file – and Bloomington, despite its urban aspirations, was (and remains) in many respects a small town, albeit home to the flagship campus of the state university. Flynn kindly co-signed for the mortgage, and we moved in.

As the weeks of job rejections turned into months and I grew increasingly desperate for income, I decided to use the tools and skills I had to earn some money. I bought an old Ford F-150 truck for $1,500 and dove into that full-scale bathroom remodel for Andrew, never having so much as replaced a toilet's wax ring. I bought a book about remodeling and relied on it for guidance. My poor client had no idea what he was getting into, though he ended up with a very nice bathroom several long months later.

Flynn was a cat man. He had a large orange tabby named Otto who took naps on his chest every afternoon. I still had my orange tabby, Teddy. But now that Flynn and I were living in a place of our own, I was itching to get a dog.

"If you get a dog, I'm out of here," Flynn said. I had a hard time taking him at his word. How could he be so adamant? Dogs are great companions. And puppies are irresistibly cute. Surely if I came home with one, he'd relent.

One day when Teddy had to go to the vet, I spotted a flier on the community message board next to the desk. "Beyond Adorable!" the flier read. Below that heading was a snapshot of three brindled puppies, collapsed in a heap and staring at the camera with huge, curious eyes. I tore off a scrap with the owner's number and called.

The following day I drove out to a farm in Brown County to see them. Melanie, who had posted the flier, led me over to the barn. She and her husband had taken in a Redbone coonhound stray they called Ruby. All sinewy muscle beneath her glossy red coat, Ruby had surprised them with a litter of puppies sired by a neighbor, a cross between an Irish wolfhound and a chow. Melanie opened the barn door and one pup clambered out on unsteady legs. He came right over to me while his littermates hung back, the opposite of Oscar, the shaggy black dog I adopted just after my training. "Hey, lady, who are you?" He sniffed my shoes and gave me a cocky look – ridiculous coming from a toddler who, even with four legs, could scarcely keep himself upright. His brindled coat and outsized front paws made him

William on his first birthday with celebratory lei.

look like a tiny monster. I melted at his mix of audacity and charm. I probably should have known better.

"That's William," Melanie said, explaining that she'd named each pup for a Shakespearian character, and in William's case, the bard himself. He was the one.

I held him in my lap as we drove home. He was perfectly content, which shocked me. Eight-week-old puppies aren't usually that chill about being ripped away from their siblings and mother.

It was getting late and I had no plans for dinner, so I stopped at my favorite place for burritos. I set William down on my seat, cracked the window a few inches and told him I'd be right back. I returned to the heart-rending yips and howls of a puppy terrified for his life. "It's OK," I cried, balancing the burritos in one hand and trying to get the car key in the lock with the other. I put the food in the back seat and held him in my lap as we drove the mile home against a soundtrack of whimpers punctuated by ear-splitting reminders that *I REALLY AM NOT AT ALL HAPPY ABOUT THIS.*

Sheepishly, I opened the kitchen door, burritos, wallet and William in my arms. "I got burritos from Laughing Planet!" I announced, hoping the prospect of good food would sweeten the impact. Flynn was in the kitchen. "Cute puppy," he said. "I'll be moving out tomorrow."

He found a house to rent around the corner, transferred his wall of LPs and his extensive collection of beer bottles from around the world, and we were done. Just like that.

My heart ached, but William immediately took up the slack, providing solace and distraction. Much as I admired Flynn's worldliness and his scientific work, not to mention his outrageous and often scatological sense of humor, he and I had never been that compatible. I was a morning person; he was a night owl. He loved to go out; I loved to stay home. He loved to travel, and often arranged to work in Europe; I wanted to work on the house and garden. William, on the other hand, was a puppy – ridiculous, and impossible not to love. Aside from sleep, he had two settings: the neediness of a baby and the swagger of a wannabe teenager. Who did this kid think he was? Most of the time his confidence was so absurd that it, by itself, made me laugh.

To minimize the likelihood that my dogs would continue to destroy the plants, I ended up laying paths of limestone that doubled as borders for the beds.

One of my earliest projects after moving into the house had been to fence the backyard with a hodge-podge of store-bought shadow panels and other parts – whatever I could cobble together or buy on sale. Even a puppy could not get out. I'd started a secret garden and built a deck off one of the bedrooms, but I soon learned that William was going to make gardening a challenge. Always looking for a game, he'd dig seedlings out of the ground and plop right down on tender foliage for a nap. But he was so cute I couldn't be angry for long.

Within a few weeks, he had my number. He knew just how to get me with a knowing look – "Come on, you always say I'm cute" – when caught chewing the neck out of my favorite jacket or running gleefully around the house with my dirty laundry, pulled from the hamper. He slept with me in bed and snuggled up when I read on the couch.

About a year after adopting William I thought he might appreciate a pal of his own. They could play together, keep each other company when I was busy with work or friends. I put him in the back seat of the car one evening and drove to the animal shelter. As I walked through to the area where they kept newly arrived puppies I saw a large crate with a couple of 12-week-old littermates. One was napping; the other was standing on her hind legs, pawing and biting at the wires. "Don't worry!" I imagined her telling her brother. "I'm gonna bust us out of this joint." I was drawn to her determination and only hoped that her brother, too, would find a good home. I filled out the paperwork and took William home to wait the mandated 24 hours in case I changed my mind.

The next evening we drove back to the shelter and officially adopted the black pup. She looked like a bear cub, so I called her Winnie, short for Edwina. They had her down as a Great Dane mix, due to her large paws. I was pretty sure she was just your basic black Labrador crossed with something less beefy than a purebred Lab. Her fearlessness changed instantly to worry when I picked her up in my arms, but as soon as I put her in the back seat with William, she breathed a sigh of relief: *One of my own! I have an alpha dog!* For his part, William was delighted to have a playmate – all the more so because he could dominate her physically and boss her around.

My shop at the time was in the small garage next door to my house. I'd made a habit of taking William with me to work there sometimes for a bit of variety. The two dogs together were too much for the small space, so I took them with me on alternating days. Within a week it was clear that Winnie came home with heightened confidence on the days she spent with me. She'd stride into the kitchen, head high, and give William a look that said "I spent the day with Mom in the shop – not you, dolt." I watched her sense of power grow with her weight and height. She still deferred to William, but I realized there could be problems between them down the line.

William and Winnie in the living room.

***

Some time after Flynn moved out, he understandably wanted to buy a house. To relieve his credit report of the weight of the co-signature for my loan, I was going to have to get a mortgage in my own name. As a self-employed woman with relatively low income, I was not eligible for a conventional loan backed by the secondary market. A neighbor, Elizabeth Cox-Ash, who worked as a loan officer at a locally owned bank, offered to write a loan in-house. It came with a higher interest rate, thanks to the statistically heightened risk. If I remember, it was something like 9 percent – hard to imagine at a time when rates hover at less than half that. My higher expenses were going to require more income.

The only solution I could come up with was to rent out part of the house. The ground floor had two bedrooms at the back with a full bath between them, a setup that was near-ideal. I wrote up a formal lease with the usual terms and customized it for each tenant. Would I have preferred to live alone? You bet. But that was an indulgence I could not afford. And there were advantages to having a tenant. Although I had just four renters over the six years I lived in the house, every one of them was thoughtful and quiet. I could arrange with them to keep an eye on things if work took me away for a day or two, in exchange for a reduction in the next month's rent.

For the tenants' sake as well as my own, I made clear that the lease applied to the back of the house, which had a deck off one of the bedrooms for convenient access to the backyard. They were free to use the kitchen, but the rest of the house was mine.

The tenant who stayed the longest was Eric. Eric had come from California to work on a doctorate at the Indiana University-Bloomington School of Education. A large man with curly hair, he drove a bright-orange BMW, which he parked in the driveway behind the garage. He was gentle, polite, moved slowly and kept to himself – desirable qualities in a housemate. His culinary habits, on the other hand, were less desirable – at least, for me, a longtime vegetarian. Eric ate a lot of meat, which meant there was usually some bloody hunk of beef or pork on his side of the fridge. He rarely used any herbs or spices, which ensured that the smell of cooking body parts would hit my nostrils with unadulterated force. Eric's cuisine was all about the meat, perhaps with a few spears of steamed broccoli or asparagus on the side.

One summer day I was reading in the little nook I'd added to a corner of the kitchen when in trundled Eric, clad in nothing but a pair of skin-tight trunks. It was sweltering, despite the central AC, which I always set with an eye to keeping the electric bill affordable. Sweat was dripping down his face, chest and back. The sweat and tiny trunks made for an unforgettable image. He retrieved a large piece of pork from the fridge, plopped it in a pot of water and turned it on to boil.

As the water became hot, the floating mass swelled and turned gray. You can't unsee such a sight. As for the smell, I can't describe it; I found it nauseating. I took my book upstairs, leaving him to enjoy his meal.

But Eric was great with the dogs. Not only did he appreciate their personalities, I could count on him to spill the beans if they did anything bad when I was away. A perfect example was the time I built a set of Shaker-inspired cabinetry for my friend Nancy's kitchen. Another of Nancy's friends was a scholar from Turkey who'd come to work at the university in Bloomington. She'd taken a trip with him to his homeland and returned with a trove of hand-painted plates called *cini*. The plates were the stuff of dreams (at least, my dreams), with mouthwatering colors and patterns. We agreed that three of them would make up a small part of the payment for my work.

I brought the plates home and unwrapped them that night. One was a platter with a stylized floral pattern in scarlet and grass green, a color combination I have always loved. Another was a classic Mediterranean blue and white. After admiring them I put them back in the bubble wrap and stashed them on top of a low cabinet for safekeeping.

Because that summer was so hot, I'd moved my bed downstairs to the living room. The dogs always slept with me on the bed. Sometimes William would get up for a drink of water in the middle of the night, leaving Winnie and the cat by my side. I'd just be starting to fall back asleep when he'd trot mindlessly back in his William Hiller way, poised to jump up on my side, and all hell would break loose.

DON'T EVEN THINK YOU'RE GETTING BACK UP HERE,

snarled Winnie, pounding across my body to the edge of the bed.

OH YEAH? said William; *WHO THE HELL DO YOU THINK YOU ARE? MOMMY CHOSE ME BEFORE SHE GOT YOU, AND SHE GOT YOU* FOR *ME. I OWN YOU, BITCH.*

With that he'd leap up and there would be a full-blown dog fight right over my naked body – barking, growling, flashing teeth. At times I feared for my safety. It was stupid and maddening, completely unnecessary. Winnie now matched William in weight, yet William always won. Five minutes later they'd be curled up beside me, snoring, leaving me to at least an hour of cortisol-fueled insomnia.

The day after I got the *cini*, I came home from work, set down my bag and went to find the dogs. The living room had two entrances – a 15-light door just off the front entryway, and a pair of French doors in the cased opening between the living and dining rooms. I always kept them firmly shut when I left the house to keep the dogs out while I was gone. Without my oversight, the living room promised too much temptation for ~~fun~~ destruction. On this particular evening, I found the small door open. Strange; Eric must have come into the room. Not a problem in itself, but if he was going to come into my space, I wanted him to close the door behind him. Then I saw the bubble wrap on the bed. It was the thick kind, with big bubbles, the stuff I find irresistible to pop. How had the bubble wrap come to be on the bed?

That was when I learned that Winnie shared my bubble-wrap addiction. I walked around to the other side of the bed and saw my two favorite plates on the floor, in shards. These were handmade plates, painted by artists. The thought of this work being destroyed – well, it was a crime against all art and craft.

How had Winnie managed to get into the room? I knocked on the door to Eric's part of the house. "Did you go into the living room and leave the door open?" I asked.

"I would never go in there," he replied. "It's Winnie. She knows how to open doors. I've seen her; she stands on her back legs and paws at the knob until it turns, then pushes the door open."

Her determination to avoid being locked in or out evidently had its downside. I told myself to be grateful the exterior doors opened inward and pieced the *cini* back together with epoxy as well as I was able.

The dogs developed a habit of running around the perimeter of the backyard as soon as I let them out, so I stopped trying to grow things in their path and let them have at it. Before long, the track, as I called it, had the best tilth of any place in the garden; no sooner had I mulched it with chips from the shop than they'd work the fresh material in. With my monsters ever on the rampage, I had to fence off an area to grow basil and a few tomato plants. I built a wire enclosure and secured it with a shop-made wood-and-wire gate. That worked fine until a mother rabbit made her nest below the patch of thyme – a safe spot to hide offspring, thanks to its fragrance, which masked the animals' scent. Tragically, William and Winnie sniffed out the nest, and Winnie used her problem-solving skills to get in. The dogs tore through the house and ran ecstatically up to my office. Hearing the unmistakable sounds of baby bunny terror, a cross between a shriek and a raspy moan, I ran upstairs behind them. Each dog had multiple bunnies – it was like one of those sales where you get 15 percent off everything you can stuff into a brown paper bag. *WAIT! I THINK I CAN GET ONE MORE BUNNY IN MY MOUTH! THIS IS THE MOST FUN I'VE HAD IN AGES!*

Yelling "NO!" at the top of my lungs, I got them to drop the rabbits. But the carnage was complete – dead bunnies were strewn across the floor. I took the babies outside and buried them with apologies and a prayer, then added a keyed lock to the latch I'd thought impervious to Winnie's wiles.

My fun-loving pair also wreaked havoc at the back of the garden. I'd enclosed a back corner on three sides to use for a compost pile. Between garden debris and kitchen scraps, the pile grew fast. William ran up and down the pile many times a day, quickly packing it into a solid mass. Once compacted, it sloped steeply upward from ground level at the front to some four feet high, making an ideal lookout post for William as people walked up and down the alley. He was fine with grown-ups – they were boring. But he had a thing about children. So small! What are they, 3/5 scale? Members of another species? A pair of kids would be walking home from school and he'd bound to the

Mother and baby. Rae and one of her offspring.

Graphic evidence that William's boldness exceeded his intelligence. Good things typically do not follow when a 45-lb. dog barks ferociously at a fully grown bison bull.

top of the pile, stand fully upright and balance his weight against the fence, barking ferociously. Kids were terrified, and no wonder – from the alley he appeared to be 7 feet tall, The Hound of the Baskervilles brought to life in Small Town Indiana. For William, their shrieks were positive reinforcement. He became a neighborhood terror. No one in their right mind would want to mess with such a beast.

***

In the autumn of 2000 I left my cinder-block garage for a rented shop about 8 miles from town. The new place belonged to a businessman who got my number from the guys at the paint store on the Square (sadly, no longer in that location, which is now occupied by a nail salon or martini bar). He'd seen a personal ad somewhere, placed by a woman carpenter looking for someone to accompany her on hikes and go canoeing on the lake. The guys at the store thought I might be the one who'd placed it. I wasn't, but when this stranger called, we struck up a conversation. He sounded thoughtful and interesting. During the call I mentioned my inadequate shop situation, and he told me he had a shop at his farm in the country. He'd built it for himself but was still too busy with work to use it.

Several weeks later, he called again. Might I consider renting his shop? I was aware that I was violating a city ordinance by using a garage to build furniture and cabinets as a business. My neighbors and I had formed a neighborhood association to strengthen our ties and protect the area from unwanted development. I knew that some might see my behavior as hypocritical, even though neighbors assured me that my business was not the kind they minded. Renting Alan's shop for $200 a month was more appealing than worrying about running into trouble with my neighbors or the authorities.

Alan's shop was on a farm where he raised buffalo. It was late September when I went to see the place, a hot end to a long summer. I took the dogs with me; they would come to know the last mile of the drive so well that once we turned onto the road, my vehicle itself appeared to be barking the rest of the way, alerting Alan and all the neighbors to my

The built-in I made for the dining room of Rick and Joy Harter's home in the late 1990s. (Photo: Spectrum Creative Group.)

impending arrival. On that first visit William found the buffalo intriguing and tried to play with one, which earned him a swift kick. Winnie, of course, knew better. I agreed to rent the shop.

Having 1,000 square feet to myself was a luxury I had never known. I moved what machines I had to the new place. I was glad to get the old 12-inch Crescent jointer I'd bought from a woodworker in North Carolina out of my friend Ben Sturbaum's storage building and put it to use. I loved that the dogs had a place to run around.

Alan often came out in the evenings, when I was still at work, and almost always on weekends. He was constantly working to improve the farm, hauling away a dumpster's worth of demolition garbage tossed into a sinkhole by the former owners. He sowed and cut hay; he built electrified fence around endless acres. He'd bought a used band-saw mill and restored it to working condition; to dry the boards, most of them sawn from logs cut on construction sites, he'd built a solar kiln. He had a barn full of equipment to go with his astonishing variety of practical skills. This man was a paragon of Getting Things Done. I couldn't not admire him, and as time passed, I admired him more and more. On top of all this, he was ruggedly handsome, with blond hair, piercing blue eyes and skin tanned from working in the sun.

As winter approached I bought a propane heater for the shop, which had no other source of heat. The fumes were noxious, the noise a nuisance. I was paying rent, so maybe Alan thought there should be a better source of heat. He'd planned to install a woodstove whenever he was ready to have the shop back for his own use, but one weekend morning shortly before Christmas I was excited to see him show up with one, a Jøtul, along with a buttery Kringle he'd ordered from a bakery out of state. He unwrapped the pastry on the table saw outfeed table and we each had a slice with coffee.

After Alan had installed the woodstove he asked for a hand with the buffalo. A young female had been sick, and despite his efforts to help her get well, she had not responded. She had diarrhea, could hardly eat and was wasting away. He was going to put her out of her misery.

He'd moved her into a pen by herself. I felt an obligation to witness her death. We were fellow mammals. This was about kinship.

As young females, the ailing buffalo and her "sister" had been sold to some people who had no idea how proficiently buffalo can jump. I'd watched Alan's buffalo BOING over obstacles and sometimes levitate into the air repeatedly for fun. It's an absurd sight, giant animals with springs in their feet. After the young pair escaped, the owners decided they couldn't keep them. They knew about Alan and called him. Would he help? If he could catch their girls, he could have them.

He'd driven out to their property with a cattle trailer and some tasty hay. Relying on what he'd learned about buffalo behavior at conferences and through experience with his own herd, he thought up a way to lure them into the trailer. His method took a couple of days, but it worked.

Introducing these new members to Alan's existing herd was a challenge. After watching the buffalo for just a few months, I recognized some key dimensions of their dynamic. There was one dominant male; Alan had named him George. A magnificent animal, he'd gained my admiration for his gentle way of managing his extended family. There were challengers, of course, younger males, a couple of them close to George in size. One day I watched one rival stage a coup attempt: He rushed up to George and mounted him from behind, the ultimate insult. George swung around, bellowing, and chased him all over the field. Up and down, around and around, the sight was like something in a cartoon – but in this case the characters were live, raging beasts, each weighing around a ton. The ground shook beneath their hooves; I could feel it from the shop. George won that round, though some months later Alan discovered him dead; he'd lost his footing on a steep slope and fallen, his enormous head downhill from the rest of his body, a position from which he hadn't been able to get up.

The adult males were the first to get hay, or grain at the trough. But close behind them was a seasoned female I called Rae, in honor of Alan's late mother. Rae had one intact horn; the other had been damaged, so it was shorter and deformed. She had been the most prolific bearer of living offspring, which seemed to have won her this valuable position; another female had had as many births, but at least one of her offspring had died. After Rae came the other mature females who had mothered offspring, followed by the older youths.

The two young females were pretty much ostracized. I felt for them. Their predicament seemed awfully similar to the new kid at school whose parents just went through a bitter divorce, leaving her traumatized, awkward and shy, with an old flip phone when all the other kids have the latest Apple product, and hand-me-down clothes from her siblings. I'd had more than enough experience of being the odd one out by the time Alan asked me to help put the sick buffalo down. I was going to witness this unfortunate animal's release from her pain-wracked body as a matter of principle.

It happened in a flash – the blast of the gun, the buffalo's fall. I heard the "NO!" that flew out of my mouth as though from another body, and the next thing I knew, Alan had me in a tight embrace, the canvas of his Carhartt jacket stiff against my cheek.

We developed a serious relationship and talked about moving in together. He initially said he would move into my house. I was in love with my home, which had become a kind of partner to me over my years of living there, effectively on my own. Truth be told, I had a hard time envisioning Alan living there with Winnie, William and me, considering that Alan would be moving into what was undeniably William's territory. They were both extraordinarily strong-willed. In the end, Alan decided we should move into a house he owned on the edge of town, a place he had previously rented to others and was ready to sell. If we lived in it for two years, he could sell it without paying capital gains tax. My interest in the relationship won out. I rented my house to a chef and her partner and continued to maintain the garden in my spare time.

William and Winnie were grudgingly allowed inside at the place on the edge of town. Some of the time they stayed in the backyard, then came into the garage at night, an abrupt change for all three of us. I sometimes took them to work with me, so they had freedom in addition to my company. I knew that William was badly behaved – I'd raised him to think he could get away with far too much. His dual personality, which alternated between stubborn and hilarious, had won my heart. That was manageable when we lived alone, but Alan reigned over our household with a strong hand. William resented the new authority figure and the changes to his previously ~~spoiled~~ happy life. One day, when I was gone, Alan demanded that William get out from beneath the dining table. William refused, as much from canine instinct as from uncertainty about what was likely to happen with Alan, in particular. The battle of wills ended when Alan reached under the table – always inadvisable with a wary dog – and William bit his hand.

Alan might just as soon have shot him, but he called me instead. "William just bit the shit out of my hand," he said, leaving me panicking about how this new drama might end. That night he took William out to the garage and beat him with a 2x4 as Winnie watched in horror. Winnie had always been afraid of Alan, who rode big, loud machines – a tractor, a Bobcat, his rumbly diesel truck – and carted bales of hay as big as a Smart car around the farm. She'd seen him corralling the buffalo, enormous monsters she knew better than to mess with. Alan joked that Winnie called him "the tractor man." Now the tractor man had exceeded her most terrified imaginings as she witnessed William resist the beating. Had he been a kid, he would have been yelling "I CAN'T EVEN FEEL IT, YOU BASTARD." I winced in the living room, deeply conflicted about the harsh punishment while knowing I'd done William a disservice by failing to give him the kind of training he should have had, and sorry about the injury to Alan's hand.

I felt overwhelmed and torn. Clearly Alan and my dogs were not a good mix, but what should I do? Alan was a good man who had raised steady, intelligent, accomplished sons. Several years earlier, I'd left my marriage to Kent. Over the intervening time I'd concluded that I hadn't tried hard enough to save it. Sure, my former husband and I had our talks; we discussed seeing a therapist, but I was the only one who went. I would not repeat my mistake and let this relationship fail. Alan had started to build the house at his farm and planned to move there with me. I loved and admired him and wanted to remain part of that dream.

Maybe two dogs were too much. I said I would try to find Winnie a new home; she would be the more attractive one to a prospective adopter. Alan agreed that was a good idea. I put an ad in the paper. A woman called, prompted by the sweet description, all of it true. I told her more; she said she wanted to meet Winnie and would probably take her home.

That was all it took – I couldn't go through with it. Winnie was a sweet, intelligent dog, loyal to William and to me. I would not betray her trust. I apologized and told her that in the end, I couldn't bear to let her go.

As time went on, I became deeply depressed. Alan didn't even really know me, though he insisted he did. We'd discuss our problems; the fault was always mine. This was quite a winning streak I was on when it came to men. I didn't want to travel with him – at least, not as often as he would have liked, nor to the particular places he wanted to visit. I didn't want to go canoeing; nor did I ski, though I went with him on a skiing vacation to Montana with his sons, during which we spent some time with Kent, his wife, Mary, and their first son, Ethan. What I really loved to do was build things, garden and write.

The problems were all too familiar from my marriage to Kent and some of my shorter-term relationships. Early on, I'd accompanied Alan – once in winter, then in summer – to his family's cabin in the north woods; both visits were a treat. I'd gone to an air show and been awed by aircraft from the Grumman Goose to the Flying Fortress and F-14s. I took part in family occasions with his sons. I was making an effort, but it seemed as though nothing I did would ever be enough.

When I confronted him with my perspective or told him that he often seemed to forget there were two distinct people in the relationship, each with our own interests, wills and talents, he insisted he was aware of that and knew himself very well. In effect, this translated to "I hate to say this, but you're the one with the problem." Like William, I'm not much of a quitter, at least unless I'm thoroughly convinced that leaving is the right decision. So I doubled down on my efforts to bear the way things were and stayed.

One day it became too much. I can't recall the particular circumstances. I don't even think it was anything specific, but rather the grinding, low-level sense that my partner really wanted someone other than me, despite his protestations to the contrary. I now appreciated Kent's devastating "I hate you. I don't love you. I wish you'd leave" as liberating for him and me, both. In contrast, Alan's unhappiness with me, coupled with his denial that he wanted to be with someone who was not-me, made for what my friend Veda called "a crazy-making situ-

R.I.P., William Hiller. Three months before he died, we had no idea that William was ill. Mark took this picture on the front porch of his house. (As usual, Winnie was merely tolerating her adopted brother/oppressor.)

ation." By staying in the relationship, I was being irresponsible to myself and my animal friends.

But as exasperating as I found our relationship at times, I genuinely loved Alan. I admired him as a father, exceptionally hard worker and businessman. He had helped me in many ways, allowing me to use his shop at no charge after we became a couple, working alongside me on several jobs, then declining to charge for his labor. I felt an obligation to keep trying after both of us had invested so much and made sacrifices to be together.

Lurking in the background was another, less admirable reason to stay. I had grown up in a culture obsessed with romantic relationships, one in which women who were dedicated to their work and happened to be unattached were too often seen as "difficult" or, as one relative put it decades ago, possibly infected with a "social disease." The implication was that if you made an effort to stay in shape (and didn't "let yourself go"), were even minimally intelligent and knew how to cook, you should be married – it wasn't that hard. (Tell that to any of my single female friends and you can expect to be booted straight out the door.) At times the pressure to be in a relationship felt like a game of musical chairs – find someone, and don't be too "picky" or you're going to be left out. I had heard women older than my mother joke about having gone to college not to get a B.A. or an M.S., but an "M.R.S." Esse had stayed in her marriage even after her husband started to see a younger woman – a relationship that went on for years and became a marriage after my grandma's death. When we were teenagers, Maggie had overheard Esse tell her sister-in-law that she'd thought about jumping off the balcony of their 20-something-story apartment.[2] Even as the women's liberation movement was challenging longstanding norms and prejudices in the '60s and '70s, our own mother, like many mothers of our friends, had in effect made clear through her actions that she depended on being in a relationship with a man.

Already twice-divorced, I had been told repeatedly that I was joyless and unlovable. I was in my mid-40s, an age at which a vast corpus of popular publications assured me I was unlikely to marry again or even have another long-term relationship. I wanted a partner; there was so much in life to share – not just sex, but good food, fires in the woodstove, gardening, walks, books and movies, other friends – and I have always loved the basic mammalian comfort of sleeping next to someone I love and trust.

Faced with the prospect of what so many presented as failure, I decided that I would simply remove myself from the equation. A friend had

---

[2] This is not to deny that there are often good, loving reasons to remain in a relationship where others are involved, as ended up happening with my grandmother, but rather to acknowledge the internalized social pressure many women have felt to stay, regardless of how destructive it may be for their health.

taken her life many years before. I'd do it the same way. I knew I could find the necessary materials at a locally owned hardware store.[3]

But just as I was feeling perversely comforted by knowing I had a plan, it hit me: If I went through with it, William would be toast. No one else would take on such a willful, uncooperative dog – and certainly not Alan. I was going to have to suck it up and find a way to go on, if only to ensure William's welfare.

---

[3] In honor of Kieran Binnie and so many others, I urge those who are even thinking about taking their life to seek help. You can contact the National Suicide Prevention Lifeline at https://suicidepreventionlifeline.org or 800-273-8255. I know from personal experience that an hour – and even sometimes a minute – can make all the difference, and as in my case, life can become richer than we can often imagine when we're in the grip of depression-induced despair.

10: Lizzie, Part One (2004-2020)

THE OLD cat perches on the chair next to the woodstove, eyes closed, in a shaft of sun. It's spring, 2020. She's tiny now, skin and bones – a shadow of the majestic gray tabby she was in her prime.

She has lived many lives. For more than a decade, she was an indoor cat with outdoor privileges; her canniness about the road kept her on our property, even as she hunted right up to the boundaries, which at one time included a busy road. Five years ago she nearly breathed her last when ravaged by a dog; blinded in one eye and left with a broken jaw, she pulled through thanks to her favorite activity, eating. She threw up almost daily. We'd hear an eerie howl – *a-wow…a-wha-wha-wha-wha-wow* – followed by retching so violent that I sometimes feared the spasms would kill her. Sometimes there was a hairball, sometimes not.

In 2018, she grew so thin and frail that we thought her time had come. As it turned out, she had an overactive thyroid gland; transdermal medication twice a day renewed her lease on life. Two weeks ago she still climbed up the stairs to yowl at us for breakfast, but for the past few days we've been spared those demands. Three days ago she ate her last food and spent the day sprawled luxuriantly on her chair. Life was still good.

The next morning a fog descended. She lay head-up, eyes pressed shut, to all appearances focused on minimizing her discomfort. To look at her now is to see myself on the bathroom floor, propped against the wall, putting all my effort into staying in that elusive space between nausea and surrendering to its urge.[1] When her eyes open, they're

---

[1] For the sake of others who may be contemplating chemotherapy, let me add that the last time I felt so nauseated was years before my diagnosis of cancer.

Lizzie napping in her ninth life.

LIZZIE, PART ONE (2004-2020)

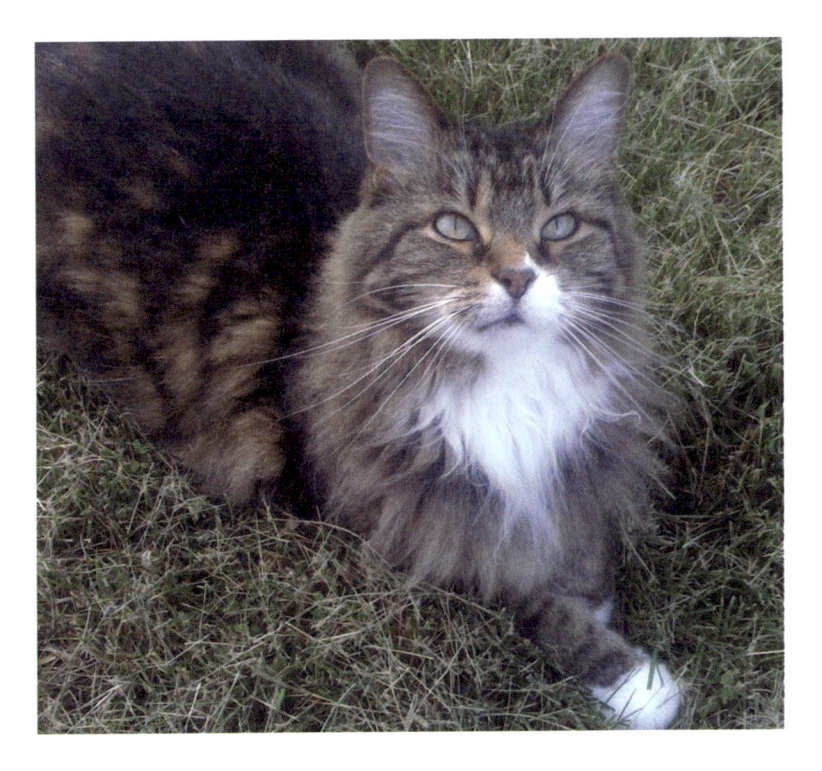

In her prime Lizzie was a beautiful tabby with long white socks.

glazed. I lift a cup of water to her chin. She drinks. Every few hours she climbs down to the floor and makes her way weakly to the water bowl in the pantry to take a long draft for herself, as if to say *I can still do this*. Back at the fireside, she pauses and looks up at the chair, the seat's 15-inch height now beyond her reach. *Can I make it?* asks her expression. I lift her up and lay her gently on the fleece.

Lizzie's story – at least, the part that involved me – began with an earlier cat named Joey, around the year 2000. I was at a locally owned building-supplies outfit on the edge of downtown, buying some framing material for a project at home. Bob, who ran the lumberyard, had just finished slicing through a stack of 2x8s with the 12-inch radial-arm saw, its blade fully exposed. By law the saw should have had a guard. But this was a contractor's yard, frequented by seasoned builders, not the kind of folks who streak upstairs from the basement on mistaking a piece of old duct tape for asbestos, then call their handyman to remove the "life-threatening" find.

It was a glorious summer day. I'd just told Bob about the death of my cat Teddy, who'd escaped through the kitchen door of my bungalow and been killed by a car, despite years of effort to keep him safely inside the house. "Ah've got an orange cat for ye, if ye want him," he said in his southern Hoosier drawl. "Well, he's more butterscotch'n orange. Barn cat just had another litter. Come back tamarrah; ah'll have him back in the lumber rack." He tipped the brim of his cloth hat and got back to work.

The kitten was there when I stopped by the next morning. Bob pointed to a dark corner in the back, where a ball of pale-yellow fluff, locked in a coon hunter's cage behind the stacks of glass bead and chair rail, was mewing for his mother. "Take the cage," said Bob. "Just bring it back tamarrah."

"Can I give you anything for him?"

"Goodness, no! Yer doin' me a favor."

At the time, my shop was the unheated cinder-block garage next door to my house. It had one small window for natural light, a "man door," as they're called in the trade, and an overhead garage door. I carried the bulky cage inside. The kitten cowered at the back.

"Hi, kitty!" I whispered. I couldn't wait to snuggle him in my arms. He hunkered down. I unlatched the wire door and tipped the cage forward, hoping he'd come out. He grabbed onto the wire for dear life and wouldn't budge.

Two could play at this game. I left the shop for a few minutes, hoping he'd relax and come out on his own. He did. But as soon as I opened the door, he darted behind a stack of boxes, hissing and puffed up like a hairy balloon. I called him sweetly, kneeling on the floor. No joy.

I walked next door to the house for a can of cat food and pulled off the lid as I got back to the shop. Suspicious eyes peered through a slit. I waved the can through the air, hoping he'd notice the aroma. He glanced around the corner, then took a few halting steps – it might be a

Joey the Cat in the kitchen of my bungalow in town.

trap. When he was a few feet away I put the can on the floor. He wasn't about to come closer. I gave the can a push in his direction. He sniffed the meat, licked it and dug in.

The magic of canned food was all it took to transform Joey the Cat from feral to tame. I brought him into the house, where he got along fine with William and Winnie. From that moment on, he loved to be held, came running when I called his name and turned into one of the most affectionate cats I've ever known.

It was a few months after Joey came into my life that I became involved with Alan. Joey moved with us to the house on the edge of town, where we would spend the next few years. I didn't want to let him out for at least a few weeks, until he was familiar with the new location. "He'll be fine," Alan assured me as he let him out the front door. It was still early enough in our relationship that I wanted to believe him.

Joey was the most dog-like, affectionate cat I have known.

Joey explored the suburban neighborhood and came home late each afternoon. The house was on a cul-de-sac with little traffic, which I was relieved to find he avoided.

Things were different when we moved to the house at the farm in the spring of 2004. There, Alan didn't allow the dogs inside, though he sometimes let them in the mudroom off the backyard. He fenced in part of the yard and built them a doghouse. They had never lived outside; now we were in a rural location where coyotes and small wildcats took down deer and even the occasional buffalo from Alan's herd that was young or weakened by ill health. William kept us up at night with his barks and howls.

I felt terrible about the dogs' exclusion. I was betraying members of my family who depended on me. I told myself that most dogs lived this way; in fact, those who did were the lucky ones, with a roof over their head and plenty of food. I told myself to stop being a baby; I knew I'd spoiled my dogs and let William, in particular, get away with all kinds of bad behavior. The property was Alan's, not mine, and I should live with his decision. Still, I felt torn, aware that I was acting as my mother sometimes had when forced to choose between respecting my wishes, or Maggie's, over those of George, her erstwhile boyfriend in London, or later, our stepfather.

As I had when we first moved into the house on the edge of town, I asked Alan to keep Joey inside until he'd familiarized himself with the new place. Again, he refused. The first couple of times I came home to find Joey gone, I called "Jo-ey!" in the high-pitched voice that had always brought him running. It was a relief to see him tear up the hill to the house in response. Still, I didn't like it; everything I'd ever read about moving with cats recommended keeping them inside for at least a couple of weeks, until they were used to a new place.

One day I came home and couldn't find him despite my calls. Alan said he'd let him out, the act and his straightforward acknowledgment of it just another implied expression of how unreasonable I was being and how little my thoughts on the matter meant to him: *Of course I let him out; that's what regular people do. You're not normal, and I'm tired of accommodating your views.* I walked around the yard calling, to no response. A few days passed. I was distraught – not just at Joey's disappearance, but at Alan's lack of respect for my concern. I hoped that Joey might show up out of the blue.

By this time, it was late spring. The grass was thick and green, the trees lush with leaves, the garden bright with lilies, daisies and delicate blue catmint flowers. I walked out to the road to get the mail, as I did most afternoons. Our neighbor Bill was sitting on his front porch across the road. Bill was a retired excavator who sometimes pronounced that word "escalator," a malapropism I loved. Cheerful and round, Bill was always friendly and ready to shoot the breeze. I crossed the street and asked whether he'd seen a pale orange cat. "Oh dear," he answered. "Was that yours? Poor thing came over here one day and stood on the roof of our car, crying. We felt sorry for 'im. A couple of days later I found 'im out here on the side of the road, hit by a car. I threw his body over the hill out back."

It was the latest of too many insults. This would be the last time I betrayed an animal friend because of a man. I was over Alan's complaints about my ill-mannered dogs and his refusal to let them come in the house, over the marginalizing of my abilities as a woodworker, as well as my opinions on so many subjects. I was done with his resentment that I failed to share his love of canoeing, skiing and travel and preferred to spend my time gardening – back then, my greatest joy. His resentment of the hours I spent in the garden was so intense that when I came home one evening that summer after working in the beds I was establishing at my new shop property, he pulled up a row of blooming sunflowers I'd grown from seed and tossed them on the ground to die. It was time for him to acknowledge that I would never fulfill the role he'd imagined for me early in our relationship, when he'd looked into my eyes one day and said, "You are the other me," a statement I'd wanted to see as romantic, even though I recognized it as a giant neon sign flashing POTENTIAL NARCISSIST ALERT. "I'm lonely," he'd lament. The therapist I'd consulted in an effort to address my deepening sense of despair suggested a golden retriever might be better suited to provide the kind of companionship Alan wanted than a woman with passionate interests and values of her own.

By now it was dusk. I sat on the stacked stone retaining wall I'd built to create a terraced garden and watched the moon rise. This was the straw that would break the camel's back. There was no way I could stay with this man.

I'd sold my bungalow in town the previous year, so I couldn't go back there. Much as I'd wanted the relationship with Alan to be permanent, a part of me felt conflicted and insecure – not because we had different interests or different thoughts about how to do things (we did, as do partners in many relationships), but because of how I felt he leveraged the imbalance of power between us. Far more successful in business than I, his income was much higher, and while he was generous toward me and had given me hands-on help with my work on many occasions, the flip side of that generosity seemed to have become a loss of respect. I sensed a general attitude that, in return for whatever help he gave me, I owed him compliance. But compliance wasn't right, either. This was something that he honestly considered more benign: He wanted me to want what he wanted. Looking back, I can say "That was nice of him" and mean it sincerely, even while recognizing a turd in a punchbowl. Sidney, our childhood dog, had taught me a more respectful way of relating, in which both partners allowed each other to be who they are. The fact that I had my own professional and ethical priorities was an inconvenience that Alan and I never managed to negotiate. Plainly put, he wanted to be with someone who was not me, despite his insistence that I was wrong about that, too.

Little wonder, then, that as soon as I'd closed on the sale of my bungalow I started dreaming vaguely about buying a property in the country, someplace where I could have a shop of my own – and go to live, if things fell completely apart. In October 2003, several months before we'd moved to the farm, I'd bought the most affordable place I could find.

The place was one acre with a decrepit house and a small wood-frame garage. I thought about using the old garage for my shop and restoring the house, a Snuffy Smith[2] structure built to the most basic standards during the Great Depression, mainly out of materials gathered directly from the land. Piers of dry-stacked limestone, pulled from thin topsoil on the slopes that creased the surrounding acreage, supported beams of rough-sawn poplar. Native hardwood studs framed the roof and walls, which had originally been covered with board-and-batten siding; the circular saw marks on all of these parts were still visible. The north wall had apparently housed a fireplace until it was retrofitted with a gas heater vented through a limestone chimney.

By the time the place went up for auction it had suffered decades of improvements made by people who had no understanding of how to work with the structure's primitive skeleton. First they'd removed the battens and covered the oak boards with a layer of Homosote insulation, topped by sheet-asphalt siding. Later, in a remodel that replaced the original wooden window sashes with vinyl, the exterior walls were

---

[2] Snuffy Smith was a character in a long-running comic strip by cartoon artist Billy DeBeck. A moonshiner in the Appalachian hamlet of "Hootin' Holler," he lived in a crude home-built shack.

furred out with softwood, insulated with fiberglass and sided with vinyl. You could scarcely have devised a better recipe to retain moisture and cultivate mold. At some point the garage had been added, just a few feet from the house's north wall, which created a dark, damp corridor between the two structures. No surprise the beam supporting the north wall (and the roof) had succumbed to rot. The couple who had owned the house were retired and had apparently been unable to afford repairs. When I took a walk through the interior to see how much work it might take to make the place livable, the north wall was so near collapse that there was a slope of more than a foot across the living room floor, which, like the rest of the house, was strewn with clothing, shoes, convenience-food wrappers and old magazines.

I bought the property with proceeds from the sale of my bungalow in town. Not only was this the only affordable place close to Alan's, I'd fallen in love. A statuesque native persimmon tree, the biggest I'd ever seen, stood in the front yard, and a grand old catalpa stood on the house's south side, where its heart-shaped leaves provided shade in summer. Scattered around this pair, which had the feel of guardians, were traditional Midwestern shrubs and flowers: viburnum, forsythia, rose of Sharon, peonies, surprise lilies and a drift of daffodils dotted with grape hyacinths, all evidence that generations of people had loved the place.

Alan and I agreed that the cramped, uninsulated garage, which listed at an angle, would never make a decent shop. Ready to have his own shop back, he was willing to build me one for the cost of materials and his crew's labor. My shop would be 30 feet x 40 feet on a single level, with one corner walled off for dust-free finishing and some space in the attic for storage. Meanwhile, I'd spoken with a builder who specialized in restoring old houses about putting this old house right; a good foundation, repairs to the north wall, better windows, new wiring and a new roof would be the minimum required, and all I could pay someone else to take care of. I could do the rest in my spare time. I was giddy at the prospect of restoring a modest wreck to a well-loved home.

Alan had other ideas. "I can't let you keep that house," he told me a couple of days before the restoration contractor was set to begin. "With your asthma and allergies, it will kill you. Let me build you a new house. It will be healthier and far more energy-efficient than this old one could ever be. I'll do it as affordably as possible, for the cost of labor and materials, and you can finish out the inside in your own time." Then, he suggested, I could rent it to someone else to help cover the mortgage.

I was stunned. On the one hand, how could I not appreciate the generosity of his offer, which was based on his concern for my health? He was right about the daunting task the restoration would be when I had a business to run, not to mention the risks to my health. On the other hand, his proposal felt like an imposition. I understood that any time I devoted to working on the decrepit old house would be time away from him. He usually followed "I'm lonely" with the old saw about how it's bad enough to be lonely when you're on your own, but when you feel lonely in a relationship, there's something *really* wrong – and it's the fault of the person who's not complaining. By this point in our time together the implication was indisputably clear: I was the problem.

Compounding my dilemma, I'd been active in our local preservation community for many years, urging others to repair their old wooden windows, to restore their crumbling houses and barns. I had signed a contract with Chris Sturbaum, the restoration contractor. Now I was going to pay someone to raze a sweet example of roll-up-your-sleeves, we-can-do-this Depression-era gumption?

I called my friend Duncan Campbell, a preservation consultant with a fondness for modest structures. He and his wife, Cathy, live in a pre-Civil War-era house they've restored over decades, largely with their own hands. If there was anyone whose opinion on this matter I respected, it was his. He drove over, looked around and said, "Bring on the bulldozer." I paid his consultation fee of $75, a small price for a less-guilty conscience.

A few weeks after Joey disappeared, my pole-barn shop was up and insulated, and the wiring had been run. All that remained was to hang drywall. Then I could bring over my workbench, tools and machines, and start working in the new location, my first official shop of my own at 45.

I wanted a cat. And I was going to have a cat – not just for my sake, but in Joey's honor. In fact, I'd be doing my small part to honor all of

Not long after I adopted the cats, Tom was diagnosed with feline infectious peritonitis, which he did not survive.

the world's underappreciated cats. But before I could get a cat, I needed a place for it to live. The drywallers were still a few days out from starting my shop's interior. I told them to prioritize hanging the finishing room. They didn't need to know why, and they certainly didn't need to pass the word on to Alan, who worked with them on a regular basis.

I went to the animal shelter in search of a kitten. I had in mind a black and gray tabby. A receptionist led me through a door into the cat room, where cages were stacked several-high. I'd just put my name down for a 2-month-old male when someone in the adjoining room let out an exasperated cry: "Oh, Sparkle!" Looking through the doorway I watched an adult cat in one of the higher cages bat her freshly filled bowl of food to the front of the crate, shooting kibble all over the floor.

"She does this all the time," the woman told me. She had a drawn

LIZZIE, PART ONE (2004-2020)

Lizzie and Tom got along surprisingly well, considering that they were thrown together immediately after I adopted them both from the shelter.

face and pale complexion, the kind of look anyone might develop after the years of hope and resignation required of those who care for animals at a shelter with limited space.

"What a personality," I remarked, amused that any animal in a shelter who had been given food and a safe place to live would be so picky. The attendant half-smiled. "Sparkle has been here for months," she told me. "Most cats get less time. But she hasn't been adopted, and we just have to keep her in the hope she'll find a home. She has such spirit." I was sorely tempted.

Could I take two cats? I already had William and Winnie. It would mean hundreds of dollars more per year in food and veterinary expenses alone. I really wanted a kitten. I was going to adopt a kitten. But there was no way I could not also adopt this adult cat.

The drywallers still hadn't hung the finishing room. The shelter was overburdened; I had to bring the cats home. Alan would probably be mad if I said anything, so I had to keep them secret. I cobbled together a crate for the cat and kitten out of scrap wood and chicken wire, leaving a flap through which I could pass food and the bottom half of a plastic lunchbox filled with litter. I hid the cat coop behind my lathe and a stack of offcuts under the attic stairs in the rear corner of Alan's shop. "Bear with me," I whispered the first night when I put them to bed. "It will get better." I prayed that Alan wouldn't notice them; when he stopped by the next day I distracted him from the view beneath the stairs by pointing out something fascinating at my bench.

The tall gray tabby had long white stockings that looked like go-go boots. Despite this potential bimbo association, she was too regal for a dimwit name like "Sparkle." I decided to call her Elizabeth – Lizzie for short – after my grandma Esse's sister, who was intelligent, poised and urbane. I named the kitten Tom after the Beatrix Potter character. I'd worried that the cats, who were strangers, might get in a fight as a result of being holed up in such close quarters, but as I came and went, I found them surprisingly at ease with being cooped up.

As soon as the finishing room was drywalled I installed a pre-hung door and moved the cats over. They would be safe in that room while the drywallers hung the rest of the shop.

By fall, things between Alan and me had deteriorated further. I moved my old bed, a poplar pencil post made as a prototype, over to the finishing room and took to sleeping there some nights. William, Winnie, Lizzie and Tom all slept with me on the bed. My friend Peggy had camped out in the basement of a barn she was converting into a house; I took her cue, adding a microwave and kettle to the shop bathroom, which had a utility sink (still not plumbed in) and no toilet. There really was no need for a toilet at that point; the shop was on the edge of woods, so I had plenty of privacy. I drilled a hole through the wall between the finishing room and the bathroom, where the phone jack was located, and ran a landline extension to the jack so I could call someone in an emergency. The only person who called at night was Alan. He called repeatedly as the weeks wore on. The conversations started out cordially enough, but often reached a point where he said he couldn't understand what had happened to our relationship after we'd both invested so much in making a life together. I didn't know what else to say; I'd said it all before, so many times. We usually both grew angry. Sometimes, after telling him what I was about to do, I hung up. It seemed to be the only way to end the terribly stressful madness.

One morning that November, I got ready for a meeting with a couple of prospective clients who'd been referred to me by one of my former professors. I brushed my hair and dressed, wondering whether they might have thought better of hiring me, had they been aware of where and how I was sleeping. I shouldn't have worried; when I walked into their kitchen the tension was so thick you could have cut it with a knife. It felt familiar.

Sometimes Alan and I stayed together at his house. My furniture and possessions were still there. I went "home" to work in my office, even after my shop was up and running. I also appreciated the opportunity to take a bath or shower a few times a week.

By mid-December the shell of the house at my shop property was complete. The drywall was hung, taped and ready to paint. There was no trim, no doors between rooms, no cabinets. Nor were there any plumbing fixtures. Those would come in the following weeks and months. For now, I would stick with the ~~drywall bucket~~ chamber pot and get water from the standpipe near the road. I had the important things: electricity, a roof, a furnace, lockable doors. It was more obvious by the day that Alan and I were going to split up for good and this house would become my home.

One evening when I was at Alan's, things turned exceptionally bad. I have no memory of the details; I only know that I had reached the end of my rope. Furious and despondent, I was in the little loft outside our bedroom, where he kept a shotgun. I grabbed the gun and started waving it about. It wasn't loaded, and I would never have used a gun against anyone other than myself (had I even known how to shoot one). "We have to get you moved over to that house," he said, as though addressing someone of feeble mind. I'd been so determined to keep this relationship going that I had, as my friend Peggy put it, turned myself into a pretzel. I was a rat in a Skinner Box, thwarted from affecting our relationship in any positive way, short of getting a personality transplant. Even though he'd insisted until now that he wanted to be with me, he didn't. You can't want to be with someone when you don't even know who she is.

There were no finished floors in the new house, just sheets of raw OSB subfloor nailed over joists. I was going to lay the floors myself, as time allowed – lauan underlayment topped with classic kitsch vinyl composition tile for the kitchen and bath, 3-inch-wide hickory flooring everywhere else. I'd start with the living room, to get one room ready for relatively comfortable habitation.

I spent my first night in the new house upstairs, my bed a piece of upholstery foam on the OSB floor, topped with a sleeping bag. William, Winnie, Lizzie and Tom surrounded me like potatoes and carrots arranged around a nut roast, their familiar press a comfort. As I closed my eyes, I became aware of a bright light outdoors. It was one of those infernal security lights at the property line, the kind Kent used to threaten to shoot with a BB gun to reclaim the dark. Like a full moon, it shone through the window straight into my face. But unlike a full moon, this interrogation light did not budge. I still had no curtains or rods; I was too exhausted to get a hammer and tack a moving pad over the window, so I did my best to hide my face in the sleeping bag.

The next morning I called the power company and asked them to disconnect the light. Their records showed no indication that a security light had ever been installed – apparently it was another instance of can-do ingenuity on the part of previous property owners. They sent someone over to disconnect it. My next bill had a month's charge for a security light. When I disputed the charge, they said the light had been up for years, even though I hadn't been living there or had any knowledge of it, and the least I could do was pay for one month. Welcome home.

11: Winnie (1996-2010)

WHEN WINNIE, William, Lizzie, Tom and I officially moved into the house next to my shop in the winter of 2004-2005, I kept the dogs confined to the laundry room and kitchen instead of giving them free run of the house. Not only was I loath to see any repeat of the destruction at my bungalow in town; I had begun laying the hickory floors in my spare time, and it was an unimaginably slow job, done on my hands and knees.

Alan had kindly loaned me a flooring nailer. It was the manual type you whack with a dead-blow mallet. I tried it repeatedly, but the hickory was so hard it just bent the nails. Once a nail was bent, it was far more time-consuming to remove from the dense wood than it would have been to drive by hand. A pneumatic nailer might have done the trick, but I didn't have one, so I bought several pounds of large finish nails and recalibrated my expectations. I had to pre-drill the tongue of each board about every 18 inches along its length to keep it from splitting. I drove the nails with a hammer and finished with a nail set. It took a week of spare time to lay the floor in the 13 x 18-foot living room, but as I watched the hickory spread slowly across the OSB subfloor, I was thrilled by the transformation in my surroundings.

After the living room I moved down the hall to the bedrooms, then hired my friend John Hewett to sand the floors. I applied two coats of Waterlox Original tung oil just before driving to Florida with a kitchen full of cabinets for Maggie and her new husband – the tung oil was so heavy on the solvent that I didn't want to be in the house while it cured.

Considering how much work the floors took, I was not about to see

Bathing beauty. Winnie's Labrador genetics drove her to find water wherever she could.

Cramped quarters. When she saw this stock watering bowl at Alan's farm, Winnie climbed right in to cool off.

them scratched up by the dogs' claws, so I decided to confine them to the kitchen and laundry room, rather than allowing them the run of the house.

***

Every so often someone complains that I'm too protective of material artifacts, whether the floors in my house, the top of our kitchen table or the quilt made by our friend Kim, a gift when Mark and I were married – "Use the delicate cycle! Those are Kim's hand-sewn stitches!" These criticisms, which are often veiled, pit things against people (or things against dogs, in the case of my floors), implying that I value the former over the latter.

I get it. When I was around 10, Esse, gave me a melodica, a hybrid between a wind instrument and a keyboard. You blew into a mouthpiece, pressing keys to produce different notes. The resulting sound struck me as artificial, and the instrument itself was mostly made of plastic. It didn't seem like a serious instrument. I had no idea back then that the melodica was good enough for the coolest of professional musicians, like Jon Batiste on "The Late Show with Stephen Colbert." I was touched that she'd bought it for me, but not that interested in learning to play it.

The gift of the melodica coincided with the influx of hippies living in our yard. From them I learned that attachment to material things was bad. "You gotta let it go, man. Free yourself," they'd say – not about my melodica, but about other, grown-up things. Their happiness living with few possessions impressed me. I wanted to follow their example. So one Saturday morning, when a couple mentioned they were going to a swap meet to divest themselves of still more possessions, I asked if I could join them. It would be an exercise in renunciation.

I set the melodica down with a bunch of other people's stuff on a fold-up table in a dusty parking lot cooked by the Florida sun. I think I priced it at $25. Eventually someone haggled me down to $8. The money wasn't important; what mattered was that I was letting go of another object I didn't use. I was training myself to avoid attachments. I overrode the pang of guilt as I took the cash – my dear grandma had given the instrument to me – and told myself to grow up. When I told my grandma, she was hurt. "I bought that for *you*," she said. "It was a *gift*." She wasn't trying to make me feel bad; she was expressing how she felt. I've been troubled by my superficial take on the melodica ever since.

As I thought about that experience over subsequent years, I came to see "things versus people" as a dichotomy that's false and destructive. You can't even *have* things without people; we're interdependent. People make things, whether they do so on a factory production line or in a one-person workshop. Then other people put them to use. Beyond this, things are more than mute material; they express their makers' dreams and values. This connection between maker and made object is most visible in artifacts crafted by individual makers to their own designs, or designs they've adapted significantly – think Megan Fitzpatrick's Dutch toolchests, or

The Peggy Shepherd Pottery Collection (at least, most of it) now lives in my office. The whisk brush was made by Aspen Golann.

Danielle Rose Byrd's bowls. But even anonymous workers on the production line at Toyota or General Electric are expressing their dreams of a good life, albeit less directly, as they cut, weld or assemble parts to other peoples' designs using tools and equipment they don't own.

Material artifacts are also repositories of memory. They keep people and places alive. In my office I have a Victorian bamboo étagère, its shelves filled with antique ceramics. The stand and all of its contents — a Dutch urn resembling an antique from Greece; two sugar-and-cream sets from Japan; pitchers and vases from Germany, Romania, England — once stood in the entryway of my friend Peggy's house, a converted timber-frame barn. She'd bought the barn in pieces and made it into a home filled with character and natural light. I always coveted the pottery collection (and kicked myself for doing so, because it was hers). After Peggy died, her daughter held a barn sale. I bought the shelf and the ceramics — not only because I loved them, but to keep those things together as the Peggy Shepherd Pottery Collection. Peggy lives on in these artifacts, as well as many others in our home: the curvy black metal chair she gave me at Christmas in 1998, the funky painted cabinet a former boyfriend of hers had cobbled together, the beautifully upholstered chair she gave me after I built cabinets for her barn-house kitchen. "You didn't charge me enough," she said. "I want you to have this."

The World War II-era sofa in our living room, which I bought from Peggy many years ago, reminds me to be thankful that we're not hiding in bomb shelters while subsisting on tinned meat, chicory "coffee" and other rations. The salvaged leaded-glass window I built into our bathroom wall carries forward the legacy of a client's family home that was demolished as part of an airport expansion. The ceramic model of a terraced house on my office bookshelves reminds me of my first woodworking boss, Raymond, who gave it to me when Patrick and I were married, adding "You've always said you want a house of your own."

When we buy things from those who make them, we not only support those craftspeople, we also do our part to keep craft traditions alive. In the factory-made Arts & Crafts-style cabinet I bought tenth-hand from a back room in a Bloomington grocery store in 1995 lies a silver cheese knife made by Hart Silversmiths in Chipping Campden, England, the lone surviving enterprise from Charles Robert Ashbee's Guild and School of Handicraft. Mixed in with blue-green ceramics bought at yard sales and junk shops is a vase bought for me by my former husband, Kent, and his wife, Mary, on a visit to the Van Briggle Pottery & Tile. There are small pieces by Ephraim Faience that I purchased at The Omni Grove Park Inn and a Granny Smith green cabinet vase I bought from Scott Draves of Door Pottery in 2015, when we were in neighboring booths at a show in Chicago.

Even mass-produced artifacts deserve more respect than we generally give them, at least in the States. We have a famously materialistic culture in which too few people have more than the most superficial, consumerist understanding of material objects. As Elaine Scarry pointed out in her 1985 book, "The Body in Pain,"

> ...*anonymous, mass-produced objects contain a collective and equally extraordinary message: Whoever you are, and whether or not I personally like or even know you, in at least this one small way, be well.... Whether they reach someone in the extreme conditions of imprisonment or in the benign and ordinary conditions of everyday life, the handkerchief, blanket, and bucket of white paint contain within them the wish for well-being: 'Don't cry; be warm; watch now, in a few minutes even these constricting walls will look more spacious.'*[1]

Instead of "things versus people," it would be more fitting to appreciate how things embody important characteristics of their makers, as well as memorialize others.

The things we live with also shape us in ways we often don't even see. They impose their own demands on our behavior: We have to learn how to use the new email platform, drain the compressor, grease the sander's gears, prime the pump. Many things, from the humble kitchen whisk to the thickness planer, bicycle or car, become extensions of our bodies, magnifying our abilities, for better or worse, and sometimes leading us to imagine ourselves more powerful than we are. (All it takes to prove the validity of this statement is a power outage.)

In the case of my floors, I had simply invested a lot of hours and energy; I wanted to honor that labor by keeping them pristine for a while.

***

---

[1] Scarry, "The Body in Pain" 292.

Daniel O'Grady came to work with me at the start of 2005.

Daniel O'Grady came to work for me that winter. A cabinetmaker friend, Tom Replogle, had hired him for a months-long contract to make institutional furniture. The deal fizzled, so when I asked if I might hire Daniel for a few hours a couple of times a week, Tom was glad to let him become my employee instead of his.

William was less happy about having a new man in the shop. A few days in, he made a point of catching Daniel's eye, then cocked his leg on the planer, leaving a big streak across one side. *Dude. You may work here now, but make no mistake – this place is mine.*

Desperate to stay busy enough to cover the bills for my business and home on a single income, I took every commission I could get. Consequently, 2005 turned out to be a busy year. We did three kitchens with highly customized cabinets – one incorporated salvaged hardware and leaded glass; the second was a set of mid-century-style cabinets in curly birch; the third, painted cabinets for a turn-of-the-century Queen Anne. We built bookcases and an armoire for other customers, linoleum-topped kitchen tables that sold around the Midwest (Daniel made weekend deliveries in his Volvo station wagon, which by then had traversed nearly 200,000 miles) and a lot of other stuff I can no longer remember without hunting through old records in the filing cabinet. The year was further distinguished by my clean break with Alan after he disappeared with someone else at a party he'd attended as my guest. It was terribly painful, but after I had allowed our breakup to drag on for so many months, it was also a relief to see him develop a relationship with someone who was not me.

In my spare time, I worked on the house and garden. I'd built and installed the casework for kitchen cabinets, but they were still skeletons, albeit with counters and a functioning sink. Simply having countertops, which I made from linoleum with a retro-style aluminum edge, felt luxurious – who needed doors and drawers? I later paid Daniel to build those. I added a storage cabinet in the bathroom with a tall, salvaged door, and continued to work on trim and interior doors for the rest of the house.

Beyond the work I was doing to finish up my home, I accepted every invitation, whether to coffee with a customer or the annual Easter

The kitchen cabinetry that Daniel and I made for Lee and Eric Sandweiss. Daniel was the primary cabinetmaker on the job. (Photo: Spectrum Creative Group.)

The cabinetry we did for Fritz Lieber and Donald Maxwell in 2005. White oak with salvaged hardware and leaded glass. General contracting by Bert Gilbert. (Photo: Spectrum Creative Group.)

In the first iteration of the kitchen in our house I stained the cypress cabinets dark; I wanted to experiment with a new finish. I made the counters out of veneer-core plywood with linoleum tops and a retro aluminum edge and laid vinyl composition tile on the floor in a four-color pattern. The enamel-top work table came (with permission) from the rental house where Kent and I first lived in Missoula.

Flower child. Winnie with daylilies circa 2003.

party our friends Bert and Amy hosted at their place. I wanted to meet new people and deepen my existing friendships. Whenever a girlfriend came to visit, William did his best to impress her. Winnie would look on from the laundry room, figuratively rolling her eyes, as William grabbed one of the pillows I let them sleep on and started to hump it frantically. He outdid himself one time, going at it with such intensity that he somersaulted across the kitchen floor.

The finality of my breakup with Alan was wrenching. I grieved the good parts of the relationship and missed the simple pleasures of having a companion. Even though I worked with Daniel every day and spent time with friends, I felt alone and depressed. One day, while reading a magazine, I saw an ad for dog food in which a woman was gazing at her golden retriever. The joy in her expression felt completely unrecognizable to me; I could no longer imagine how it felt to be that happy. I cut the ad out and stuck it on the fridge as a reminder that someday I would almost certainly feel that way again.

As hard as that time was, it made me appreciate just how deeply I had absorbed the message from Alan that I was inadequate, unlovable and incapable, whether or not he had meant for me to feel that way. It was a message that had also been delivered loudly by my stepfather and other boyfriends along the way.

***

As with any relocation, the move to the house at my shop property brought with it new logistics. When the dogs had to go out, I could simply open the back door for Winnie, who ran down the steps and stayed responsibly close – she wasn't going anywhere without her alpha dog or me. William, on the other hand, could not be trusted. I set up a run for him just off the steps, with a cable strung from the big catalpa to the far corner of the yard.

The following year was no less busy, with a variety of freestanding commissions and several kitchens, among them the cabinets for some clients in Washington, D.C. Immediately following our kitchen installation in D.C. I taught my first class at Kelly Mehler's school in Berea.

I was scheduled to do a photo shoot for my first project article in *Fine Woodworking*, a simple Arts & Crafts-style wall shelf, that fall. I had based the design on a piece spotted in a book, where the shelf was mounted on a bathroom wall over a clawfoot tub. I'd done two articles for *Fine Woodworking* before this one – a two-page spread on the design of an Edwardian hallstand, on which I worked with

(RIGHT) One wall of cabinets in the kitchen Daniel and I did in 2006 for clients in Washington, D.C. The bank of base units includes pull-out refrigerator and freezer drawers. The countertop is solid cherry. Daniel was the primary cabinetmaker on this job. (Courtesy photo.)

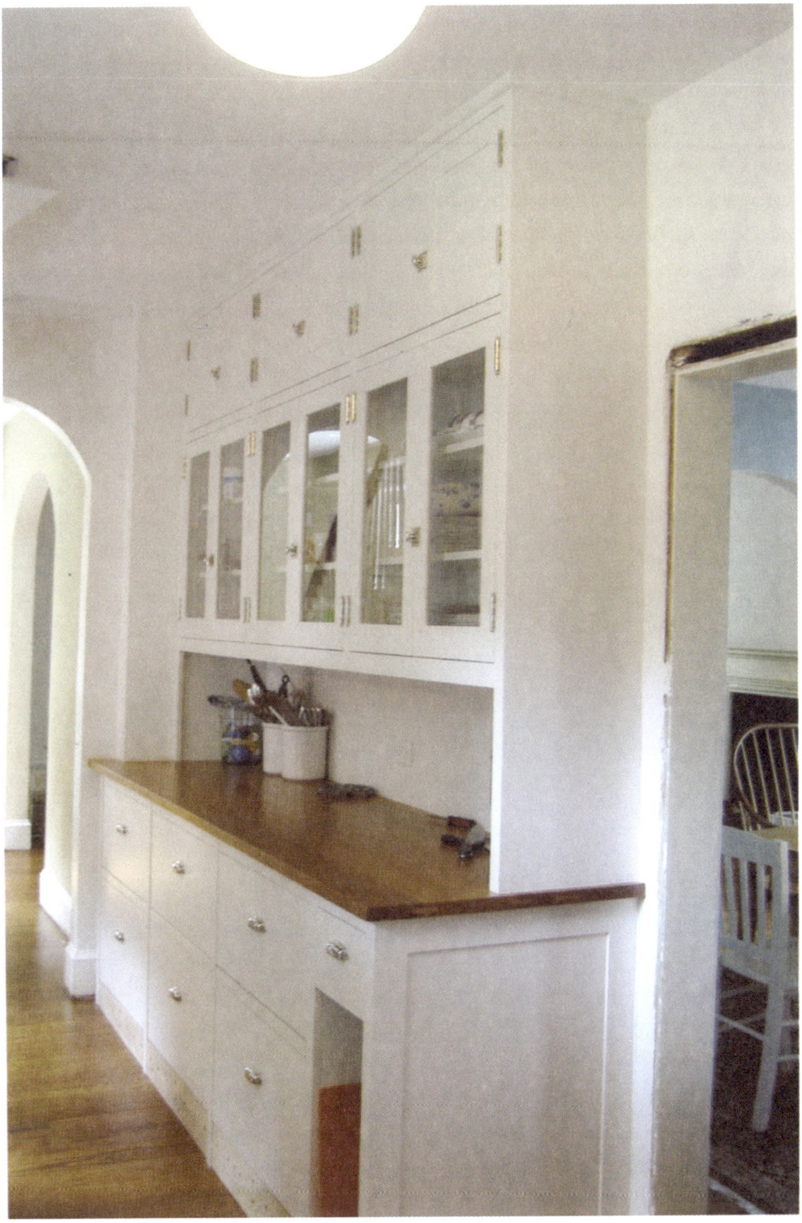

editor Karen Wales, followed by a feature with Bill Duckworth about designing built-ins to fit their architectural context. But this would be my first project shoot.

The week of the shoot, my attention was focused on preparation. I'd finished the prototype but still had to make a partially assembled version of the cabinet, as well as a variety of parts we would use to show the joinery, inlay and other processes. We were also going to do a companion feature about the multi-part finish I use for this style of work.

But first, the story of how I met my husband, Mark, which is closely bound up with what follows.

Mark and I had run into each other at an appliance store around 2003. The store was one of those family owned businesses with knowledgeable salespeople who understand the importance of customer service. We, too, valued customer service and were each there to check on orders for clients. I recognized him right away because the local paper had recently published a feature about the energy-efficient house that he and his former wife, Patti, had built.

"You're Mark Longacre," I said, mentioning the article.

"And you're Nancy Hiller," he replied. "I recognize you from your articles in *Fine Woodworking*."

We were both involved with other people – I with Alan, he with our friend Mary Beth. We each took care of our business, then said our goodbyes.

Our paths crossed every so often over the next few years. He always struck me as a thoughtful, kind person – one who was also very good at building and remodeling, and continually sought the latest recommendations for energy- and space-efficient design. More unusual, he seemed to be free from the kind of ego over-investment that makes the occasional builder (or designer, or furniture maker) hard to be around.

When Alan and his crew were building the shell of my house in 2004, Mark had invited me over to look at some features of his, in case they might be helpful. I wanted a woodstove, but it would have to be tiny; the footprint of my house was around 900 square feet, and I didn't want to cook myself right out of it. I made a note of his Jøtul, the smallest model available. He had also incorporated ideas from "A

Pattern Language" into his home, among them the suggestions in a chapter titled "Raised Flowers."[2] The gravel path along the west side of his house was bordered on one side by a raised bed filled with ferns, hostas, bleeding heart and several native plants he'd moved from the woods – bloodroot, goldenseal and jack-in-the-pulpit among them. I made a similar raised bed in front of my house and said I would credit him with the idea.

A week before the shoot with Anissa Kapsales and Mike Pekovich, I had laparoscopic surgery to remove an ovarian cyst. (Luckily, it proved benign.) Before the surgery, Daniel and I had cobbled together fence-like barriers to keep William in the backyard while I recovered; there was no way I'd be able to wrestle him on a leash when I had fresh stitches. All I needed was to be able to let him and Winnie out to do their business, then lure them back with Milk Bones.

One evening that week, Mark invited me over for dinner with his son, Jonas. He made salad, garlic bread and spaghetti; we ate at the little table in their kitchen. Jonas was around 7 and attended elementary school in town. His class had been studying local trees, and the sassafras tree he'd made from cardboard and construction paper presided over the table. I liked these two. Mark and I had found ourselves working alongside each other on a couple of projects for customers we had in common. I admired his proficiency and his calm sense of humor in the face of problems; he also had a sweet-awkward laugh. That summer, he had mentioned what he called a rough patch in his relationship. He and his partner seemed to have agreed to go forward as friends, as they had been for years before they became romantically involved.

After dinner we put the dishes in the dishwasher and Mark asked if I'd like to watch a film. We went into the living room and sat on the futon, which doubled as a couch. He put on "Toy Story II" – not the kind of film I might have imagined, but I had never seen it, so I decided to consider it a way of gaining insight into what kids were watching at that time in place of my generation's "Gilligan's Island" or "The Mickey Mouse Club."

[2] Alexander, "A Pattern Language."

Within 10 minutes, both Mark and Jonas had nodded off. *So, I thought; I guess I just keep watching and hope that one of them wakes up before long?* I checked their faces periodically. Both were fast asleep. After about half an hour, Mark stirred awake, and I took the opportunity to convey my thanks. We said goodbye in the mudroom, and I walked out to my truck in the dark alone. He didn't even come out to say goodbye? Clearly this man had no interest in me whatsoever.

The first morning of the shoot arrived. Anissa and Mike showed up at my shop door with multiple suitcases of photography equipment. It was Anissa's first shoot out of town, so Mike had come with her to show her the ropes. We worked through the first day, then the second. That night an email from Mark showed up: "Short notice, I know, but want to celebrate 50 years?" I asked Anissa if we'd be done in time for me to join him for a birthday dinner. She couldn't be sure. I promised to make that day's shoot as efficient as possible. I really wanted to join Mark for dinner.

The rest is history. But as a result of that synchronicity, Anissa has pretty much felt like a consummately professional member of my family.

That Christmas, Mark and Jonas gave me a dog door for the shop, so that the dogs could get to the crudely enclosed backyard without me having to let them out. Winnie swooped through right away, an otter diving gracefully for fish. Before long she was running in and out, in and out, for fun. Or maybe she was gloating – William was completely spooked by the mysterious portal that had appeared without warning on the back wall of the shop. He watched Winnie push it with her nose, and the next thing he knew, she was gone. *Where'd she go? She might've been abducted. No way I'm touching that floppy rectangle.*

It took a few weeks for him to summon the courage just to poke his head through. He'd push the flap open and stand there, his big, hairy head outside, the rest of him parked safely in the shop, not unlike a semi[3] stranded on a humpback bridge. It took months for him to jump through the dog door.

---

[3] A semi in the States is an articulated lorry, or sometimes a juggernaut, in Britain.

WINNIE

When Daniel moved home to Milwaukee at the start of 2007, I went back to working alone. That summer, Mark asked if I'd like to move in with him and Jonas. I spent some time getting my house ready to rent, then made lots of trips to move stuff over in my truck. For my birthday Mark paid a moving company to deliver the few really heavy pieces of furniture.

I felt like I was floating on air. I was 48, and this man I'd admired for years before we'd even met wanted me to move in with him. Even better, he had an 8-year-old son, a boy who loved learning, whether at school, at summer camp, or on his own at home. Jonas was a pro at entertaining himself when necessary, but he also enjoyed the company of adults, even those of us who were technically old enough to be his grandparents. He was constantly inventing things and experimenting artistically with new materials – building a papier-mâché sphere, using an old railroad spike to carve a Latin inscription in limestone, making films with elaborate storylines involving figures he represented with coins, rocks or deadheaded coneflowers. And he seemed to like me. How had I lucked into this household?

Mark shared many of the best qualities of my parents. He maintained close, caring friendships with former girlfriends, in addition to his former wife. He had an open mind. He appreciated people others called "difficult," learned their backstories and did his best to be a supportive friend. He wasn't concerned about what others might think. He worked at being patient and nonjudgmental, and when he did indulge in a bit of selfishness or especially mean snark, he was willing to be called on it. He wanted to be and do better, and his willingness to put in the necessary work made me want to do the same. He was the builder/maker/gardener/poet of my childhood exemplars; he even had a ponytail and a beard.

As soon as I moved in, I promised myself that whenever I was on the cusp of doing or saying any of the things I knew had hurt me in my relationship with my own parents, I would count to three and come up with a kinder, more thoughtful response; I had seen and experienced enough damage caused by the kind of toxic behavior that, left unchecked, shapes one generation after another. I really wanted to

My first version of this sideboard based on a 1903 original by Harris Lebus of Tottenham, London was in plainsawn red oak. I built the second version, shown here, in quartersawn white oak, with art glass by Anne Ryan Miller and pulls by Adam Nahas, for my book "English Arts & Crafts Furniture: Projects & Techniques for the Modern Maker." (Photo: Al Parrish.)

avoid contributing my family's quota of crap to Jonas. (Every family has its own.)

For me, the move proved a life-saving plan. My business, along with many others, slowed dramatically in the lead-up to the official years of the Great Recession. If business continued not to come in, as seemed likely, I would not be able to pay my mortgage, business and household expenses and might well have lost my property. The move meant I could keep my shop and take care of the garden at my place while others covered the mortgage and lived in the house.

With fewer commissions for shop work, I took on more writing as a source of income. I worked on a book about Hoosier cabinets that I'd agreed to write for the Indiana University Press, along with essays and articles for local and national magazines. One day I was stopped in my tracks by a sideboard in a home that I was hoping to write about. The sideboard belonged to Russ Herndon, who thought it had been made for Liberty, the literally fantastic department store in London. I asked if I might take measurements with a view to building a reproduction. He said yes.

I built my first version of the sideboard in plain-sawn red oak, because the original piece had lots of plain-sawn oak mixed in with quartersawn. Meanwhile, Russ had discovered the sideboard's maker: Harris Lebus. I looked the company up and was intrigued to learn that it had once been among the largest furniture manufacturers in the world. In 2008 I proposed an article about Lebus to *American Bungalow Magazine*; the editor and publisher were on board. I scheduled a trip to London for a week to research the company. Then I contacted my first boss, Raymond, and asked if I could visit him when I came over. "Let me pay for your ticket!" he insisted. "And you cahn't just stay one week; you've got to stay at least two. You c'n stay with us." The trip would be in October.

In the meantime, William slowly took on a changed appearance. His mouth and neck seemed swollen. I waited a couple of weeks, but the swelling didn't go down. His energy level was falling, too.

I took him to Jim Koch, husband and business partner of Mary Alice Cox, who had euthanized my dog Oscar 15 years before. Dr. Koch did some tests and came back with a diagnosis of lymphoma. He thought William had just a few weeks to live. We went home, where Winnie gave him that *Ugh, you went to the vet?* sniff, then went back to whatever she'd been doing.

We did our best to make his last weeks rewarding as his energy declined and his eyes grew dull. Our friend Aaron dug him a grave – more of a challenge than usual, as the summer had been so hot and dry. William's appetite disappeared. One morning he wouldn't even drink water. We had reached the end. I made the appointment.

I was not going into that final trip precipitously, as I had with Oscar. I decided to spend the rest of the day with William, just being together and thinking about the 13 years ~~I had endured due to my own bad "parenting"~~ we'd shared. We walked slowly down the driveway to Mark's shop and went inside. Sitting on the concrete floor with my back against Mark's wall of tools, I stroked William and told him some of my favorite stories from his puppyhood. An hour later, it was time to go. I drove him to the vet and we went in.

I steeled myself as Dr. Koch entered the room. He put William on the table and looked him over. "You know," he said, "there may be something we can do."

Prednisone, he explained, can sometimes give a dog a few more weeks of life. It doesn't always work, but he was happy to send me home with a bottle of pills if I wanted to try. The caveat: Even if the steroid worked, the cancer would come back – and when it did, it would return with a vengeance.

Of course I wanted to get a few more weeks! We'd started the day believing it would be William's last, then gone home with new hope. I gave him the first dose that night.

The next morning William was a changed dog – bright-eyed, head up, back to his insufferable, entitled self: *Where's my breakfast? Get to it, woman!* It was deeply gratifying. I covered his empty grave with a scrap sheet of CDX plywood, knowing we were probably going to need it before long.

We had a great month together. About three weeks in, Mark went sailing in Canada with his friends Jim and Anne. We talked about what I should do if William's condition went downhill while he was away. Amazingly, William remained in good shape. Mark came home and I packed for my trip to England. This time, Mark would be the one to make the decision, should William's condition plummet while I was gone.

On the morning of my departure I went downstairs to feed the dogs and found William barely able to walk. His eyes were glazed, his stare vacant, his mouth as swollen as it had been the last time I took him to Dr. Koch for euthanasia. I opened the back door to let him out. He shuffled, tripping, down the steps and crawled into the gravel under the mudroom – the kind of small, dark place dogs go to die. I had nice clothes on – I was going to the airport in a few hours, then to London – but I couldn't just leave him there. I got down on my knees and crawled in behind him. I had to drag him out; he was that far gone.

We needed to get him to the vet, and right away. Mark climbed into the passenger seat of my truck and I put William in his lap, on top of a towel. Dr. Koch came out to the truck with his battery-powered shaver, alcohol and syringes. He'd been William's vet for 13 years; it was at his office that I had seen the flyer with the heading "Beyond Adorable!" He shaved William's forearm and gave him the first shot, then the second. As William took his final breath, his bowels gave way on Mark's lap – his final outrageous act.

We put him in the back of the truck and drove home. After digging out the dirt that had fallen in from the edges over the previous few weeks, we lowered him into the grave. There's something so final about putting a loved one into the ground, then hearing the impact of that first shovelful of soil. Winnie watched, with no expression. She and William had had a complex relationship, one in which she looked to him constantly for her lead, even as she resented his bullying. We'd give them each a bowl of food, only to see William scarf his down, then move on to Winnie's. Sometimes she fought back. Blood often flew. But William always prevailed. After every fight he'd whimper petulantly as if to say *I didn't want to do that. You made me. Why can't you just be like a normal bitch and submit when I lay claim to what's mine?*

Winnie was well acquainted with our rules and understood my expec-

Winnie thought this recycling bin made a good place to hang out.

tations. When we were alone in the garden, she stayed by my side. But when she'd been with William ... well, all it took was a gate left slightly ajar, and she'd tear down the road after him. "Look out!" my neighbor Paul Ash would say when we lived at my bungalow in town. "Nancy's crazy dogs are on the loose!" In the country, they'd be a mile down the road before I caught up to them with our friend Charlie Savage's help. So we worried she'd lose her mind, now that her tormentor/enabler/alpha dog was gone.

I grabbed my suitcase and backpack and threw them in the truck. I

Picture of contentment. Winnie in the garden at my shop property where Mark and I now live.

could make it to the airport if I left right away. The timing was ideal – I was so preoccupied by the trip that I had hardly a moment to be sad.

"Please take care of Winnie," I told Mark.

"She'll be fine," he said. "I'll take her to work with me so she won't be alone."

Mark was right. Winnie was perfectly fine. Far from falling into despair, as we'd feared, she blossomed. It was as though she'd been waiting for this moment her entire life, which made me feel guilty, considering how much of William's abuse she'd endured. She became the most loyal companion, practically glued to my side on walks. In evenings and on weekends she loved to join me in the garden. She'd figure out where I was likely to be working, then plop herself down in the grass, adjusting her location as I made my way around each bed.

Mark's son, Jonas, loved Winnie.

As she grew older, her gait became stiff and I started to call her Penguina because of her shuffling walk and her pointy face, the only part of her black body that had gone gray.

How do you measure a dog's quality of life, especially when that dog is well-behaved and seems more interested in feeling grateful for what she has than demanding more? During her last two years there was a sameness to Winnie's days that might have struck many as stultifying. Get up, go out, eat breakfast. Make sure Mom, Dad and Jonas are safely off to work and school, then take a nap. Watch robins hop through the grass. Go out when Mom comes home for lunch, then have a biscuit. Wave goodbye to her at the door, then take another nap. Greet the family when they come home in the evening. Eat dinner! Hang out under the kitchen table while they talk, then go sit in the living room. ("Mom, is it OK if I get up on the couch with you?") Go out in the

Winnie lived her best life after William was gone. (Photo: Mark Longacre.)

dark and tell the coyotes they'd better not even *think* about coming into the yard overnight. Have a bedtime cookie and a drink. Lie down with Lizzie near the woodstove for the night. A basic life of responsibilities, simple rewards, a loving family and rest well-earned.

To all appearances, Winnie saw her life as full. Only those who have been spared serious loss and hardship could see a comfortable home in a loving family as anything less than rich. I let her appreciation sink in. Who needed the interminable striving?

I did, still.

Early in 2010 she began to have problems with her kidneys, which were failing. We fed her a special diet, which helped, but by summer she'd lost most of her interest in food. I tried to tempt her with homemade soup, but after a few weeks she quit eating altogether. As with William, I was determined to stay with her until it was clear she no longer took pleasure in being alive.

One evening she had a seizure. She was in pain – I heard her yelp – but recovered quickly. The next day she had a seizure in the morning that I feared would kill her. She stayed in the same spot on our bedroom floor for most of the day, then picked herself up and went downstairs in the evening. It was time to call the vet.

That summer the ground was baked too hard to dig, so we had her cremated. A few weeks later, I picked up her ashes from the vet's office. It was the first time I'd held a container of bodily ashes; I was startled by their weight and whiteness. So much bone.

I spread her remains over William's grave at the bottom of the hill on the edge of the forest and felt my grief for both of them well up. But no sooner had I begun to anticipate the relief of a heartfelt cry than I squelched the impulse. My dad was visiting.

12: Louis, the Mayor of Louisville (2006-2019)

ON A Friday in the fall of 2006, I was driving up State Road 37 to interview Philip and Phyllis Kennedy about their history as experts on the once-common piece of kitchen furniture known as the Hoosier cabinet when my eye was caught by a small animal on the shoulder. An emaciated baby squirrel, it was heading toward the slow lane, where it would certainly be flattened. I didn't expect a wild animal to let me get anywhere close, but I still had to pull over. As soon as I got out of the truck, I realized that the squirrel was a small ginger kitten.

I imagined he would run away, but he let me pick him up and put him in the truck. Then he broke into a yowl that would go on for most of the day. I stopped at the next gas station to buy a bag of cat food, along with some litter. The kitten showed no interest in either.

It was still too hot to leave an animal in the truck, so when I arrived, I asked the Kennedys whether I might bring him in. Sure, they said, as Phyllis found us a cardboard box. The kitten sat inside the box, next to my chair, and cried the entire time, which made the interview far more challenging than it should have been.

On the way home I stopped at the vet in case the cat had an identifying chip. There was no chip. They'd asked me his name when we arrived; when I said he didn't have one, they typed "37" on the bill for the exam. I took the kitten home and named him Louis after my great-grandfather Louis, who, my mother had told me, had had a stylish pale-yellow suit.

Louis as a kitten, shortly after I brought him home, here on the old couch that I had re-upholstered late in 2004.

***

    I had wanted to interview the Kennedys for the book I was going to write about Hoosier cabinets, which were developed around the turn of the 20th century and became a central fixture in North American kitchens. Although my sister and I had grown up with a Hoosier cabinet, I would never have dreamed of writing a book about the genre had it not been for a design-build job the previous year.
    In 2005, Daniel O'Grady and I did a kitchen for Lee and Eric Sandweiss, who lived in a near-pristine mid-century ranch. They'd hired me after a preliminary discussion that covered the spectrum from one local designer's inflated ego through arguments by 20th-century French philosopher Paul Ricoeur on the significance of authorial intent to the

valid interpretation of a text. In this case, the text was a room within a house; the interpretation revolved around the history of this particular kitchen and how we might rework it in aesthetic and practical terms to suit the family who now lived there.

As with any other room, the design of a kitchen usually reflects prevailing styles and cultural values. Even most of those who decide to rework their kitchen in a period-sensitive style are responding to a trend (albeit a long-lived one – and long may it continue) to respect their home's historic architectural character instead of obliterating all traces of the original layout and materials, then replacing them with a pale-gray-and-white "open concept" plan.[1] The family who had had this house built in the middle of the 20th century had evidently recognized the centrality of the kitchen to their life. This one was designed to be spacious, with plenty of room for preparing meals, then cleaning them up. It also incorporated a built-in breakfast nook where family members could converse with the cook while drinking coffee or eating lunch. In contrast to many kitchens of the time, which were cramped and closed off from public view, the architect who planned this house intended the kitchen to serve as the corridor from the attached garage to the home's interior, which ensured that every member of the household would be exposed daily to the kitchen and its operations. This openness to seeing the work done by family members made it a modern kitchen, in contrast to the compartmented spaces where servants had labored behind closed doors a century before. In fact, this kitchen was by far the most public of any mid-century kitchen I could remember.

The original cabinets had been painted steel, with metal-edged yellow laminate counters. A few of those cabinets were still around, put to new use in the sewing room and garage. One option would be to replace the standard brown "Colonial" cabinets installed by a previous owner with new retro-style cabinets that would be as similar as possible to the original ones, bringing the old kitchen back to life. Most other elements of

---

[1] In the United States, this embrace of original architectural character got going in force during the 1970s. The *Old-House Journal* is one of the popular publications that has encouraged and guided period-sensitive restoration and design since the movement's inception.

the original room were intact: the split-cedar ceiling tiles, laid with their grain in opposing directions to create a checkerboard pattern; the pale walnut veneered walls; the dark green-and-white resilient tile floor. The weight of intact original fabric seemed to argue for restoring the room to its original cheerful kitsch.

On the other hand, Lee and Eric pointed out, we should consider the house's bathrooms. The two full baths still had their original glass wall tile, colored plumbing fixtures and rolled-glass privacy partitions between toilet and vanity; they were as glamorous as those featured in full-page magazine ads for Pittsburgh Plate Glass in the 1930s. The exceptionally high caliber of the bathrooms' aesthetic prompted Lee and Eric to ask (and I quote), "Shouldn't we bring the kitchen up to the level of the bathrooms?" In this house, the rooms dedicated to the least-glamorous activities enjoyed an elegance worthy of Hollywood.

In the half century since the home's construction, kitchens had become important gathering places for family members and guests. Women might still be the primary cooks, but their socio-economic standing had changed markedly. By the 2000s, most (at least, in the U.S. and many other Western countries) had moved from being full-time housewives whom manufacturers courted by designing cabinets and equipment that were "colorful" and "gay" to professional careers outside the home; to many, kitsch now felt condescending. There was an argument to be made for elevating the aesthetic of the cabinetry and counters. The bathrooms won. The three of us agreed that Paul Ricoeur would probably not object to our interpretation of the text.

At one point in the job I showed Lee a copy of *Fine Woodworking* that included an article I'd written about designing built-ins with their period architectural context in mind. She realized that in addition to being able to write, her cabinetmaker had a strong interest in kitchen history. As sponsoring editor for trade books at the Indiana University Press, she had to generate new titles and come up with people to write them. While looking for books in print about the Hoosier cabinet, an icon of Indiana's manufacturing history, she had found just one, the self-published softcover "Hoosier Cabinets" by Philip D. Kennedy. She'd contacted him and asked whether he would like to have his book

Kitsch no longer cuts it. Appeals to prospective customers have changed a lot since the early 20th century, when this advertisement for Sellers kitchen cabinets appeared in Good Housekeeping *magazine.*

republished in an imprint by IU Press. He had refused – not surprising, when you consider that his inexpensively produced black-and-white book was netting him a lot more than the royalties he would have been paid (and I would later be paid) to do a book for a university press. In a meeting over breakfast at a local restaurant, Lee asked if I would like to write a book about Hoosier cabinets. After considerable thought, I signed the contract.

I made an ethical decision to avoid reproducing any of the basic content in Kennedy's book. The decision was made easier by the difference in our respective areas of interest; I'm as fascinated by the idiosyncrasies of different manufacturers' hinges or latches as I am by NASCAR, which is to say, not. Sure, I pay close attention to such things when I'm building, but I have little desire to write a book about them. Kennedy had also included a brief profile and history of each manufacturer he covered, so I would refer readers to his book for further information on that front. I agreed to write my book on condition that I could place the Hoosier cabinet in the context of broader kitchen history, with a focus on social, economic and gendered dimensions of the product's design and marketing. Instead of telling readers how to restore an antique or identify their cabinet's maker, as Kennedy's book already did, I wanted to talk about how kitchens today are better suited to kitchen work thanks largely to working-class women in the mid-1800s who left their positions as domestics for factory jobs, precipitating a dire shortage of domestic help. This crisis was resolved thanks to a squad of middle-class women activists who wrote and lectured about the need to design kitchens for their fellow housewives who had taken over their own housekeeping when they could no longer find servants to manage their homes.

Writing a book had long been a dream of mine. Daniel and I were working four 10-hour shop days in exchange for Friday off each week, which allowed me more time for research and writing. That's how I came to be driving north that day on Highway 37.

Louis immediately became part of the family, taking no flak from William and Winnie. He and Lizzie pretty much ignored each other – she was the undisputed queen of the house. On the whole, he was well behaved. But the second time he peed on the chair that my friend Peg-

Louis often slept under the jointer when I wasn't working in the shop. He was well protected from potential intruders, and the chips made an ideal bed (with en suite toilet).

Louis loved to tease Joey by staying just beyond his reach.

gy had given me, he became the shop cat. With a warm shop in winter, two meals a day, high window sills from which to watch woodpeckers at the feeders and a dog door that granted him freedom to roam, he had the best of both worlds. Every afternoon at 5 p.m. he'd leap through the dog door for dinner.

  Louis's life overlapped with the period during which I rented my house to others. I came to the shop most days to work. I also took

Louis loved to nap under this hosta.

care of the garden, cleared snow and mowed the grass. All of the renters were lovely people; most of us still keep in touch. Louis, too, formed relationships with them all. He sometimes perched on the handrail of the front steps and looked through the window, asking to be let into the house. He even trained some of them to give him treats. In 2016, when Mark and I moved to what had previously been my house, he got even more attention.

Over his 12-1/2 years Louis met many dogs and performed sophisticated psychological operations on them all. He'd crouch beneath a truck or around a corner, then leap out with a startling cry. He ignored any dog that wanted to play, walking past with regal nonchalance, then surreptitiously batting at the poor sap's leg or tail to get its attention. When the dog perked up – *Oh! You want to play?!* – Louis's eyes glazed over and he moved on.

This plant pot was just right for Louis to curl up in.

He flirted with women visitors. Whenever someone arrived in a car, he jumped onto the hood and lay there, soaking up the engine's warmth. Sometimes I'd find him curled up in a flower pot, sometimes reclining sphinx-like on the arm of the radial-arm saw. He loved to nap in the shade of large hosta leaves on hot summer days.

He spent hours padding silently through the garden, which was more like a forest to him, given that he was only about 12 inches tall. I called him the mayor of Louisville because he was so vigilant about patrolling his domain. He surveyed the acre each morning, marking all the important plants. He especially loved to roll in the catmint.

As attentive as he was to the borders of his domain, he was surprisingly non-confrontational toward other cats, as long as they weren't aggressive toward him. One morning I arrived at the shop to find him sleeping on a moving pad I'd slung over a trash can to dry it out after a

In his youth, Louis jumped up onto the rim of the birdbath to drink, but as he got older he preferred to drink while standing on tiptoe from a steadier spot.

delivery in light rain. Then I turned around and saw him on the floor. Louis had a doppelgänger; the interloper had let himself in through the dog door. Louis tolerated him for several days, until our friend Amy took him to join the crew of cats at the rural property she shares with her husband, Bert.

Occasionally I'd find Louis perched on the edge of the birdbath, lapping up water, though in his final summer he took to drinking there on tiptoe, like a kid who can't quite reach the water fountain.

The cause of Louis's death remains unknown. Several friends suspect he had a heart attack. On his last night he showed no interest in his food, though he had been waiting in his usual place to be fed. When

Rest easy, friend. When Louis died, I wrapped him in this fleece and kept him in a box outside, frozen, until we could dig a hole under the catmint (nepeta, not catnip) in the garden.

I went to work the next morning, I found him curled up in his bed of wood chips, as usual, but the food was still there. He'd pressed it down with his nose, as he did when he didn't like the food I'd given him, or wasn't feeling well. I gave him some affection and went to work.

We'd been keeping the dog door closed at night for Louis's safety. Coyotes kept coming closer and closer to the shop. I'd forgotten to remove the barricade on the door before I started work that morning. While brushing finish on a cabinet, I saw him go over to the dog door. Finding it closed, he went to the spot beneath the radial-arm saw bench, where I kept a bit of sawdust for him to use as emergency litter. As soon as I was done with my brush, I opened the dog door and called him. This time, he didn't come running over with his usual chirp of thanks. I went looking for him and found him lying on the floor – motionless, with no expression, his body limp and still warm. The bright orange cat who'd followed us through the woods on walks, the small figure we'd glimpse in the neighboring hayfield waiting patiently to leap on a rodent when it climbed out of its hole – gone, in an instant. It's hard to keep up when the world changes so dramatically in a flash.

13: Lucy, As Told by Herself (2005)

MY LAST adventure began in the summer of 2005. One day the people who raised me took me out for a drive and dropped me off at the side of the road. It was a hilly spot in the country with a mix of woods and fields. I found a long meadow full of mice and voles and spent the rest of the afternoon chasing them. Most got away but I caught a couple, which made a warm and tasty snack.

As dusk fell I began to miss my people. Where had they gone? Why weren't they coming back to get me? I wandered along the side of the road and came to a driveway with a house where I could hear a dog barking inside. It was a high-pitched bark – probably one of those annoying little dogs that are basically overgrown rodents. Come to think of it, the dog would probably make a nice dinner if I could catch it. I crept up to the door and peered through the sidelight. Just then the door opened and a lady appeared. "Oh, my word," she said. "Marshall, there's a strange dog on the porch." Her husband came out and put a rope around my neck, then led me to a fenced area in the backyard.

The next thing I knew, the lady from next door showed up. "Thank you for coming, Nancy," the first lady said. "We just can't keep another dog, what with our Yorkie. She's very sensitive." Her husband brought the lady called Nancy to where I was trapped and she took the rope and led me down the driveway to the road, then down the hill and up another driveway to a building behind a house. She called it her "shop." "You can stay here for the night," she said. She brought me bowls of food and water, then took me out one more time before I went to sleep.

The next morning she opened the door and there were two dogs with her. One was a tall brown and gray dude with wiry hair – an overgrown dolt, by the looks of it, but ultimately harmless. The other worried me; she was a black Labrador mix, obviously very smart, and I immediately sensed she was determined not to let me get friendly with either the dolt or Nancy.

The three of us dogs were in the building where Nancy was working when a young fellow showed up. As soon as he came in, the black dog snarled and backed me into a corner by the door.

"Daniel, we have a visitor," said Nancy. "I've reported her to the shelter, so hopefully her people will come and get her." In the meantime, they called me Lucy. I would have preferred something heroic, like "Athena the Huntress," or a bad-ass name like "Killer" or "Fang." But I could answer to "Lucy" if I had to.

At that, the black dog attacked me. I cowered as she snapped at my neck. "Winnie! Stop that!" said Nancy.

"She's acting like a prison warden," said the young man named Daniel. So that's what I decided to call her: the prison warden.

I stayed with them a few days, but my people never claimed me. Daniel said he wished he could take me, but he already had a dog at home. And a girlfriend. He was very kind, though; he bought me a rainbow-colored collar and a nice leash.

Daniel had a friend named Paul who thought he might like a dog, so one day Daniel took me to live with him. Paul was a graduate student who lived in an apartment. He was alright, but he spent too much time at school, and even when he came home, he didn't know how to relate to a dog. When he left each day, I cried. I was lonely and bored and wished I could have a human who understood me. His neighbors told him about my crying, and the next thing I knew he told Daniel he didn't think he should keep me because he believed I had something called "seperay-shun ang ziety." So Daniel came and got me, but he said he was going on a trip for a few weeks and would have to take me back to Nancy's until he returned. Then he would take me home and I would be his dog!

Things weren't *that* bad. Nancy let me into her house a few times, but one time the prison warden attacked me in the kitchen and I fought back and our claws made some deep scratches on one of the cabinets.

LUCY, AS TOLD BY HERSELF

Other than memories, all that's left of Lucy is the collar that Daniel bought for her. Mark found it a few years ago and hung it on this fence post at the edge of the forest, where it stays to this day.

Nancy said "No good deed goes unpunished; I can't believe you two did this after I've done my best to give you each a good home," and put me back in the shop.

Every day Nancy would tell me how many days were left before Daniel came back and could take me to live with him. Finally I heard her say, "Lucy, this is the last night. Daniel's coming home from Europe today and he's going to take you home tomorrow!" I was very happy because, to be honest, living with the dolt and the prison warden was getting old.

That night Nancy took me out to the small deck outside her kitchen, where she usually fed me. She tied my leash to the railing and brought my dinner out. Then she went to her office in another part of the house to do some work. I was lying under the catalpa tree enjoying the hot summer air, content with my full belly, when out of the corner of my eye I saw a pale form dart across the street. Squirrel! My favorite thing to chase and eat! I couldn't resist; I quickly chewed through my leash and ran down the stairs, across the front yard, and into the street, drunk with the pursuit and looking forward to that juicy squirrel who was fat from summer's plentiful walnuts and acorns. Suddenly everything went dark.

I lay there a while feeling fuzzy, as if I was floating in another world. I could hear Nancy's voice. "Lucy! Lucy! Where are you?" Her footsteps were coming closer. She saw a still shape at the side of the road in the dusk. I heard her say "Oh no." She tried to pick me up but ended up pulling my lifeless body onto the grass and left me there for the night.

The next morning Daniel came to work. Nancy told him about "the tragedy." He picked me up in his arms and wept on my coat as he carried me up the hill into the forest and laid me to rest on a bed of leaves. I said "Daniel, I'm sorry. I was really looking forward to a life with you." But I don't know whether he could hear me. To this day, the collar he gave me hangs on an old black locust fence post, where Nancy's husband, Mark, put it after he found my skeleton in the woods.

14: Alfie and the Cat Whisperer (2012)

NOT LONG after I adopted Tom, the gray tabby kitten I brought home with Lizzie in 2004, he developed a terrible case of diarrhea that sent us to the vet. It turned out to be feline infectious peritonitis. I did my best to keep him hydrated and comfortable, hoping he'd recover, but his condition just got worse. I had him euthanized when we were finally past the point of hope, then buried him among the daffodils behind the shop. Fortunately, Lizzie had escaped contagion.

I wanted to adopt another male tabby. I returned to the shelter, where the cat room was again beyond capacity. To accommodate the overflow, the staff had put a couple of crates in the lobby at the front of the building, across from some monstrous rabbits, evidently bred to exceed the size of the largest Maine coon cat. Perhaps the idea behind this exercise in genetic engineering was to improve a rabbit's self-defense options by making a single bunny capable of smothering a cat to death simply by jumping on top of it.

In one of the crates nearby I spotted a small pale-gray tabby. "Alfie" was printed on the label. He was a skinny guy, his face oddly pinched. His eyes had a far-off look that struck me as wistful, as though he was begging *Take me* – though in retrospect I realize the look was a sign of ill health. I filled out the paperwork, and the next night I brought him home to be my shop cat.

When Daniel and I arrived at work the following morning we realized Alfie was suffering from some sort of digestive problem. Small brown puddles of diarrhea were scattered across the floor; the smell was so acrid it burned our eyes. "I'm not going in there," choked Daniel, reversing back out through the door. After filling my lungs with fresh air, I dashed

After Alfie recovered from his terrible gastrointestinal malady, he was a picture of health, albeit slightly smaller than he might have been, had his ability to absorb nutrients not been interrupted.

in and started the cleanup. I opened the windows and turned on a fan, but even an hour later the stench was enough to turn our stomachs.

I took Alfie to the vet, who prescribed a course of antibiotics – sadly, all for naught. The poor cat slept, ate and shat. This was no ordinary defecation. We're talking epic shitting. One of us would turn off the sander, only to hear a sickening sound like that of a sex worker at an all-night pancake place attempting to squeeze the last dregs of ketchup from a plastic bottle at 5 in the morning. Twenty years before, a customer had told me to burn a candle as an antidote to nauseating smells. I took to burning crumpled sheets of newspaper, setting up miniature pyres around the shop and lighting them as necessary, hoping my insurance agent wouldn't show up for a surprise inspection.

"You know, this is really not OK," said Daniel after a couple of weeks. "You can't expect people to work in these conditions."

A friend recommended her vet, Dr. Martinez, who specialized in homeopathic treatments. It seemed Dr. Martinez was a patron saint of hopeless causes, the local vet of last resort. I made an appointment.

"What's the matter with Olfie?" she asked, ushering me briskly into her closet-sized office. As she zipped through the paperwork, occasionally glancing my way over the top of her glasses, I described the problem and the treatment we'd already tried. "Ay!" she said, laying her clipboard on the examination table. "No wonder hees condition ees no bayter! Jou should have brought heem to me right away. Imayeen how terrible he mus' be feeleen." Unfortunately that was something I didn't need to imagine.

She palpated his stomach and back. "Jus' one saycond," she said, hurrying out of the room. She returned a moment later with a set of needles. "Acyuponcher. Thas wot he need. Please hold Olfie while I admeenster the treatment."

The cat let out an agonized moan that emanated from the deepest recess of his being. I felt punched in the gut with empathy. What was she doing to him? His moaning continued even after she withdrew the needles. I was starting to doubt this doctor's abilities and felt terrible for having subjected poor Alfie to such torment.

Ignoring the queasy look on my face, she moved on to her next angle. "And now we deescus the food. What are jou feeding heem?"

I told her I'd been giving him a dry food made by a respected national brand. *"No no no no no!"* she shook her finger at me. "The cats, they are not eentaynded to eat carbohydrate. That food jou are giving heem ees very high een carbohydrate. Here" – she pulled a small bag of dry food from the shelves above the counter. "Thees food contains only protein, as a cat would be eating een nayture."

By this point I was willing to try anything. I paid the $350 fee for the 10-minute torture session plus the small bag of food and took Alfie back home.

Over the next two weeks, Daniel and I watched Alfie continue to shrink. We'd thought we had it bad before, but now his bowel movements were downright explosive. After he splattered a newly glued-up cabinet door we took to locking him in the storage room during the day while we worked. If anything, the shop smelled even worse.

"I'm sorry. I just don't think I can keep working here," Daniel announced one day.

"I know," I said. "It's disgusting. Poor Alfie. I don't know what to do."

I called the shelter and told the director that this was the second kitten I'd adopted from the facility who had turned out to have an apparently incurable digestive problem, and as a single person who was self-employed, I could not afford to keep paying the resulting vet bills. "I hate to ask you this," I continued. "But would it be possible for me to bring him back to you?"

"That really does sound like an impossible situation," she agreed. "We can put him to sleep for you, if that's what you want." It wasn't what I wanted. But I was at my wits' end. I scheduled the appointment for lunchtime the following day.

At 11:45 p.m., with a guilty heart, I got the cat carrier down from the attic and told Daniel it was time to say goodbye. He picked Alfie up and set him on his bench. "Goodbye, little guy," he said. "I'm sorry."

Alfie stood up on his hind legs, put his front paws on Daniel's shoulders, and looked intently into his eyes. *Don't let her take me*, I could sense him thinking. *Really. I* will *get better.* The interaction was intense.

There was no way I could go through with the plan. "What are you, the cat whisperer?" I asked Daniel. I called the shelter and canceled the appointment.

From that moment on, Alfie's condition improved. I guess it could have been a delayed response to the acupuncture, but we were happy to call it a miracle. We switched back to the regular commercial food, which now unaccountably agreed with him.

Alfie spent a happy winter and spring as our shop cat. On Easter morning I found his little body lifeless at the side of the road, a sad ending after so much effort by us all.

15: Warring Parties (2011-2017)

ABOUT A year after Winnie died, I was ready to get another dog and fantasizing about a trip to the animal shelter. At the time, I was working on a job that involved refacing and modifying the kitchen cabinets in a newly built house. The place had been built on spec, so the builder had been careful about where he invested resources. The kitchen had a modified galley layout – base cabinets and uppers against the back wall, stove in the center and a capacious pantry unit on one end, all facing a big island of matching cabinetry that housed the sink, dishwasher and one of those pull-out-then-pull-up mixer stands I've always considered a stupid waste of space – and never more so than in a small kitchen such as this one. The cabinets had been built by a local shop. They were perfectly well made, but nothing that I would call craft. The carcases themselves were functional and made to cutting-edge standards, with undermount drawer slides and so on; it was the parts you could see – the doors, drawers and end panels – that were the problem.

The clients had been referred to me by one of their colleagues. Martha said they were happy with the basic cabinets, but there was something she couldn't stand about their looks. As soon as I arrived for a first meeting, I knew what it was: The cabinets were "walnut," which in this case meant maple-veneered MDF with a semi-opaque medium-dark-brown finish. Martha's eyes were used to real wood.

By way of illustration, I pointed to the cutting board by the sink. "This is walnut," I said. I didn't criticize the cabinets; I simply explained that the builder had probably chosen them because they were well made and more affordable than they would have been with walnut faces. She listed the details she wanted to have changed and I put together

Pals for a while. Henny and Lizzie in the early days, here on the couch (with a sheet to protect the upholstery).

a proposal, which she and her husband accepted. The scope of work included removing the mixer stand, which I took to the Habitat for Humanity ReStore; refacing the cabinet end panels, including those on the island; making new doors and drawer faces; and switching out the vaguely Craftsman-style brackets supporting the overhang of the island counter with more modern brackets in welded metal. I was especially keen to replace the glazed doors at the top of the cabinets along the wall; instead of making them with rails and stiles, the original cabinetmakers had simply cut out a rectangular opening in each blank of MDF, probably with a CNC router, and left the inside

"I won't be any bother. Really." Henny took a nap on a pillow after shredding some material in the shop.

corners round. In place of glass bead, they'd fastened the glass in the rabbet with flexible "glass bead" in "walnut." Ouch.

I refaced the cabinets with custom-veneered panels that I cut to size, edged and fitted by hand. I made new glazed doors out of solid walnut with mortise-and-tenon joints, proper rabbets and wooden glass bead. Then I took them to a locally owned fabricator, Heitink Veneers, to have them faced with sequence-matched offcuts from the rest of the doors and drawer faces so the grain would run continuously from the tops of those doors through the ones below.

Late in the day, I was still dreaming about getting a dog when

Henny was devoted to Mark.

Mark texted me that he had a surprise waiting at home. "Is it a dog?" I asked. He refused to say. If it was a dog, that would certainly be a wild coincidence. As I pulled into the parking area at the top of the driveway that evening, a young cream-colored dog with rusty speckles on her legs ran down the hill from the house, barking ferociously, convinced that she was guarding Mark and Jonas from an intruder. "Henny!" I cried, the name inspired on the spur of the moment by her spots, which reminded me of a speckled hen. "It's OK! I live here. I'm not going to harm your men."

   Mark told me how she came to be there. He'd been on his way home, driving along a favorite back road, when he reached a three-way intersection. The dog was standing there while two other drivers, who had each pulled over, were discussing what to do. "I'll take her," said Mark. He picked her up and held her in his arms. "She smelled like a baby," he remembers; she was perfectly clean and well fed, not the condition you'd expect in a stray. Like Lucy, she appeared to be a cross between a pit bull and a Lab.

We reported her to the shelter, certain her owners must be looking for her, but no one ever called. So she joined our household.

I often took Henny to my shop, where she dreamed of playing with Louis. In typical feline form, he refused to acknowledge her presence. She'd lie down on the floor in disappointment and chew wood scraps to console herself. When I delivered pieces of work downtown, I took her with me in the truck. She sat in the front seat and napped, waiting for my return. Though quick to bark in defense of her family, she was exceptionally ingratiating toward one person: Mark. She'd laid her claim on him the day he brought her home. With the utmost delicacy, she would crawl, not jump, into his lap, and gaze adoringly into his eyes. She grudgingly acknowledged that I was the one who shared his bed.

She was far more anxious than any dog I had known. Mark had bought a small car for fuel-efficient driving; we also used it for personal trips to town. A few months after adopting her, we went to an annual holiday brunch at the home of some of my clients, Rick and Joy Harter. It was always a fun occasion to catch up with people we saw rarely and see the latest improvements that Rick had made to their house, an 1890s Queen Anne in a historic district. They'd bought the place from a neighbor, Bill Sturbaum, who made a point of acquiring nearby houses to sell to people who would restore them and make good neighbors. Rick and Joy had gone through the entire house over the years, inside and out, turning it back from a multiplex rental to a single-family home. They'd removed aluminum siding and fixed the fish-scale shingling and clapboards. Rick, who taught high-school science, spent summers working on the house; he went around and around the outside with a terrifyingly long extension ladder, priming, then painting in multiple colors. They stripped paint from interior trim, installed replicated trim where the original material had been removed, sanded and refinished floors and turned a back porch addition into a family

"What? Did I do something bad?" Henny at the back door with a cardboard box she had shredded.

room with a mudroom on the side. They landscaped the lot and Rick created a brick patio at the back, which entailed massive excavation with a hand-held shovel followed by endless wheelbarrows-full of gravel and sand before he could even start on the brick. He then surrounded the patio with a limestone wall. He restored the garage, turning it into a workshop with a studio in the loft. With Rick and Joy, there was always something new to admire.

We took Henny with us for the ride and told her to take a nap while we were gone.

A few hours later, merry with mimosas and happily sated following a meal of savory casseroles, quiches and holiday desserts, we ambled

Mark had to persuade Henny that it was safe to get into the crate we bought to keep her from destroying the house.

out to the car. No sooner had Mark unlocked the doors than we realized things looked different. Stricken with anxiety at finding herself left alone, Henny had expended her nervous energy on the interior. The upholstered back of one seat was ripped, the cowl around the gear stick, gone. She had chewed all the buttons and knobs and pried off the gear stick handle, baring the crash-test-dummy-like works beneath the familiar finishes of a contemporary car.

Back then, we didn't have a fenced yard at Mark's house. Henny was good about coming when we called, but we never left her running loose outside. Sometimes Mark tied her to the post that supported the shed roof on the small deck just off the mudroom while we were inside, to

Henny loved to nap in Mark's chair.

let her watch the birds on the edge of the forest. She'd lie down, her eyes closing in contentment as she was warmed by the setting sun.

One evening Mark and I were inside watching the animated Pixar film "Up" when we heard Henny barking madly, followed by a loud BANG. I ran out the mudroom door to find her still tied to the post, but the post was no longer attached to the house – she was dragging it across the lawn, completely panicked. Above us, a hot air balloon lazily puffed "SHOO … SHOO" as its pilot lit the gas, controlling his descent to a nearby field. *MOMMY!* she seemed to be thinking, *A DRAGON IS COMING TO GET US. GET OUT OF THE HOUSE! NOW!*

I'd been up in a balloon once. It was shortly after I moved to Alan's shop. Alan's friend Wilbur was a pilot who flew a small plane and had his own balloon. I'd always been fascinated by hot air balloons, so when Alan suggested I ask Wilbur if he'd consider taking me up for a ride, I did. He said he would be happy to take me. It was October, one of the best ballooning months in our area. I drove to the designated spot around dawn, and with a couple of helpers, Wilbur prepared the balloon. It was an exercise involving stakes, ropes and an elaborate laying out of what balloonists call the "envelope." We climbed into the basket, and off we went.

It was glorious. The air was crisp, the sky pure blue. We floated up, up, and over miles of rolling hills, fields and forest. The silence came as a surprise – how could you cross so many miles without making any noise? Of course, the silence wasn't complete; it took the occasional jet of hot air to keep the balloon aloft, and it was sobering to realize that the flame could potentially burn a hole in the balloon, dropping us to our death. But what I found most surprising was the reaction of cattle and dogs on the ground. We'd spot a herd of cows, and the next thing I knew, they were running – they were unmistakably aware of the balloon, and it was obvious that for cows, hot air balloons were Not A Good Thing. Dogs were even stranger; as high as we were, they were mere dots on the ground, but at every blow of the jet, they barked. It's weird to be so far away, yet hear barks that clearly. I'd never known how readily sounds travel upward from the ground.

So it was perfectly reasonable for Henny to panic at the monstrous flying beast that was a balloon. The problem was, you never knew when they were coming – especially when you lived near the airport, as we did.

In 2012 our cattle dog mix, Joey, joined the family. He and Henny got along famously at first, when Joey was smaller and she could easily assert her dominance. She loved having a playmate. As Joey grew, their relationship occasionally became contentious, but on the whole, we had a happy family.

One Friday evening in October 2014, Mark and I were watching another film in the living room. Henny and Joey were curled up on the floor; Lizzie was in Mark's lap. At some random, unremarkable moment, Lizzie sat up, stretched and gave Henny a sideways glance that said *In case you hadn't noticed, I'm the one in Daddy's lap.*

Henny lunged. Lizzie immediately leapt to the floor but could not escape. There was a sudden, terrifying blur of snapping jaws and yowling cat as Lizzie, whose unknown former person had had her declawed, was unable to defend herself. I jumped up and tried to restrain Henny. Somehow, Lizzie got away and shot up the stairs, leaving a trail of blood.

I ran after her. She was in the laundry room, huddled in the crack between a sleeping bag and the leg of an old table we used for folding clothes. I pulled her out and held her to my chest, collapsing on a rolled-up futon we kept against a wall for guests. I cradled her and sobbed, afraid she might not survive the stupid, brutal attack. Perched on the futon, looking out the little window at the night sky, I was reminded of the night 10 years earlier when I'd sat on the limestone wall in the garden I was making at Alan's place, where I'd watched the clouds scud by, their undersides silver with the rising moon, and thought *This is definitely not OK*. Henny wasn't so much loyal as possessive; she wouldn't allow anyone between her and her Mark. She tolerated me only because she understood she had no choice in the matter. Throughout the time we'd had her, she had become increasingly prone to violence. We had no idea why. She'd taken to warning those who might pose even the slightest threat to her position with a nip. We always told her "no"; before long we crated her when anyone came over. While a nip on the wrist or ankle may mean nothing to a farmhand, it's serious business to a guest at the dinner table, never mind a young child or someone in frail health.

The vet would not be open again until morning. We honestly didn't know whether Lizzie would make it through the night. I took her a litter box and some water, set my alarm so I could be at the vet's office before it opened and retired to bed, where I got little sleep.

I found Lizzie in the basement, lying on a cushion. One side of her jaw was drooping, and she'd been injured in one eye; there was a big blob of clotted blood on the "temporary" OSB treads of Mark's unfinished stairs. I wrapped her and the pillow in a soft blanket and drove her to the vet.

Her jaw was broken. That much was certain. It was still impossible to

After her violent encounter with Henny, Lizzie was a little lopsided, but she still enjoyed life to the full.

know the extent of the injury to her eye, though I was pretty sure it was now blind. Our options included euthanasia; short of that, the vet said she could wire Lizzie's jaw to encourage it to heal in the proper alignment. There was nothing they could do about her eye; we would just have to wait and see whether she'd been blinded. Some cats don't survive the jaw-wiring, she warned. I asked what would happen if we did nothing other than nurse her and keep her as comfortable as possible.

"She'll probably heal, as long as it doesn't get infected," said the vet. "Of course, she'll look weird and won't be able to chew on that side."

I opted for no jaw wiring and took Lizzie home with a bottle of prescription eye drops, some pain pills, a course of antibiotics and a plastic syringe for feeding mashed-up food. We set her up in the second-floor bathroom, away from the dogs. She had a cozy bed, a litter box and a bowl of water. Several times a day Mark or I would mix some canned food with water, fill the syringe, and push it into the good side of her mouth. She was fine the first night. The second day she indicated that she didn't need the stupid syringe; she'd be happier licking the food straight from the plate, as she always had, though the process would now be more of a challenge. She improved by the day and even resumed her trips outside, prowling the property to keep rival strays from getting ideas. She was a champ.

Henny, though, was something else. Alarmed by the viciousness of the attack, I thought she was the one who should be euthanized. Mark was adamantly opposed. We found a trainer who came highly recommended and started taking her for lessons. She was responsive during classes, but the training did nothing to change her hair-trigger propensity toward violence. She and Joey started to get into fights so intense that I feared they'd both wind up dead. Equally matched in size and weight, they were inseparable once they got started. In place of two dogs, they became one: a snarling, jaw-snapping, teeth-baring monster of muscle, froth and flying fur. Short of letting them kill each other, which we did not want to do, we had no choice but to pull them apart. As someone whose livelihood depends on her hands, I knew better than to reach for a collar; I went for a tail instead – usually Joey's, as he was less likely to react by attacking me. At least their tails were the farthest

When we moved to my house in 2016 I built this gate to keep the dogs separated. I didn't realize it was curly maple until I had already surfaced the board.

point from their mouths. In the end, we learned the safest way to get them apart was to drag one through a doorway, stop at a reasonable breaking point between the shape-shifting heads, and close the door. It was painful for me to slam a door on someone's face – it had to hurt – but I knew of no other way to save their lives.

We took to keeping the dogs apart. One could be with us while we kept the other outside or in a crate. When we sold Mark's house and moved to mine, Mark fenced in a dog yard and built a deck with gates that would allow us to have one dog on the deck while the other was in the yard. Inside, I built a gate for the opening between the kitchen and mudroom so that one dog could be there and the other with us.

One Sunday afternoon Mark and I were talking in the shop when we happened to see Henny trot past the window. A perfectly normal sight – just a happy dog passing by. But this was Henny. She had found a way through the fence, straight to freedom. We called her inside, then Mark found the gap she must have squeezed through and patched it with wire hog fence.

A month or so later, I was working in the shop, with Henny in the fenced yard and Joey tied to the serviceberry tree in front. Our former neighbor, Abe, drove up the driveway, all 112 pounds and 90-something years of him. As I came out to say hello, I spotted Henny out of the corner of my eye as she nimbly climbed the fence and bounded our way. The reason for her interest didn't matter – there was no telling whether she was overjoyed to see her former neighbor or wanted to tear his throat out for trespassing. With Henny, excitement could turn deadly in a flash. I opened the shop door and pushed Abe through it so hard that I worried I might have knocked him to the floor.

She swung around and jumped on Joey. One minute she was on his back, teeth at his neck, the next, on the ground. Joey was tied in place; he couldn't get away. Unless I grabbed Henny's collar and pulled her off, she would kill him. She wasn't motivated by a desire to be violent; this was beyond anything you could meaningfully call "motivation." It was some kind of instinct gone haywire. I was terrified, knowing that if I grabbed her by the collar she might turn on me. But I was not about to let her kill Joey.

I reached for the collar and yanked with all my strength. Tied to the tree, Joey had to let go. I pulled Henny briskly to the backyard. For whatever reason, she didn't turn her rage on me. I shut her behind the gate and went to check on Abe. He was fine. I was shaking.

Mark put an adoption notice on the website of a group that specializes in finding homes for "difficult" dogs. We got no response. Her obsessive devotion and potential to serve as a killing machine would have made her an ideal partner for a hermit, or even better, a rare human survivor of apocalypse. The shelter would not want a dog who had proven herself destructive to property and prone to violence. It would be grossly irresponsible not to disclose these features of her personality to any would-be adopter. And with two escapes behind her, she seemed to be viewing the fence less as a barrier than a fun new challenge. Our neighbors across the street had several foster children. What if Henny got out and went after one? We'd done our best to understand her, having no knowledge of her life before she came to us, and to work with her constructively. We were at our wits' end.

It's a terrible thing to end the life of an animal at the pinnacle of health. Following the incident with Abe, two years after Henny's attack on Lizzie, Mark agreed that we should have her euthanized. We both accompanied her into the exam room. She was shaking with fear; until that moment, only one of us would ever have been with her at the vet's office. A powerful dog who was probably capable of taking down a full-grown buck, she crept tenderly into Mark's lap. The vet shaved her forearm. Henny looked into Mark's eyes. It was hard not to feel she was pleading. Logically, as far as Henny knew, she might just be having blood drawn for labs. She couldn't read our minds. Or could she? Until that moment, she had never seen us both in tears. We told her we loved her.

It took a millisecond for the taut muscles and racing heart to melt across Mark's lap. Our feeling of unbearable responsibility was far heavier than Henny's 50 pounds.

Lizzie had outlived yet another member of our family. She would go on to outlive others. But in the spring of 2020, she made clear to us that her time had come. We took her to the vet, who told us to meet her in the parking lot behind the office, where we'd have more privacy than in front. We got out of the truck and stood together, close enough for the vet to reach Lizzie while we all did our best to stay safely apart. All three of us had tears rolling down our cheeks behind our masks as we set Lizzie free. We brought her home and buried her beneath the catmint on the north side of the garden in front of the house.

16: Joey Walker Kangaroo Tail (2012-present)

TUESDAY, NOVEMBER 27, 2012, afternoon.

I was working at the lathe when I glimpsed a dog rolling in the pile of wood chips I'd dumped outside the door at the back of the shop. Of course – it must be Polaris, my tenants' dog. At that point, Kristen and her husband were renting my house. Polaris must have thought she'd won the jackpot when she spotted the deep pile of scratchy maple, the perfect texture for a good roll.

Then again, this dog looked small for Polaris, and its black spots were different from hers, as well. I switched off the lathe and went outside for a look. The dog, a male, was on his back, eyes shut, wriggling with joy while a pair of unrelated puppy companions looked on. Just another set of strays to keep in the shop while I tried to reunite them with their people. I picked up the black-and-white one and carried him in, hoping the others would follow. They didn't. By the time I was back outside, they were well up the rise of the neighboring hayfield, wagging *See ya!* to their pal.

I clipped a puppy leash to the dog's collar and called Kristen to come check him out. She pointed out his awkward gait – he ran less like a dog than a rabbit, his hind legs curled up beneath him. He was also weirdly lopsided. The more I watched him walk, the more likely it seemed that his hips or back legs were malformed. Unable to find any identifying information, I called the animal shelter and left a report on their answering machine in case someone was looking for him.

That night, I stopped at the shelter on my way home. I carried the

Always ready to help.

puppy in with me. As soon as we walked through the door, he began to shake violently in my arms. Had he been there before? No one had called to claim him. Nor did he have a chip that might have led us to his owner. The attendant took a photo, added more information to my earlier report, and I brought him home, stopping at the grocery for a bag of puppy chow and a fleece throw.

"We don't need another dog," said Mark when we arrived. "Don't even bring him inside the house." A bit harsh, considering the late-November weather. I made the pup a bed in the back of my truck. Our friend Betsi had given us her late dog, Martha's, bed with a fleecy cover; that would provide several inches of insulation between the dog and the frigid steel of the truck bed. I fixed some scrambled eggs to warm the little guy up. He was a sweet boy with soft, floppy ears and soulful brown eyes. Before eating, he gently cupped my chin in his mouth; it may have been a dog's instinctive request for its mother to regurgitate food, but to me it felt like thanks. After a late-evening walk I put him to bed with a hot water bottle, the new fleece throw and my old down jacket from Vermont wrapped around him, hoping we weren't going to wake up to a frozen puppy.

Each morning I took him for a walk around the woods behind the house. I took him to work at the shop, then put him to bed in the truck each night after the same routine. When I tried to take him for a walk on the road, he got as far as the neighbor's house and sat down. Strange. I had never met a dog who didn't want to walk. On the bright side, he seemed to know how to sit on command.

Days passed. No one called to claim him. I stopped at the pet supply store one evening on the way home and bought him a red collar and a tag engraved with my address, phone number and "JOEY," after my most-affectionate-ever cat. Mark still didn't want another dog, but this dog was too sweet for me to let him go.

Joey had only been with me a few days when I had to deliver a desk for a show in Columbus, Indiana, about 1-1/2 hours away from my shop. He still smelled gamy – no surprise, considering he'd been running around the woods, living rough, eating (and no doubt rolling in) whatever wild animals he could catch, as well as their scat. As with most dogs, the smellier, the better. But having him on the truck seat next to me for this drive was more than I could face. There was a car wash on the way with a sign advertising a self-service dog shower; I pulled over and parked, then took Joey into the building and set him up on the rubber-covered counter. I pushed some coins into the automated machine and sprayed him with warm water. He let out such a howl that anyone passing would have thought I was trying to drown him, so I made it quick. He refused to stand still for the hairdryer, so

Joey loves to nap in the jointer chips. His peg leg is on full display here.

I rubbed him down with an old towel, put him back in the truck and went on my way.

We were about a third of the way to Columbus when, prompted by the movement of the truck, he puked in my lap. This would make a fine professional impression on the people at the gallery, walking in with dog barf between my legs.

I took Joey everywhere – to the shop, to my customers' houses. At the shop he napped in the pile of wood chips at the end of the jointer. He also came up with several ways to play solitaire with a tennis ball while I worked: He'd drop the ball in the middle of a coiled Shop-Vac hose and kick the springy hose to make the ball jump out, as if of its own volition, so he could chase it. Sometimes he put the ball in a shoe, then nosed the shoe to knock it out and make it roll across the floor. *Look! It escaped! I'd better catch it and put it back.* He'd place the ball on the shelf under my workbench, then push it off so he could retrieve it and put it back. The wood chip pile offered another variation: Drop the ball in the pile, then dig through to make a channel so the ball would roll. I had never known a dog who entertained himself this well for hours; I was used to puppies like Oscar and William, who pestered me and turned into agents of destruction when I kept working.

As the days passed, it became clear that something really was wrong with Joey's hind legs. On December 7, I took him to the vet near our house to get him treated for worms and have his back checked out. He could still walk but was getting wobblier by the day. The vet X-rayed his hips, legs and spine; nothing appeared wrong with their development and there was no sign of injury. Based on the leg X-ray, he estimated Joey's age at 4 to 5 months. He chalked up the pup's troubles to growing pains. On the bright side, now that Mark knew we had a gimp on our hands, he softened and let Joey in the house. We already had Henny; she was about 1-1/2 years older than Joey, and as the new member of the family he was happily submissive toward her. We loved to watch them play.

Joey's condition continued to worsen. Another couple of days and he was even weaker. He'd walk 10 or 20 feet, then sit down to recover. Another three days and he simply could not walk. He could still stand up, barely, but his legs wouldn't hold him. I started to carry him everywhere. One morning, after more than a foot of snow had fallen, we shoveled a path from the back steps into the yard and took turns, Jonas, Mark and I, supporting Joey's hind end while he used his front legs to move forward. He started pooping while lying down, pulling himself forward as he went. Clearly frustrated by his incapacity, he became more vocal, with grunts, whines and an ear-piercing yip when he needed to go out. At least he was a good communicator.

What was going on? Was he going to keep going downhill until he died? Would he be one of those dogs with paralyzed hind legs who need a cart to get around? Just in case, I found a GingerLead,[1] a kind of sling-plus-leash designed for dogs who can't quite walk; it supports

---

[1] https://www.gingerlead.com/

them while allowing them to move their legs, insofar as they can. But I wanted another vet's opinion.

On December 14, I took him to my longtime vet, Jim Koch. After a thorough exam, he was inclined to agree with the other vet: growing pains. But that still didn't feel right. The dog was becoming paralyzed. There was no telling whether the paralysis would spread. It was the end of the day; the practice was closed, with no new patients to see. Jim called in his partner, Mary Alice Cox, for another opinion. Between them, they decided it was probably not growing pains after all, but possibly a virus or neurological disorder – myasthenia gravis, thymoma or polyradiculomyelitis, the last commonly known as "coonhound paralysis." Or it might be Lyme disease.

They weighed the possibilities. It's inspiring to watch a couple of seasoned veterinarians discuss potential diagnoses. They bring a lifetime of experience to the analysis that we can only wish for from overworked general practitioners of human medicine. The localized nature of the paralysis argued against myasthenia gravis. They were doubtful about the thymoma tumor, as it's rare; in more than 50 years of combined veterinary experience they had seen just one example. They ruled out Lyme disease because Joey's temperature was normal and he seemed healthy in all respects other than the weakness in his hind legs. The localized weakness, along with his general condition – energetic, alert, able to feel stimuli in his tail – suggested polyradiculomyelitis, a temporary paralysis usually caused by contact with saliva from an infected raccoon. The prognosis was guardedly optimistic: Once the condition reached its nadir there would be a temporary stasis, followed by a slow upturn. At least we had a diagnosis, if tentative.

By this time I was ready to deliver some tables and install a set of built-ins for customers who lived north-west of town. I took Joey with me, leaving him in the cab of the truck, which was more comfortable than the frigid bed under a thin aluminum cap. At lunchtime I carried him outside for a constitutional, then put him back. With food, water and a blanket, he seemed happy as long as we were together.

At home we kept him on an old blanket or towel in case of accidents. It was touching to see how gentle Henny was with him, how aware she

The job northwest of town included this cherry work table for the kitchen, a dining table in walnut and burly silver maple, and built-ins for a room just off the kitchen. (Photo: Spectrum Creative Group.)

was of his condition. She'd get a bone or a ball and drop it within his reach. He'd grab it, then they'd play tug-of-war under the coffee table.

Mark took Jonas to Elkhart on December 21 to visit his family for Christmas. It was the first time I'd been alone with the dogs and Lizzie, our cat, and the first time the dogs had a fight. For more than three weeks, Joey had been with me almost every waking hour. With Mark gone and only the beta dog – me – available, Henny apparently felt the need to assert her position in the pack. The spat was alarming, but on the bright side, Joey managed to sit up.

On Sunday, December 23, I wrote in my diary: "I detect in the most tentative way a small improvement. Yesterday afternoon Joey sat up more; lately he has just been lying down all the time. This morning he has sat up a couple of times, perfectly erect, and at one point he tried to stand up so that he could play with Henny. Walking Joey with the GingerLead, he stood up the whole time and moved his legs, sometimes in a bunny hop, but sometimes walking like a dog. He still can't bear his own weight, but this seems to be an improvement."

Mark and Jonas came home that night. The next day, Christmas Eve, Joey stood up for the first time and took several steps. It was one of my best Christmas presents ever.

Joey regained his strength over the following months. Before long, he was chasing balls, more agile than we'd ever seen him. Watching him run was a little painful – he'd trip and fall, then get up, unfazed; sometimes he'd go head over heels. In our sloping backyard, he learned to use his right hind leg as a brake by dragging it behind him. As a result, the upper surface of that foot is often stained green from being pulled, upside-down, across the grass. Joey is oblivious. All that matters is having fun.

Unlike his hind legs, his ears were in fine form. I'd always had floppy-eared dogs, but not long after his arrival, his ears became cocked – stiff at the base, then bent outward about halfway up, a good look for a cartoon character. His ears kept growing, at one point suggesting a cross between a dog and a giant moth or bat. Finally, they stopped, fully erect and pointed, and the rest of his body caught up. His tail, too, transformed rapidly from a stringy extension of his spine to a beefy tool for balancing, as well as expressing emotions. Mark came up with a new nickname: Joey Walker Kangaroo Tail.

I continued to take Joey with me to most jobsites, including a small project I did for the dining room of the Glossbrenner Mansion in Indianapolis. The property, a Tudor Revival built around 1910 in brick and limestone, had more than 7,200 square feet on two upper floors and an extensive basement where servants had once run the show. Many of the formal rooms were paneled in wood; there were stained glass doors and windows, elaborately carved limestone mantels and a ballroom in the attic.

The dining room was paneled in book-matched Circassian walnut, sequenced so that you could follow the sawyer's progress through the log as you went around the room. One of the panels beneath a window had been removed when a former owner adapted the house for use as medical offices. Mark Dollase at The Indiana Landmarks Foundation asked if I would recreate a panel and fit it into the space. He also hired me to unearth a stately pair of stained-glass doors that met in a Tudor arch; when the former owner had converted the formal dining room to an office, he'd a carpenter close off the doors behind a built-in bookcase. For a few days I worked there with John Dehner, a skilled carpenter who worked for Mark most of the time. We rode up in my truck, Joey sitting between us on the seat. I took Joey out periodically, but he spent most of the time napping on the hardwood floor while we worked. He has turned out to be among my most patient dogs. He allows me to work without interruption but is always ready to go home once the work is done.

When Joey was still a young dog, I took on a project for *Fine Homebuilding*. Senior editor Chuck Bickford, with whom I had worked on an earlier article, contacted me to ask whether I would be interested in collaborating on a project article and video about how to design, build and install a floating vanity. Unlike many floating cabinets, this one would not be built in an alcove; instead of relying on the walls at each end, in addition to a hanging cleat at the back, it would be supported entirely by the back wall, which called for extra-beefy brackets. I bought Hebgo brackets through Häfele, tweaked the original architect's

Joey sensed my nervousness as I prepared to leave for a shoot of the floating vanity installation for Fine Homebuilding.

drawing to improve the proportions and puzzled through how to build the piece, which had to incorporate a removable door section between the drawer columns for potential future ADA compliance. Once we'd agreed on the details, Chuck booked flights for himself and a videographer. I would get all the parts ready, they'd film the whole process, then I'd crate the carcases, doors, drawers and hardware, and ship the lot to the headquarters of Taunton Press.

  One day I was walking behind Chuck at my shop when I noticed he'd adopted an awkward gait. His left leg moved forward as usual, but he swung the right one out in a semi-circular motion, keeping his right knee locked. Without mentioning a thing, he was impersonating Joey, and his unannounced impersonation was spot-on.

After the shoot, which lasted a few days, several parts for the job wouldn't fit into the crates. I packed them in my suitcase, wondering what the TSA staff might make of the Hebgo brackets, veneered drawer faces, door pulls and tools. I flew to the Tweed New Haven Airport, which was housed in a charmingly compact building that reminded me of some minor airports in the Caribbean where we'd occasionally flown in the '60s when my father was working in that part of the world. So much saner than a multi-terminal hub, such as Heathrow or JFK. I rented a car, threw my suitcase and satchel in the back and set out.

When I arrived at Newtown, I found the Taunton campus, parked and asked for Chuck. He walked me around, introducing me to people, then showed me the Project House, where the vanity would go. It looked very different in person from the carefully framed images I'd seen published in the magazine; the place has been used to shoot so many diverse projects that it no longer has an architectural identity beyond "Project House."

We began the installation the next morning. The Project House was chilly, and the forecast was for a wintry mix of snow and rain. I was coming down with a sore throat and head cold, perfect conditions for a high-stakes shoot. Fortunately the job went off as well as I had hoped. The vanity looked good and was solid as a rock. The hot lunches that Chuck arranged to have delivered were just the inspiration I needed. I will always be grateful to Chuck for offering me that opportunity, because it was so much fun to work with him (and no one does a better impersonation of Joey's walk).

***

Joey is now almost 9. His eyelashes have turned from black to white, as has with most of the bandit mask that once covered his face. I think he's aging faster than he might have, had he not had that encounter with an infectious raccoon. Then again, it was his growing weakness due to that encounter that brought us together; without it, he would surely have run off with his playmates the day the three of them showed up.

Sometimes it hurts to watch him go through the labored steps re-

The project article about the floating vanity was republished in this special-interest publication from Taunton Press.

"Can we keep her, Mom?" Joey with Anissa Kapsales.

Joey in the spring of 2021, poised for me to throw his ball.

quired to lower himself onto his bed or the floor. He can't walk up or down the stairs in our house, and sometimes even has trouble with the four steps up to the front door. But when he falls, he just picks himself up and tries again.

He is the least demanding and most appreciative dog with whom I've shared my life. He has a special, elated bark when he hears Mark's truck about to turn into the driveway – *It's Daddy! I'm going to get him to throw my ball!* Mark puts his satchel on the old wooden armchair by the door, takes off his shoes and goes out to play. If Joey were a human, he'd be a medal-winning soccer player; he dashes after the ball, sometimes catching it before it hits the ground. He leaps and twists, and sometimes falls in ways that make us cringe in empathy for what we can only imagine is pain. He cannot get enough.

Fifteen minutes later, he comes crashing through the back door to get a drink of water. Turning around to go back outside, he gives me a look that says *We are having so much fun! Mark is the best dad ever!* then dashes off.

Joey's skill in accepting what is, and finding ways to be happy, strikes me as an example of pig-level enlightenment. This is not to suggest that he's immune to the allure of certain behaviors he knows we don't approve, such as exploiting the opportunity presented by a gate left ajar to cross the road and see what That Goddamn Neighbor Dog is doing, the one who takes a shit in her front yard in full view of our house (how dare she?) … or helping himself to cat poop from the litter box, as evidenced by the grit outlining his nostrils and dropping like silver bakery sprinkles from his lips. No one can be a saint all the time.

17: Pedro (2000-present)

PEDRO WAS an unwanted member of the family who lived across the alley from one of my clients in the late 1990s. While working in my client's garage or carrying things in and out of her house, I often heard a raucous voice shouting, or talking on the phone; occasionally the person would cry. It sounded like the voice of an old woman who was a few blades short of a pack, so I concluded that the neighbors had a multi-generational household and were living not just with their twin daughters, but also an elderly grandmother or aunt. Lovely, and commendable. It was only when I happened to meet the wife of the house one day in the alley that I got a chance to ask about the conversations I'd overheard. I learned they were the "songs" of the family pet, a yellow-naped Amazon parrot.

Her husband, Derick, had bought Pedro as a hatchling and raised him by hand. Pedro was about 10 years old. Unfortunately, he was devoted to Derick, but not to Derick's wife; an opera singer, she would do her best to practice scales, only to find herself one-upped by an out-of-tune impersonator. I overheard both parts of the performance on multiple occasions, along with many other words and sounds.

Penelope, the wife, said they were getting ready to move and had considered finding Pedro a new home. Would I like to adopt him? I thought the bird was brilliant and hilarious and would make a fascinating addition to my two-dog-and-one-cat household, so I said yes. I had no idea that Penelope was going to keep this plan a secret from her husband. The truth came out when I arrived at the designated time to pick up the parrot. It was a wrenching, tear-filled scene that unfolded while movers carried the family's possessions out of the

I made a perch for Pedro to hang out on in this wallpapered nook in my bungalow kitchen. The wallpaper is from Bradbury & Bradbury.

house and loaded them into a truck. Even as I insisted I had no interest in taking the bird away if he wanted to keep it, Derick acceded to Penelope's arrangement. He'd fought too many battles. The time had come to give in. It was a move with which I would become familiar.

Once I had Pedro transferred to my bungalow in town, I put him in one of the back bedrooms, which had a door to the fenced garden. That way I could take him easily out to the deck to enjoy a sunny day or a rain shower, which I knew he loved – while working across the alley from his former home I'd often heard him singing in the rain.

My tenant Eric came to live with me around the same time. The bedroom where I kept Pedro was one of a pair on either side of the bathroom at the back of the ground floor, making a suite of rooms the tenant could use. The bathroom and other bedroom were for Eric's exclusive use. I encouraged him to use the second room as a living room but reserved the right to keep Pedro there at least some of the time, as well as pass through the room to take him outside to the garden.

One night I came home from work to the sound of a baby crying. I mean, this kid was upset. "Do you have a baby back there?!" I casually asked Eric when he came into the kitchen. It seemed unlikely, given that Eric had never so much as brought over a girlfriend.

"No," he answered in his unflappable monotone. "It's Pedro. There was an ad on TV with a baby crying, and Pedro just joined in."

Before long, Pedro had added several new songs to his repertoire, among them "Gleeful Five-Year-Old Opening Long-Awaited Toy" and "Nine-Month-Old Throwing a Raging Fit." Thanks to his sojourns on the back deck, he also mastered the unique bark of every dog in our neighborhood and was building a songbook of local and seasonal birds.

Arguably less benign, though no less entertaining, were the songs Pedro had learned at his previous home. While those included the sound of twin girls crying (no doubt Penelope's twins were the original source of that performance; perhaps Pedro even thought those family members from his early years were nearby when he heard their song on TV), they extended to the occasional record of domestic distress unfiltered by norms of etiquette. *"DERICK!"* was one example, the single word shrieked at the top of Penelope's lungs. "What're You Gonna Do About the Goddamn Bird?" was another. When I mentioned this genre of parrot song to a friend, she exclaimed "You're hearing all of that family's secrets!"

Another friend, Dan, would stop by occasionally on his way to or from the hospital. A plumber who had switched professions to become an ICU nurse, he worked nights, so our schedules were reversed. One evening I took Pedro out of his cage to introduce them. Pedro was quite comfortable walking around on the floor; one of his wings was clipped to keep him from flying. William made a threatening move toward the bird. Pedro swung around like a puffed-up drill sergeant and strutted single-mindedly in William's direction, prompting him to flee. What dog expects a bird 1/25th his weight to give him the Kamala Harris *"Excuse me.* Excuse me, I'm speaking" treatment?

"I've heard of bird dogs," said Dan, an avid hunter. "But this is the first time I've seen a dog bird."

I'd met Dan at the plumbing supply shop, where I had gone in search of some parts for a kitchen. It was one of those old-fashioned businesses with a popcorn machine, coffee and doughnuts every morning, and a row of vinyl-upholstered stools printed with a manufacturer's logo – a cross between a hardware store and a diner. Merle, who handled wholesale orders, sat at a desk in the back corner below a poster of a pretty girl, her blouse pulled up above her waist, cut-off jeans below her navel and a bunch of red roses – *"Aw, thanks, sweetheart!"* – clutched in her arms with a pair of beers, one for him and one for her.

One of the guys behind the counter made a crack about the coincidence that two customers were driving brand-new trucks. I had recently bought my first new vehicle ever, a dark-green Toyota Tacoma (no mod cons like power windows or an extra-cab; it was a two-wheel drive with a four-cylinder engine – bottom of the line, but it's a good line), so I asked who the other person was. He pointed to Dan, who'd just bought a red Ford F-150 (with many mod cons). We struck up a conversation. I loved that he had left plumbing to become a nurse and wished I could hear more about what had prompted that career switch.

I wasn't seeing anyone at the time, so I asked him out for coffee or a beer. He was funny and intelligent, good looking in a cowboy-like way and had a boyish, innocent charm that came from his sincere desire to be and do good. I had a major crush on him, but the attraction was one-way, so we stayed friends.

One morning my friend Peggy dropped by unexpectedly with a cup of coffee on her way to work.

"Hi, Peggy!" I said as I opened the door. "What are you doing here so early in the morning and wearing sunglasses?"

"You haven't heard?" she replied, lifting her glasses. Her eyes were

The simple wooden swing I built for the front porch at my bungalow.

red. She'd seen my friend Bill's obituary in the paper and rushed over to console me. I hadn't even picked my paper up yet.

It took all day to absorb the shock, and I will always appreciate that Peggy came over to break the news. We hugged each other and she went to work. A few minutes later there was another knock on the door. It was Dan; he happened to be passing by on his way home. We went out to the swing I'd built for the front porch and sat down.

I told him about Bill, who had kept alpacas for years. Being from Wisconsin, Bill called them the Packers, after the football team. He would often leave for conferences where he learned about every aspect of contemporary alpaca-culture, from acreage requirements and shelter needs to negotiating with spinners of wool. He was at least 18 years my senior, had an advanced degree in physics and worked in the Indiana University-Bloomington physics department. In addition to raising alpacas, he had spent many years in the cooperative grocery business where I often shopped. He had a daughter and a son, and appreciated the diverse cultural offerings to be found in a university town. We'd had a brief romantic relationship a few years before and remained friends. (Translation: I thought he was really admirable and cool and a survivor, plus handsome and intelligent. He said I reminded him of his second wife, who'd left him for a farrier, which made me scary.) He had started riding a motorcycle, sometimes for long distances. He was on one such ride when he hit a patch of gravel or sand, or maybe it was a sharp curve – I can no longer remember – and the bike went down. The coroner said he would have died instantly.

"When your number's up, your number's up," Dan said. I stared at the porch floorboards and tried to square that perspective with Dan's work as an ICU nurse. He wouldn't say such a thing lightly; he was a devout Catholic who spent his vacations as a volunteer firefighter out West because doing good really is his idea of fun – especially if doing good involves outdoor adventures involving copters and Pulaskis. There was a wisdom in those seemingly glib words, a recognition that we can do our best and then some, and still meet defeat, however we define it – and at that point acceptance becomes a graceful move, whether you're the one facing death or the nurse who just lost a patient.

Once again I regretted that Dan did not share my romantic interest.

But back to Pedro. A year or two later, I moved with Alan to the house on the edge of town, the place where William and Winnie had to sleep in the garage and William bit Alan from under the table. It was not a happy time. Pedro lived in his cage suspended from the ceiling, next to a sliding glass door that gave him a good view of the backyard. This was a suburban neighborhood, so Pedro was learning new birdsongs and dog barks. It was summer, so we often had the sliding door open with just a screen to keep out bugs. We were constantly going in and out.

PEDRO

One day it dawned on me that every time Alan walked past, Pedro would lunge at him from his perch, making a sound of disgust. That was strange. Maybe it was some kind of Penelope holdover, but in this case Penelope was Alan?

That didn't stop *me* from getting along with Pedro just fine. In the evening, Alan and I would sit down in the living room with a beer. I'd let Pedro out of his cage and carry him over to sit on the couch. Pedro would walk across the back of the couch to where I was sitting and bend his head down, his way of asking me to rub the back of his neck. I'd hold him on my chest and scratch gently as he fell into a trance. My heart melted every night when I went to cover his cage and heard him making Derick-is-whispering-bedtime-stories-to-his-twin-girls sounds; then he'd respond with coos, as though he was talking himself to sleep by invoking these songs from his youth. I had never known that birds could be so affectionate toward people – how members of our two species, so different, could form such a bond.

My friend Elizabeth, the most parrot-centric person I know, had taught me how to handle him and explained the meaning of parrot responses such as telescoping pupils. Having been bitten a few times early on, I did not take Pedro's trust in me for granted – the bird's beak has the strength of bolt cutters; it might as well be a cross between a can opener and a pair of channel-lock pliers. At every step of the way he'd worked himself into my heart.

Between the dust created by having a caged bird and the cacophony that grew noticeably worse whenever Alan was around – the barking, the hooting, the whistled tune of "The Andy Griffith Show," not to mention the repulsive retch/growl of an angry parrot – it didn't take long for Alan to decide I should find Pedro a new home. I resisted at first; Pedro and I had developed a real relationship. I couldn't bear the thought of giving him away. I'd been entrusted with his care. On the other hand, it couldn't be good for Pedro to be living in close proximity to someone whose very presence provoked such a violent response. I hoped the whole question of me finding him a new home would disappear, just fade away. It didn't.

I thought of an ideal location for a parrot and a pair of people who

My father with Lottie, one of my parents' now-late dogs.

might be into taking him: my parents. They lived on an island in Florida. Their house had a screened porch. What was not to like? This is not to say that I liked it, but for Pedro's sake, I wanted to like it. I repeated a silent mantra: "It will be better for him." Luckily, they said yes. Pedro would still be in my family, so I wouldn't be violating Derick's trust in any meaningful way. Now I just had to get him there.[1]

As it happened, my sister was getting married – the perfect opportunity. I would fly down with Pedro for the wedding. I booked the flight and paid the extra $80 to take him with me on the plane.

---

[1] Although Penelope and Derick gave me their contact information when they moved, I couldn't reach them when I tried, hoping to make sure it would be OK for me to move Pedro to Florida. I have tried to get updated contact information for them through friends, without success.

PEDRO

Before we drove to the airport, I put Pedro in a cat carrier made of rigid plastic. Once we were on the plane, I covered it with a towel and stowed it under the seat in front of me, hoping that Pedro would go to sleep and not try to bolt-cut his way out. Every so often I heard him gnawing the edges of the ventilation slots and felt a mild sense of panic; it would be a complete disaster, with injuries and probably lawsuits, if he escaped and went marching around the cabin.

When we changed planes in Atlanta I stopped at a bathroom. As soon as he saw a room full of women with perfume, makeup and colorful clothes, he broke into wolf whistles. Derick had trained him to whistle, then follow up with something that was garbled in translation – it sounded like "That's a ground round." Perhaps "That's a brown cow." Or maybe "That's a bow-wow." I had no idea what Pedro was saying, though it was unmistakably an expression of appreciation, probably for Penelope's appearance when getting ready for a night out without the kids. I made my apologies and found a stall.

My mother picked us up when we landed in Daytona and drove us northwest to Lake George, where my parents lived at the time. She'd bought him a larger cage than the one that came from Derick, and furnished it with several parrot toys. My heart was heavy with the awareness that I'd be leaving him when I went home.

My sister's wedding took place a couple of days later. She and her fiancé had arranged to have the ceremony and festivities at an architectural salvage yard that had a bar, indoor and outdoor stages and a fenced courtyard with tables under the stars. It was a great place; I'd been there before to buy old tools or hardware. But I was in no mood for a wedding. I had let Alan prevail on me to find Pedro a new home. Even if it was a good home, with my family, it felt like a betrayal. So I was already depressed and on the brink of tears when we arrived at the venue. I walked into the courtyard, only to find myself face-to-face with a yellow-naped Amazon parrot in a cage against the wall. What a cruel joke from the universe. The bird belonged to one of the people who worked at the business. I stood there and communed with the parrot, unable to stop crying.

Maggie gave birth to her daughter, Wyatt, several months later. She

One wall of the built-ins I did for my sister's kitchen, with Maggie and her daughter, Wyatt, in 2005. Daniel drove to Florida with me to help with the installation.

and her husband, Chip, bought a 1910s house in DeLand, Florida. They kept their former home, a tiny two-bedroom in Orange City, as a rental; Chip called it The Chateau de Poverté. The new place needed a lot of work. They hired me to do the kitchen.

Once the bulk of the work around their house was done – interior woodwork restored by their friend David Heeren, shades on the windows, improvements to wiring and plumbing – their home was stable enough that my mother and Maggie decided Pedro would get a lot more social interaction if he moved in with them.

His cage went in the living room, where he could hear almost everything that went on in the two-story interior. Inevitably, this included

"Must you go?" My parents' current dog, Rooster.

Wyatt's crying. My niece grew up with a bird who was irresistibly drawn to share her every song, especially the song with which he was most familiar, "Furious Crying Child." There is something cosmically unjust about being a 3-year-old in mid-meltdown and having every last shred of your self-righteous anger co-opted by a bird who hasn't the faintest idea why you're crying but feels compelled to join in. "I HATE THAT BIRD!" she'd shout.

One day, while feeding Pedro or cleaning out his cage, my sister spotted a tiny egg, cracked, on the newspaper lining the floor. "I'm looking around the room, thinking 'Who did that?'" she says. "I'm looking at Pedro and asking 'How the hell did that egg get in your cage?!' Is that

Pedro in her cage at my sister's home.

from you?" She thought someone was playing a practical joke. Then it dawned on her: After all the years Pedro had been in our family, and in Derick's before, no one had realized that he was a she. The idea took months to get used to.

When Maggie and Chip separated in 2013, Pedro moved with her and Wyatt to the tiny cottage behind the house our parents had moved into when they left the island; the logistical demands of remaining in their remote location into their 80s and beyond had proved too great.

PEDRO

Today Pedro lives in a corner of Maggie's bedroom with views through windows on two sides and often spends time in her second cage on the upstairs porch, monitoring our mother's comings and goings with Rooster, her lone surviving dog. Sometimes Maggie lets Pedro out to explore the room on the floor. Pedro, who is now about 30, struts around looking for things to chew or tear and objects loudly when Maggie tries to restrain her. The high point of her days is a trip into the bathroom for a shower; Maggie sprays her with water from a bottle while Pedro clings to a perch on the wall, stretching her wings, preening and singing non-stop, occasionally letting out a screech followed by a laugh that sounds suspiciously like my own.

18: Missing in Action (2014)

IT WAS obvious right away that something wasn't right when I got home after work on January 2, 2014. A Thursday, it was the first official workday of the year. We'd had a late and rather cranky start that morning after a couple of hours repairing the clothes dryer. Jonas was still in bed, happy for any chance to sleep in, so I was the smallest person available to get wedged behind the laundry appliances and fiddle with the hose and clamps. Between us, we got the dryer back in operating order and turned our attention to work. Mark was in the middle of a bathroom job for which I'd just started building a simple vanity and a tall storage cabinet for toiletries and linens.

Much as I love my work, I have always had a hard time with January 2. Not only is it the Monday of the year, it comes after months of festivities – for many of us, the sense of anticipation, the dinners with friends and planning for holiday gatherings start with Halloween at the end of October. Even in years when I've spent most of that season at work, the general mood – a time of coziness, reflection and visits with family and friends – has always brightened my days with a glow that leaves me a little bereft as the calendar turns and we face the chill expanse of a new year. So even though my workday had been shortened by my time behind the clothes dryer, I was ready to quit at 5 p.m. I forced myself to drive to the gym for a workout. By the time I reached our driveway at Mark's house, night had fallen.

As part of their divorce, Mark and his former wife, Patti, had agreed to share custody of their son, Jonas, and devised a schedule that gave each of them equal time with him. He usually spent Thursdays at his mother's house, but on that night he was going to stay with us; we'd

Jonas and Mark on a railroad trestle in 2007.

Always happy to learn new skills, Jonas used a railroad spike to carve this Latin inscription into a piece of locally quarried limestone.

swapped weekends so he could go to Elkhart the following day for a belated holiday celebration with Mark's family.

Jonas was 15, old enough to be left at home with a list of chores to get through on his own schedule. The list that day included shoveling snow from the walkway, moving a pile of split logs at the edge of the woods up to the back porch in the wheelbarrow, then stacking them beside the house. Over my six years with them, I'd seen Jonas change from an occasionally whiny little boy to a young man in the making. He understood that things work best when everyone chips in, and he enjoyed contributing, whether by weeding the garden, vacuuming or getting a fire started in the woodstove. He was also becoming a good cook – he loved to help make persimmon pudding with fruit from our trees, was learning to bake bread from scratch and produced a mean *pico de gallo* with fresh onions, tomatoes and herbs from the garden. A self-motivated learner, he would happily spend a weekend alternating between reading, building his own constructed language and helping around the house. He was also learning to play the piano and guitar; his interest in guitars led him to make his own proto-instrument from a board of red oak, a short length of PVC plumbing pipe and some strings.

Not surprisingly, given his fascination with language, Jonas wanted to learn Latin. He signed up for classes and started a Latin club at his high school, though he may have been the only member. He often came to me for advice on how to convey an abstract idea or treat a point with the requisite nuance. We shared this interest in details, the subtleties of meaning that so many whose first language is English take for granted.

I was struck by a fundamental sanity to his motivations, which were quite different from my own. Throughout my formal schooling and for decades after, I'd been driven by a desire to prove myself to others. Jonas was free from such baggage; his parents had agreed from the start to raise him with love, kindness and all the patience they could muster. They involved him in all sorts of household work that many delegate to hired help – cleaning the bathroom, weeding the garden, picking horn worms off the tomato plants, taking vegetable scraps out to the compost pile, mowing the lawn, shoveling snow. Sometimes he chafed at these responsibilities – who doesn't? – but he understood that he was learning

Proto guitar. Jonas made this instrument out of scrap materials, inspired by the film "It Might Get Loud."

important life skills. The three of us shared all of this work, so he didn't feel uniquely put upon.

    Patti and Mark gave Jonas the time and space to be alone, to engage in reflection and express whatever creative impulses might strike him. Without instilling neuroses, they guided his ability to discern a worthwhile risk from one that was irresponsible, and affirmed his sense of self-worth without resorting to praise for just showing up.

    Jonas went to school in town, so it was usually easier for Mark or me to pick him up from Patti's house after work on nights when he was going to stay with us than for her to drive him out. One of us would stop by her place in the late afternoon, usually before Patti got home from her job as a therapist in a town about an hour away, and watch Jonas say goodbye to their dog, Lucy, lock the doors and lug his overstuffed backpack out to my truck. We often had to stop at the grocery store; because my truck had a regular cab with a bench seat, there was limited

Jonas with William on a walk, 2008. (Photo: Mark Longacre.)

space for groceries, especially on days when I'd filled the bed with tools from a job, leaving no room to cram bags between the portable table saw, compound miter saw and boxes of other equipment. Jonas would get in the passenger seat and I'd pile grocery bags around him and, on big shopping days, right on his lap, until he was almost buried. "You look like a bloated tick!" I'd tell him. We'd laugh at how ridiculous it was and head home.

Although Jonas didn't seem that interested in learning to build furniture, he sometimes came over to my shop. One of his first visits was when he and I were making cookies, which required a rolling pin. I couldn't find one in Mark's kitchen, so I said "Let's go make one." He was game. I cut a blank of super-dense white oak, chucked it in the lathe and turned a fat cylinder, which we used to roll out the dough.

Jonas with Lucy, the dog who lived with his mother, Patti. (Photo: Mark Longacre.)

On a hike with Winnie in 2008. (Photo: Mark Longacre.)

In 2008, when I was working with Anissa Kapsales on an article about milk paint for *Fine Woodworking*, Anissa and Mike Pekovich agreed it would be useful for readers to have a selection of color samples finished with wax on one half and Danish oil on the other, to illustrate the effects of different topcoat products on the appearance of milk paint colors. One evening I asked Jonas to come over and help. We got through as much as we could, then brought the samples home. He applied the second coat of milk paint at our kitchen table while I cooked dinner.

We had fun together and sometimes collaborated on surprises for Mark. Even though Jonas seemed destined for a career in computational linguistics, he appreciated art and design; prints by well-known artists and paintings by family friends decorated his room, which was furnished with a pine bookcase Mark had built, an electronic piano he was learning to play and a desk covered with schoolwork and mysterious science experiments that looked and smelled disgusting. When I'd moved in with them, I'd brought my dogs, William and Winnie, and Lizzie, our cat, as well as most of the furniture from my house. Daniel had helped me carry an old china cabinet upstairs to Mark's bedroom; that evening I filled it with the collection of family heirlooms and pottery I had stored in it at every place I'd lived since I'd bought the cabinet in 1995. That night Jonas peeked into our room, saw the explosion of blue-green-pottery, and shouted *"COOL!"* We all know that seeing a parent develop a relationship with a new partner can be hard on kids. I'd certainly experienced that in my teens. I was grateful that Jonas made me feel welcome.

A couple of years later, when I shared my secret plan to replace the cabinets in the kitchen, he was all in. The first step was to remove the massive island in the center and put a table in its place – something more appropriate to a house inspired by the modest L-shaped farmhouses in northern Indiana, where Mark had grown up. I had turned the legs and assembled them with an apron, added a pair of drawers, then glued up a top of exceptionally wide and clear cherry boards. The table was ready to deliver. All that remained was to remove the island. One afternoon when Mark was at work, Jonas and I took apart the cabinets that made up the island and carried them down to the

Jonas was almost always ready to help when we asked. Here he is brushing milk paint on color samples for an article in Fine Woodworking.

The kitchen at Mark's house after I changed the cabinets with help from Jonas and built a dining/work table in cherry and mahogany. (Photo: Spectrum Creative Group.)

basement. The floor that had been under the island wasn't finished, so we grabbed the rug I'd had in my office and laid it over the area, like a toupee on a bald spot. We laughed at our ingenuity. Later that evening Mark came home and we brought the table in from my shop. It was a true family project.

Mark and Patti had built the house together as a comfortable, energy-efficient place for three people. They'd subdivided their original five acres, then handled the construction while living in the property's old farmhouse, a two-bedroom bungalow just down the hill. The place had an old barn that Mark used as a shop for his contracting business, along with a small structure on limestone piers and poplar beams that had originally housed chickens and stored feed.

They designed the new house with help from an architect friend, Jim Rosenbarger, who pointed out the best siting for views. Other inspiration came from Sarah Susanka's book "The Not So Big House." The main floor had a good-sized living room, full bath and spacious dine-in kitchen; they also added a library/office/"away room," as Susanka calls it, with French doors and large windows on three sides – a good place to go when you wanted some time alone, with a view of the apricot tree heavy with white blossoms in spring or the fiery gold maple on the southwest side in fall. Upstairs were two bedrooms, a laundry room and second full bath. Mark and his crew worked on the project daily; Mark often continued into the evening. His brother Dan, a skilled carpenter, came down from Elkhart to help, as did Patti's brother Peter and both of their dads. Jonas was still a toddler when he and his parents moved in.

The house was partway up a long hill that rose to one of the highest spots in the county. That January afternoon, we'd had several inches of snow, and despite my effort to get a good enough start to power my two-wheel drive pickup over the bad spots, I eventually surrendered to the icy patch formed by my spinning tires and left the truck in the middle of the drive. Mark could park his truck at his shop next door, as he often did. We had a system for locking the doors and turning on particular lights. At bedtime, or any time we would all be away, we put the dogs in crates in the mudroom. If it was late in the day and one of us wouldn't be home until after dark, we also left the outdoor light on so that whoever was coming home could see the way up the path and avoid twisting an ankle.

Trudging up the gravel path with my satchel over my shoulder and a bag of kindling in my arms, I wondered why the porch light wasn't on. When I reached the back door, I put down my load and tried the knob, expecting it to be locked. It was not. Jonas must have run outside for a moment – he always had some project going, as often as not involving twigs, berries or chunks of limestone.

Inside, the house was dark and the dogs were at large. "Jonas?" I called, to no reply. He must've been upstairs working at his laptop with earbuds on. Perhaps he'd fallen asleep on his bed while reading a book. He was a teenager, I reminded myself, six weeks shy of his 16th birthday. I set out to find him, switching lights on as I went.

"Jonas?" I called again as I started up the stairs. "Where are you?" I flipped on the light in the upstairs landing and looked into his room. Through the doorway in the semi-darkness I saw a figure. It looked like Jonas, but the skin was gray and the figure appeared to be hanging from the closet door. *He's made a life-size dummy of himself and hung it from his closet door to freak us out,* I thought; he loved practical jokes, though he didn't usually play them on us, and he was so artistically and mechanically inclined that my initial take seemed plausible.

"Jonas?" I said, moving closer. "This isn't funny."

And then it hit me: He was dead.

I flew down the stairs to get my cell phone from the kitchen, then ran back up while dialing 911.

I know exactly what I said on the call, because the emergency dispatch department gave me a copy of the recording several weeks later at my request. Hyperventilation. Screams of horrified disbelief. I was kneeling on the carpet at the top of the stairs, looking into Jonas's room while the dispatcher kept me on the line. Was Jonas still breathing? No. He told me to try CPR. I was loath to touch that gray body, let alone put my mouth to its face. *But this is Jonas,* I told myself. *You have to.* I touched his shoulder, then his arm. He was stiff as a board. In a spasm of cognitive dissonance, I shouted hoarsely "THERE'S NO LIFE IN THIS BODY."

Seconds dragged. This could not be happening. Random sights crowded my eyes with details I would recall only later: His feet were on the floor. He was fully clothed, arms by his sides. The abstract painting on glass that our friend Chris Blackwood had given to Jonas was leaning against the wall behind his feet. There was a rope around his neck, padded with a rolled-up t-shirt.

I was frantic with worry about Mark. How would he survive? Jonas was the light of both his parents' lives. The first time I'd visited their house, Mark had shown me Jonas's room. Pausing at the door, he said "I don't know what I'd do if anything ever happened to my little boy." He and Patti were devoted to their son; when they split up, they agreed to put his welfare above their own interests and grievances. They shared custody 50/50 and were flexible about altering the schedule to allow for vacations and trips to visit family out of town. Just one week earlier, we'd spent Christmas morning at Patti's; without realizing it, she and I had bought Jonas the same present, a used copy of the classic "Latin Dictionary" by Lewis & Short.

An ambulance and sheriff's deputies were on their way. The first vehicle arrived while I was still collapsed upstairs on the landing. The dispatcher spoke. Yes, of course – I would have to move my truck; it was blocking the driveway. I ran down the stairs, phone in hand, and threw Henny and Joey in the backyard, which Mark had recently enclosed with a fence. By the time I reached my truck there were flashing lights piercing the dark at the end of the drive. Mark was running up the hill, panic-stricken, shouting "WHAT'S GOING ON?"

I couldn't tell him. Everything so far was already too much; I couldn't add another thing. In my most authoritative voice I shouted "EVERYTHING IS UNDER CONTROL," which was true, as far as it went, and got in my truck.

My heart broke as I backed down the hill. I knew what Mark was going to find. Again – this just could not be happening. I pulled off the road, parked and screamed uncontrollably at the top of my lungs. Neighbors ran out to see what was happening. I was in no condition to talk to anyone; I ran straight back up the hill to the house. On the way I called Jim Krause, one of Mark's best friends. Jim and his wife, Anne, had lost their older daughter a few years earlier to a fall. Now, they were on a sailboat with friends off the Gulf Coast, enjoying some end-of-the-year rest and relaxation. But they had to be the first to hear this news.

The rest of the evening was a blur of sounds and light. One after another, sheriff's deputies tramped snowy boots across the hardwood floor of the kitchen, then up the stairs. One stood at the doorway to Jonas's room, arms and legs spread like a big letter X, preserving the body and the scene against potential disturbance by members of the family. For the first time, I realized that our home was being viewed as a potential crime scene. I went out to the backyard and called my mother in the falling snow.

We answered questions and followed orders. Stranger after stranger came out of the dark into the brightness of our home: more sheriff's deputies, a social worker, the coroner's assistant. The snow was falling heavily now, on top of freezing rain. Traffic was slow; many cars slid off the road that night. The detective was on her way, but it would take her an hour to reach our house.

Why would Jonas have killed himself? It made no sense. He was a happy, considerate young man who knew how much his parents, extended family and friends loved him. He thrived on adventure, especially when it meant spending time outdoors and learning primitive skills such as camping under the stars, or making fire with no more than friction from a stick and a length of string. But he took rules and safety with a seriousness more typical of an adult. He had no interest in alcohol or drugs and excelled in school. He could not have cared less about being popular; instead, he had a few good friends. He read college-level books about brain science and constructed languages not because he had to (they were well beyond the curriculum at his school), but because he loved learning and was utterly fascinated by the mind. How did this human body come to have consciousness? Could there be anything more amazing? He'd been looking forward to seeing his cousins in Elkhart. He had even been excited about going back to school the following week.

Mark and I were in shock. Every time we had a moment to ourselves, we looked at each other and quietly said "Patti." I offered to call her. Mark said he had to be the one. Jonas should have been with her that night. Instead, he was with us; he had died on our watch. *Died*, though? How could that be true? We must be living in an alternate reality; we'd surely wake up at any moment. But strangers kept trudging through our house. After what felt like hours, Mark called her, opening with "There's been a terrible accident."

When Patti and her friend Leah arrived, the deputies refused to let them in Jonas's room. They barred her from the door. The detective, Jennifer Allen, finally showed up; she and the deputies turned Jonas's room upside down and took his cell phone, laptop and anything that might shed light on what had happened. Out of respect for his son, Mark had lifted the body away from the door and laid it on the floor before the sheriff's deputies reached the room. No further tampering with the body would be allowed – not even an embrace from his mother.

I was sitting downstairs in the away room when they finally let Patti into his room. There is no name for the sound that came out of her body, a bone-deep, agonized moan. She could look but not touch. She looked at the body she had grown from two cells, carried nine months and fed with her milk for three years. Her joy, this bright life she had created and continued to nurture – her future, as well as her present. Now his body had been claimed by the authorities; he was not just a victim, but evidence. Shortly after allowing her into his room, they wrapped him in a white plastic body bag and carried him on a stretcher down the stairs, through the kitchen, out of the house and into the snowy night.

At last the house was empty. Dazed, we brought in the dogs and turned off the lights. Mark dug a bottle of bourbon out of the pantry and poured us each a drink. There was no way either of us could stomach food. Then we began the long business of notifying family members and friends that, to the best of our knowledge, Jonas had hanged himself. We had no idea why.

I quickly checked my email in case there was anything pressing concerning work. While scrolling down the page I saw one of those suspicious names among the senders, the kind that are so unlikely that they seem made up, and usually accompany a bogus invoice or business proposal. I usually delete them, but recognizing that shock was impairing my judgment, I let this one stay.

We went to bed and hardly slept. In the middle of the night I was seized by anger at Jonas for taking his life.

Friday morning dawned crisp and blindingly white. Crystals glinted off thick powder all the way up to where the hill behind the house met the cloudless blue sky. Our good friends Lee and Betsi, whom I'd notified by text the night before, showed up at 8 a.m. with a basket full of food and busied themselves making coffee, slicing bread for toast, cracking eggs into a pan. Mark sat at the head of the table, face in his hands, wracked by sobs interspersed with moments of stunned disbelief at the enormity of what had happened.

From midday on, new people streamed into the kitchen, tracing strangers' footsteps from the night before. Again, we put the dogs in the yard to minimize their barking. Friends and customers brought bags of groceries, bottles of whiskey, casseroles and pies. We sat around the kitchen table and talked into the night. As darkness fell, I was sitting in the away room with our friend Carrol Krause, when, in her peculiarly incisive Carrol way, she mentioned choking. She said it was something that kids and teenagers did to get a momentary high, though it sometimes killed them if they were doing it alone. Choking? I had never heard of it. I filed the word away. Late that night, when the last friend had left, I ran to my computer and Googled.

Jonas fit the profile perfectly: intelligent, athletic, mechanically minded and a respecter of rules. For kids, this practice is a lethally easy DIY. They do it for the rush – that moment when you just begin to regain consciousness after passing out. Although many choking deaths are recorded as suicide (strictly speaking, they are suicide in the sense that the player causes his or her own death), the distinction between intentional and unintentional self-harm is too important to ignore – at least, for those left behind. There are organizations around the world dedicated to educating parents and teachers of the risks of this practice, as well as persuading law enforcement professionals of how important it is to differentiate between suicide and accidental death by choking.[1]

As I read, a pair of details came flooding back: the padding – a favorite T-shirt – wrapped carefully around the rope, his feet planted squarely on the floor. Both seemed inconsistent with intentional hanging. Why would you try to make yourself comfortable if you were ending your life? And if you did want to hang yourself, surely you wouldn't think you could do so by simply standing on the floor with a rope around your neck. I dimly recalled my mystification at these details when I'd been on the phone with the police dispatcher; they'd struck me as inconsistent with intentional hanging, but I had been too overwhelmed to process the potential implications.

I went upstairs and examined the door. The rope had left a pair of notches in the end grain of the poplar opening stile – one scarcely half an inch from the stile's edge, the other a mere quarter inch away.

He hadn't hung himself; he'd been engaging in this practice, one that

---

[1] The organization we found most informative and helpful is Erik's Cause https://www.erikscause.org.

seemed less incomprehensible when I remembered that my sister and I, with our cousin Jean, used to whirl around the yard at our grandparents' apartment house because we loved the sensation of dropping from dizziness, then waking back up. Jonas had evidently expected to faint to his right – the rope would slide right off the edge of the door, allowing him to fall, then return to consciousness. He wasn't concerned about hurting himself, because the floor was carpeted. Tragically, when he fainted, he slumped in the other direction.

A weight lifted from my shoulders. Of course he hadn't meant to kill himself. We'd allowed ourselves to imagine that perhaps he hadn't been the person we knew him to be. It was unbearable to think we might have missed some clue that he was in distress. I went back to the living room and told Mark what I had learned.

"It makes no difference," he said. "He's gone." Later, he acknowledged that it did make a difference – a big one.

On January 3, Jim and Anne called their New Year's sailing trip to a halt and high-tailed it back from the Gulf Coast to Indiana. "Jim and Anne are going to be there just as soon as they can," our friend Margie told us. "They're going to get snowed in with you!" We couldn't wait for them to arrive. They showed up a couple of days later with still more groceries and decamped to the guest room we'd set up in the partially finished basement. Having been through a similar loss, they went straight into care mode, cooking, cleaning and helping to plan a memorial. Just having them there, so close, living with us in our house, was deeply comforting, like when a kid asks his mother to sit with him while he falls asleep, and she does.

We held the celebration of life the following weekend. The day before, we took Joey and Henny to the boarding kennel, knowing that our house would be full of friends and Mark's relatives, most of whom live out of town. Jim and Anne organized the event, with food made by friends, multiple speakers including some of Jonas's friends, and live music. I tried to help with the obituary, but words just wouldn't come. My thoughts were blown apart. The best I could manage was a eulogy.

Friends kept Mark and Patti alive – at least, in a manner of speaking. There was no denying that part of each of them had died with their son.

Once Mark went back to work, a couple of weeks after that life-rending night, the comradery with his crew, all of them friends, and the necessary order of the workday diverted his attention from the overwhelming grief, at least to a degree that allowed him to function. But at home he would spend hours by the fire, writing in his journal, reading poetry and weeping. I'd find him staring blankly, his expression despondent. We talked about Jonas every evening after work. One evening, especially distraught, he said he couldn't see how he could go on; the worst-possible thing in the world had happened.

I get the concept of toxic positivity, but what I did next doesn't qualify. Mark needed a good shaking-up. "No," I said. "Things could *certainly* be worse. We could be in the middle of a winter like this, but with our village bombed. We could be living as refugees in a freezing-cold tent instead of a beautiful house with a fire in the woodstove, with no food to eat and no safe water, let alone bourbon, and besides losing our son, we could also have lost other relatives and friends."

In a similar way, as I write this book, I can honestly appreciate that I'm lucky to have cancer that *appears* not to have metastasized – and in a part of my body that has not yet interfered with my ability to eat and enjoy food, one of my favorite activities. So many people undergoing cancer treatment can only take liquid nourishment through a port to their stomach. Some go so long without eating or drinking that they have to re-learn how to swallow. One of my favorite traits in Mark is his capacity to take a philosophical view. Sometimes a simple shift in perspective is capable of altering the world; it doesn't erase the damage or the pain, and it certainly can't prevent death, but it can offer a kind of freedom – the freedom to see opportunity amid loss and hardship. While a shift in perspective is no substitute for action to minimize avoidable risks, right injustice and address the world's sometimes-overwhelming ills, it strikes me as a critical component in any kind of healing.

For months after Jonas died, I craved contact with his teachers and with parents of his friends – any opportunity to talk about him and hear others' stories. It felt like a way to keep him close. Meanwhile, I had plunged into investigation mode. Sure, the sheriff's department was doing the legal investigation, but I could do my own. I knew this young man and loved him. The authorities did not. He was part of my life, as well as his parents'. As broken as we all were by his sudden death, I was the one parental figure who had the luxury of a little distance. I was not the one who'd given birth to him, held a bucket while he threw up or tried to comfort his screams the first time he flew in a plane. I wanted to do what I could to help us all understand what had happened. How could such a responsible, engaged young man end up causing his own death?

But just as much, I wanted Jonas not to have died alone. I wanted to be there with and for him. If I couldn't go back in time … well, isn't time a human construct? While I couldn't save him, part of me was desperate to get as close as possible to being there with him as he died.

Over the following weeks, with help from a few friends and Detective Allen, I did my best to put together what had happened. Detective Allen called to tell me that Jonas had been recording himself on his phone when he died.[2] Based on the recording, she had determined his death was due to the choking game, and so, accidental. I drove straight downtown to the sheriff's department to retrieve the phone, then listened to the recording a couple of times in my parked truck. It was unfamiliar to hear Jonas speak so unclearly; one friend explained it was because his blood oxygen level had dropped so low. The recording started with a picture of his face, then he dropped the phone, face down. The rest was audio only. I went home and listened to the recording again, over and over, doing my best to transcribe it. Not surprisingly, no one else wanted to hear it.

The recording still made little sense to me until Betsi came over and read my transcription. "He's describing what he is doing," she said. Betsi is a scholar of media and telecommunications whose work relies on rigorously conducted studies. She knows an experiment when she sees one. All it took was her academic perspective for me to understand that Jonas was documenting what he considered a scientific experiment. The

---

[2] After listening to the recording many times, I concluded that Jonas had originally set the rope as close as he could to the edge. He shifted his position during the recording and finally fainted in the other direction, which I believe caused the deeper impression in the endgrain half an inch from the edge.

early part of the transcript, though spotty, was the same basic statement of a hypothesis that I had learned to write in undergraduate psychology. It made sense that Jonas, who was fascinated by the study of consciousness and brain science, would set up an experiment to see how it felt if you temporarily deprived your brain of oxygen. Tragically, like so many others, he had performed this experiment alone, with no one present to keep him from dying when he lost consciousness and slumped in the opposite direction to the one he'd planned.

Where had he heard about this practice? We asked for weeks – teachers, friends, parents of friends – but never found out. Patti and one of her nephews pored through the history of Jonas's internet searches. Nothing.

Considering that we had never heard of choking, and knowing the tragic potential of our not-knowing, we wanted to share our experience with others in the hope that someone else might be spared such a loss. The local paper did a story, published on a Sunday on the front-page, above the fold. Mark and Patti didn't want to read the comments, but I read them and was shocked by several. *There was obviously something wrong with this young man*, wrote one; *Sounds like a bad family*, another. Some called him stupid, or troubled. Others blamed us as parents. What struck me first was how arrogant it was for strangers to imagine that they knew Jonas. They hadn't even met him. Why did they feel entitled to state an opinion, as though they somehow understood him better than we had?

Gradually I realized that many of those who shared baselessly critical comments were almost certainly prompted to do so by fear. By casting Jonas as troubled or careless, and our whole family as – well, I don't even know what they imagined, other than that we were clearly not good parents – they were trying to distance themselves, to maintain the pretense that such terrible things only happen to others, not to good, responsible people like them. Either way, it was pathetic in response to a family's effort to inform others of a practice that remains relatively unknown, while going through a devastating loss. The whole point of doing the article had been that what we were experiencing can, in fact, happen to anyone.

A few days after Jonas died, I went back through my email and read the message from the person with the unusual name. The writer was one of a pair of scholars in Chicago; she was inquiring about the possibility of hiring me to help with their kitchen in a 1915 flat. We had a preliminary discussion by phone, then talked about setting up a site visit, though it would have to wait for some snow to melt; the winter had been especially snowy, and I didn't feel it would be safe to drive my two-wheel drive truck to Chicago until conditions improved.

That kitchen was a lifesaver for me, with satisfying period details and the kind of restored appliances I can only dream of on most jobs. I built the cabinets in spring and installed them, fitting the doors, drawers and mahogany counters, over the course of 10 days with help from our friend Duncan Campbell. The clients were appreciative; they hired me to build other pieces for their home. Thanks to the timing, which linked an especially gratifying job with one of the most wrenching losses of my life, the project and the clients are special to me.

Mark had returned to work in mid-January, so he was spending weekdays alongside friends. Even so, after the first few weeks we found ourselves more and more alone as people understandably absorbed the shock and returned to their normal lives. I could see how much it meant to Mark to have visits from relatives and friends, so we arranged to have guests most weekends. At some point in the evening we'd invariably find ourselves at the table, sharing stories about how each of us had done countless stupid things, any one of which could have got us killed. So many people. So many stories.

In my case, when I was 11 and our mother was on the road in her VW bus, our home was in full-on hippie mode. After badgering people for what seemed like months, I finally got someone to give me a tab of acid or mescaline – I can't remember which. I took it that night. Around 2 a.m. I got on my bike, with its banana seat and ram's horn handlebars, and rode down to the bay in the wee hours, alone and under the influence of a psychedelic drug. Of course my father had no idea. I stopped where a dead-end street met the water and looked out at the reflected moon, Van Morrison's "Moondance" playing silently in my head. Poetic.

About the same time, my dad and some of the hippies who lived with us took me to a rock concert somewhere in Georgia. I'd decided I

The first kitchen I did after Jonas died was this one for a 1915 flat in Chicago. (Photo: Spectrum Creative Group.)

didn't want to be defined by such cultural labels as gender, age or even species. I called myself Norman Stanley Hippietoe, denied any particular gender and sometimes claimed to be a dog. I always wore trousers, but my chest was still as flat as a boy's, so why bother with a shirt? One afternoon during that weekend I went for a walk up a sandy driveway to the top of a hill. People were camping at sites scattered around the woods. Some older guy (in retrospect, he was probably no more than 22) invited me over; he had a small campfire going just outside his tent. "Wanna smoke?" he asked. "Sure," I said. I mean, I was experienced, even if I was just 11. I'd been living in the thick of this haze for at least a year. He handed me a lighted joint. I took a puff and handed it back. I knew all the moves. We sat there for ~~20 minutes~~ one minute, taking in the awesome sunset, which glittered with dust from thousands of sandaled feet shuffling over miles of unpaved roads. Amazing.

The next thing I knew, my ears were hit by this man's voice asking "Wanna ball?" I had only the vaguest idea what he was talking about, but that was enough to persuade me that I had to get out of there right away. I didn't want to seem panicked, in case that freaked him out and made him come after me, something the movies had taught me could happen. So while he took another long drag, I casually got up, mentioned I had to get back to my friends and turned around. My heart was pounding and I had butterflies in my stomach, so I made a point to look totally chill – until I reached the first turn in the road, where I ran as fast as my legs would carry me back to the safety of our van.

When I was 12, and boarding at Brimstone Hostel, I climbed what was reputed to be the tallest pine in Sussex – not because I loved to climb trees, but because I was terrified by heights, almost to the point of paralysis. Other kids climbed the same tree like monkeys. I wanted to get over my fear. My friend Jonathan taught me, guiding every movement of my hands and feet on the way up, then again on the way back down. I climbed it often after that and would always pause at the top to picture my dead body on the grass below, to ensure I paid attention.

While living at Brimstone Hostel, I sometimes decided to walk the 5 or 6 miles from East Grinstead Station to the hostel, which was a little way beyond the village of Forest Row, instead of taking the bus. I loved the walk, largely because it was a chance to experience the joy of doing something by and for myself, instead of relying on anyone else. My leather satchel, slung across a shoulder, made an intoxicating creak with every step. I pretended I was a horse making its workhorse-like way from one place to another. Imagining the journey as I believed a horse would experience it took me out of my regular self and into another perspective. A kind of ecstasy – literally, standing outside of my everyday self – this imaginary transformation from human to horse felt like a liberation. I'd pass small forests of rhododendrons that thrived in the cool Sussex damp. I admired delicate roses, perfectly rolled grass, brick-and-flint walls. Lindens and hawthorns arched overhead, leaning out toward the road. Oh yes, the road! The A22, a major highway, with scarcely a foot between me and the vehicles that careened past the sidewalk, which was elevated from the traffic by a scant 2 or 3 inches.

I thought back to a couple of Maggie's antics when we were in primary school. One day we were getting ready to walk home from a neighbor's yard, where we'd been playing. Our house was just two properties away in the subdivision. A car slowed as it approached us; the driver, a man, rolled down his window and asked if we wanted a ride. Like all children, we had been taught at home and school never to speak to strangers, let alone get into a stranger's car. "No thanks," I said without making eye contact, only to hear my little sister exclaim "SURE!" My heart seized as she climbed in and closed the door. What the hell was she doing? She was going to be abducted and killed.

Thankfully, the driver dropped her off at our house.

Another time we were on the bus to the summer camp at our school. Someone had brought a bag of small brass bullet casings. The bus was full, so some of us were standing. A budding entertainer who loved to make people laugh, Maggie set a casing upside-down on her tongue and shouted "Look at me!" The next moment, the bus went over a bump and she swallowed the casing. *Oh my God*, I thought. *She's going to die. That thing might blow up in her stomach.* Again, she was spared (and I now know that an empty bullet casing can't blow up, but it could have damaged her gastrointestinal tract).

These are just a few of my stories. Many others gathered around our table to share their own. And these were tales of childish adventure; with every passing week, we met new people who shared that they had lost a child in other ways. There were diseases, building collapses, wrecks on icy roads. Hell, I was born with pyloric stenosis and would have died in a matter of weeks, had a surgeon not saved my life. (My father always takes pride in reporting that she was a female surgeon, exceedingly rare in the late 1950s.) When you think about it, it's a miracle that anyone reaches adulthood. Tragedy can strike any family. Why don't we, as a culture, talk about this more?

To this day, whenever I think of what happened with Jonas on January 2, 2014, I can't help recalling the movies and TV shows I watched as a child – the ones in which Flipper the dolphin rescued a drowning girl, pulling her safely across the bay to shore, or Lassie, a collie, who always knew exactly what was going on with Timmy Martin, led the grown-ups to her friend at the last possible minute, saving his life. And what about Two Socks, the wolf who hung around John Dunbar and alerted him to distant dangers in "Dances with Wolves?"

Joey couldn't go up and down the stairs because he was lame. But Henny could, and did, all the time. She loved Jonas, who reciprocated her affection in a touchingly avuncular way for such a young person. How could Henny not have known that something was wrong? How had she not rushed upstairs to save him by startling him back to his senses?

At times, life seems maddeningly durable. One night in my early 20s I had such severe bronchitis that I had to make an effort to draw each breath; I was afraid to fall asleep, certain that I would stop breathing. I was amazed and relieved to wake up the next morning. Our friend Carrol, who was diagnosed with cancer just weeks after our conversation about Jonas and the choking game, survived so many months without eating that at her memorial her husband, Frank, compared her to an air plant. How is it that life can stick so stubbornly, yet at other times be so swiftly snuffed out?

19: Harley and the Goat (2012)

BY FAR the strangest animal event at my shop took place one afternoon when I was returning to work after lunch. I was just about to turn into the driveway when I did a double take. A pair of stray dogs had trotted onto the neighbor's lawn across the street. If I was quick, I'd have a chance at catching them, calling the animal shelter, and returning them to their home.

On second glance, I realized they were not both dogs; the larger one was a pygmy goat. The goat was about 18 inches tall, fat and healthy, his hair mostly white. The dog, a gray-browed male Jack Russell terrier mix, had ribs and hip bones protruding dramatically and scabby sores all over his skin.

I screeched to a halt and set the hazard warning lights, hoping the capture would be quick. The dog was friendly enough; he walked right up to me with a trusting expression. I picked him up and set him in the truck bed, hoping to follow with the goat. But the goat had other ideas. He whinnied in distress at being separated from his friend, yet he was not about to let me catch him.

I called to him sweetly. I approached him slowly, in a non-threatening manner. I got down on all fours and even laid my head on the grass in a canine gesture of submission. Lord knows what the few passers-by must have thought on seeing a 50-something woman engaged in such behavior. The goat, bleating half-heartedly, played coy. He ran alongside the neighbor's fence, rubbing his back nonchalantly. He sprang sideways away from me, then took a few leaps forward in feigned alarm.

Meanwhile, as I looked back at the truck to check on the dog, I saw that he was about to step off the edge of the tailgate, three feet above the ground. I rushed to stop him, but before I could get there, he fell. His emaciated body crumpled on the asphalt. It was painful to watch, but the dog seemed unfazed. I scooped him up gently and carried him back to the grass, hoping to lure the goat.

Just then a neighbor, Connie, pulled into her driveway. Although she had groceries to put away, she came over and tried to help. She went inside and found a jump rope, which she formed into a lasso and tried repeatedly to throw over the goat's head, in vain.

Throughout this impromptu circus act, my truck was still blocking one lane of the road. It was time for triage. I carried the dog over to the cab, set him on my lap, moved the truck into the driveway and returned to the neighbor's yard to resume the arrest.

By this time Connie was impatient to get her groceries into the house. Holding the dog as bait in one arm, I crouched down by her van and kept still. After a few minutes, the goat ventured close enough that I was able to grab his left horn. I held on tight, and when Connie returned, she tied the jump rope around his neck.

To say the goat was not happy would be a gross understatement. He bleated and moped and refused to budge. I needed both hands to control him, so I put the dog down. With Connie in the lead, calling, "Come on, goat!" and me pulling the jump rope with all my might, we tried to urge our recalcitrant prisoner toward my driveway. He set his front feet against the ground, locking his knees in protest and screaming bloody murder. When he realized strangulation was the only alternative to compliance, he leapt forward a few feet. We proceeded across Connie's lawn in this halting fashion, then continued across the street. I hoped the dog would follow.

I dragged the staccato goat to my shop, put him inside and locked the door behind us. He rocketed around the shop in desperation, screaming while emitting a torrent of droppings, convinced his end was nigh. Having just put the finishing touches on a delicate writing table for a project article in *Fine Woodworking*, I was terrified by the potential for disaster. I grabbed some blankets and threw them over the piece, hoping the goat wouldn't vent his anger by butting it to smithereens.

But where was the dog? I had expected to find him waiting loyally at the door. Now I was worried on *his* behalf. I ran inside and retrieved the goat, leading him with the jump rope and counting on his screams to summon his friend. I could hear a dog barking in the distance. Following the barks, I rounded the corner behind the shop, dragging the goat and calling to the dog as sweetly as I could. It sounded as though he might be in the shed; I heard the echo of clumsy footfalls. Yes, there he was, clambering over the lawnmower, the stacks of plywood, the rotten old couch. I called and presented the goat, positioning him like a hostage in the doorway, but the little dog kept on stumbling through the piles of junk. That was when it hit me: He was blind and deaf. As soon as he came close enough, I gathered him up with my free arm and proceeded back to the shop.

And just like that, the goat was calm.

I shut them in the bathroom, grabbed the cordless phone and looked up the number of a wildlife rescue place a couple of miles away. No answer. Next I called animal control. No answer there, either. Then I tried the animal shelter. After wading through an endless automated menu of options and advice, I was relieved to hear a live human being answer the phone.

"I have just spent three-quarters of an hour attempting to capture a dog and a goat that seem to be wandering around together," I said in exasperation.

"Is this Nancy Hiller?" came the response. By coincidence, I had reached Susie Johnson, another neighbor; this one happened to be the head of public works.

"Susie!" I cried, "What are you doing answering the phone at the shelter?"

"I just stopped by to see if they needed help," she answered. She dispatched a pair of animal control officers.

While waiting for their arrival I returned to the bathroom to check on my guests. The room now smelled like a barnyard. There was no hiding the presence of an herbivore. The dog and goat were lying next to each other by the door, an image of contentment. I offered the dog some of the shop cat's food, which he devoured. He lapped up the cat's bowl of cream, then took a long drink of water. The goat refused to eat; he was just relieved to have his dog back.

When the animal control officers arrived, I thought I should prepare them by explaining the animals' co-dependent relationship, in the hope that dog and goat would not be separated. On hearing me describe the dog as emaciated, blind, deaf, friendly and covered with sores, they exchanged a knowing look. "Sounds like Harley," one muttered to the other.

It was Harley, a crafty diabetic who had been apprehended several times in the recent past. Mysteriously, the goat was new to them, which struck me as inconceivable considering the bond I had observed. The goat was Harley's ears and eyes, and Harley seemed to serve as the goat's existential protector.

Blessedly, the writing table was unscathed.

20: Henry (2003-2004)

"HEY, NANCE," called Alan. "Look at this. We have a visitor."

It was a fine day in early autumn, so the overhead door of the shop was up. I ran from the back of the building to find a mourning dove strutting across the floor, apparently unconcerned by the aliens looming over him. Was he sick? Injured?

I came closer. He stopped but made no sign of flying away. I grabbed a cardboard box, thinking I'd take the bird to be looked at by a vet. I picked him up, surprised he let me handle him, and placed him gently inside.

"His wing is broken," said the vet. "He'll never fly again. Would you like us to euthanize him?"

Of course I didn't want them to euthanize him. Apart from his wing, he seemed perfectly fine. Besides, it hadn't been long since I'd let Alan pressure me into finding a new home for Pedro, my adopted parrot. I missed the company of a bird. If this one was doomed to die – let's face it: when you're a flightless mourning dove in the wild, you're what's for dinner – he could at least have some kind of life with me.

I cobbled together a cage and put it in my office at Alan's house on the edge of town. The vet had recommended feeding him birdseed, so I bought some. I called him Henry.

When working in the office, I let Henry out of his cage. He showed no interest in me; for the most part he wandered around the room, flutter-hopping onto the desk and printer, sometimes gazing out the window to the backyard. He ate his food and drank his water. Cleaning up bird droppings became a familiar chore. There was never a spark of recognition, let alone affection, in his eyes – just a blank, wide-eyed stare. I still maintained that his abduction by aliens must be preferable to being ripped apart and eaten by a coyote or an owl.

I had never been so close to a mourning dove and was struck by his subtle colors and his lovely speckled wings. His pink feet were especially endearing.

The following spring, we were close enough to finishing the house Alan had built at his farm that we decided to start moving in. I was still working in Alan's shop while looking forward to having a shop of my own built on the acre I'd bought the previous autumn. I packed bedding, food, William and Winnie in the back of the truck; Joey the Cat was up front with me, in a cat carrier next to Henry's cage on the seat.

As soon as we turned on to the hilly, winding road for the final mile to Alan's farm and shop, Henry became more animated than I'd seen him. He seemed to recognize exactly where we were, like an analog radio receiving a signal and coming back to life after months of silence. All well and good, but there was no way I was going to let him out when he couldn't fly. He'd be dead before midnight.

The next morning I saw that Henry hadn't touched his food or water. He was still on high alert. Now I had an even stronger sense that he recognized where he was, and wanted to be released. For his own good I kept him one more night, but he still wouldn't eat or drink. If he kept up this fast, he was going to die anyway. From an ethical perspective, at least as far as I could tell, there would be no harm in letting him go.

With a heavy heart, I took his cage outside and set it on the deck railing. "Goodbye, Henry, I said softly. "Please take care of yourself." I opened the door. He hopped out onto the rail, then lifted himself up, testing his wings. Astonishingly, they held him aloft. He flew a tight circle around my head – think what you like, but it felt as though he was saying goodbye. Then he made a larger circle, higher up. His wing had healed, despite the vet's lack of confidence.

Tears rolled down my face. He flew higher and higher, in ever-wider circles. Finally, confident that his wings were sound, he soared over the field toward the shop, back on his way home after a long, strange dream.

21: The Cattle Dog and the Pigs

WHENEVER I take Joey to the vet, he treats me to an ear-splitting performance of terror and woe. Just getting in the truck prompts panic; although I took him everywhere when he was a pup, he has spent most of his adult life in the house, yard or shop. Over the past few years, the truck has come to signify just one thing: that terrible destination where he gets poked and palpated and has no say in the matter. We turn from Woodyard Road onto Smith Pike and all hell breaks loose: the angry barks and plaintive cries, the look – part-imploring, part-accusatory. *Mom! NO! You CANNOT take me there! PLEASE! I won't go! I can't stand it! Turn around! MOM!!!* – all on repeat.

But I've always been struck by what happens as soon as I park. His demeanor instantly shifts from avoidance-at-all-costs to single-minded resolve: *OK then, let's get this over with.*

I thought of Joey last November as I contemplated the pint or so of "Mochaccino Smoothie" barium sulfate suspension I was going to choke down between 7:30 and 8 the next morning before driving to the local radiology center for a CT scan.

How is it possible that I am doing this to myself? I wondered, as I always do when facing a frightening medical procedure. I'm still the person who, as a 6- or 7-year-old kid with an extreme fear of needles, was struck one day at the doctor's office by the realization that I had the power to walk right out the door. And so I did. As I recall, my mother and one of the nurses ran after me, but for those few moments the sense of agency was potent. It lasted until my mother informed me I'd have to swallow two pills the size of grenades if I wasn't going to have the shot. I chose the pills, which we pulverized, so I traded the sting

Relief after the vet.

of a needle for gagging on bitter chunks of crusty drywall mud. Still, at some level of my being I suddenly registered that even something as important as a doctor's appointment was only possible with my assent.

Last November, the urgency of my desire to know what was causing my vague but increasing abdominal discomfort shifted me into resolve. I followed the technician through the labyrinth of offices, radiology suites and exam rooms to our destination, where I replaced my jeans with a pair of pants that would have fit John Candy and lay down on the table. The tech stuck an IV in my arm. I followed the instructions from an automated woman's voice with a plummy Kensington accent. "Please take a deep breath and hold it," she said as I slid into the scanner, then "You may now breathe as normal," when I slid back out.

After 42 hours of waiting, my doctor called with the results: There was a mass in my pancreas, and it was likely malignant.

How do you respond to such news? As someone who has had a lifelong interest in illness and dying, I have for decades been aware of Elisabeth Kübler-Ross's theory of grief, which breaks the experience into five recognizable stages that most of us have heard about by now: denial, anger, bargaining, depression, acceptance. While Kübler-Ross's theory has helped many, I chafe at the notion that anyone other than those who know me best should feel entitled to define or even describe the nature of my experience, let alone predict my next "stage" while standing on the sidelines casually enjoying a glass of wine with friends. For anyone to imagine they have the right, let alone the capacity, to speak on my behalf (or on behalf of anyone else with whom they are not intimately familiar) is sheer arrogance, however well intentioned.[1]

None of this experience is new to me on a theoretical level, though this is my first personal brush with its full existential weight. It has never occurred to me to ask "Why me?" as though a diagnosis of cancer is unfair, or should have happened to someone else. More appropriate is to ask "Why not?" Cancer happens, and it will continue to do so

---

[1] Kübler-Ross did not intend for her analysis of grief to lead to the kind of formulaic or reductionistic take on that experience that some have made of it.

My friend Edith Sarra, scholar of medieval Japanese literature, with her late dog Genji, a Belgian Tervuren.

at an increasing rate, the more thoroughly we toxify our planet.² I've seen enough to know that tragedy can befall anyone, for a variety of random, unjustified reasons, regardless of how safe we've tried to make ourselves or how prudent we have done our best to be. As I write, the 22-ton piece of debris from a rocket known as Long March 5B has just landed in the ocean near the Maldives, without causing the kind of injury or destruction it might have, had it fallen on a place of worship, a hospital, a school or house – a big relief. But catastrophes of various kinds occur on a daily basis. There are earthquakes, avalanches, wildfires and volcanoes. Weary drivers crash into others' cars, some-

---

² This statement strikes me as indisputable. We are learning about new carcinogens every day, many of them in our homes, gardens and workplaces.

THE CATTLE DOG AND THE PIGS 325

Nefarious noshing. While I was installing the cabinetry in Judith Brown's kitchen in the fall of 2019, her recently adopted dog, Hamish, crept up onto the dining table where she was keeping her cats' food bowls (and some of her own food) out of his reach.

Nessie, who belonged to Lee and Eric Sandweiss, was one of the sweetest dogs I have known. After her death Lee wrote a memoir about her titled "Lock Ness!" "Possessing the face of an innocent angel and the stealth of a jewel thief," reads the jacket copy (and I can vouch for its claims), "Nessie, a wheaten Scottish Terrier, wrapped everyone she met around her paw, while refusing to learn the meaning of the word No." (Photo: Shannon Zahnle.) (See bibliography for book information.)

times killing all involved. People lose their jobs and homes because of a change in corporate strategy or the sale of a family owned business to a nationwide chain. Animals, domestic and wild, are killed by cars, leaving the nest of chicks carefully tended in the mailbox to starve, their beaks dried forever open like a bunch of orange tulips, or the joeys thrown from their mama possum's pouch to die of dehydration at the side of the road. Other species are being extinguished at a rate unprecedented in human history. New diseases pop up and kill hundreds of thousands, sometimes millions, as we are seeing with COVID-19.

So much of how we experience an event is grounded in our sense of agency.[3] When I was 15, my mother hired a young medical student named Judy to tutor me in biology for an hour in the evening every week or two. Judy and I sat in a pair of Thonet chairs my mom had found in a skip (a dumpster, in the States) or bought for peanuts at a junk shop. My biology textbook and notes would be spread out on the fall flap of my melamine-coated chipboard secretaire. David, our guinea pig, chewed carrot sticks in his cage on the other side of the wall; feeding him was the only way to keep him quiet. One week Judy showed up looking especially skinny, which is to say amazing; we were still in the waning years of the Twiggy era, when a woman could not be too thin. "It's true, I've lost a lot of weight," she said, "but not for a happy reason." She and her boyfriend had split up. She was heartbroken. In contrast, I was ecstatic several years later to learn on the morning of my first wedding that I had finally whittled my 5-foot-8-3/4-inch frame down to 112 pounds.

Recently a friend was mildly outraged by what he called the "execrable" spiciness of a dish he'd ordered at a restaurant; he couldn't even bring himself to finish his meal. Heat, though? Give me more. For my 14th birthday, my mother took me to see Rudolf Nureyev in a ballet performance at the Sadler's Wells Theatre – a dream come true. Before the performance, we stopped for dinner at a place called Anwar's, where I ordered a dish that was so hot it made me weep. But those flavors! I

---

[3] Which is to say, in effect, so much of the event itself, given that all experience is perspectival.

drank some tap water and went back to it. By the end of the meal I had downed eight glasses of water. I was uncomfortably full, but thanks to the pleasure of that spicy meal and my gratitude to my mother for making my birthday special, I have never forgotten the experience or the restaurant's name.

What makes veterinarians the bogeymen of Joey's dreams is not just the terror inspired by seeing someone coming at him with a hypodermic needle, or the indignity of having a thermometer stuck up his ass, but the brute fact that he has no say in what's going on. Generally speaking, Joey has strong opinions about acceptable behavior from those around him; bred to be one of those bossy types whose purpose in life is to make others do his bidding (ideally, those others would be cattle, but Mark and I make reasonable stand-ins), he wants to be in charge, or at least second in command. Sure, I can scratch his neck and call him inside from the yard. But brush him? Cue the nervous looks punctuated after every few strokes by a yipped reminder that I'm on thin ice. Bathing him takes two people – one to restrain him while the other does the washing. Even worse is trying to remove an embedded tick. He cries bloody murder; then, once the tick is off, he insists on inspecting. *What did you just take from my body? It's my body, not yours. By the way, does it smell funky? Let me check ... Wait! Don't rush away with that. I'm not done sniffing.* We no longer even try to trim his toenails; he's terrified by the clippers' decisive snip. *Help me, Lizzie. They're trying to cut off my feet,* he'd mind-message the cat. Turning to me, he'd start with a look, then a querulous warning: *GET AWAY FROM MY FEET!* If I kept going, he jerked his head. *Look, Mom, I'm begging you, please stop now. I don't want to bite you, but I may not be able to help myself.*

William had many of the same neuroses, but he was ~~completely apeshit out of control~~ less restrained. He bit me without hesitation if I pushed him too far, and usually over the same things: bathing, toenails, tick removal, administering monthly medications. My friend Amy, a scholar of religions, was visiting one day when I tried to give William a haircut with an electric trimmer. All I had to do was turn it on; at the sound of that buzzing vibration he turned into a writhing, serpent-like muscle joined to a set of choppers that would do a Tyrannosaurus rex

Maggie visited when William was a few months old. The look in his eyes here hinted at the willfulness to come.

proud. "It's like Jacob wrestling with the angel!" Amy laughed. At least Joey apologizes, in a way. William just trotted off, indignant.

Before my diagnosis, I found solace in noting that for every loved one who has died, I could be happy that they hadn't seen the kinds of subsequent events that would have made them rage or weep with despair. My maternal grandpa's cousin Joe Baum developed Windows on the World, a restaurant in the north tower of the original World Trade Center. Because he died in 1998, he was spared the heartache of seeing that creation (and so much else) destroyed with the toppling of the World Trade Center on September 11, 2001. My second husband, Kent, died in 2016 of glioblastoma in his early 50s, leaving behind a beloved wife and two sons; that fall, as I grew despondent at the inability of so many Americans to recognize such previously agreed-on facts based on shared observations as "the earth is round" and "the sky is blue on sunny days," I told myself that at least he'd been spared the heartbreak of witnessing the potential demise of American democracy, which depends on a modicum of widespread agreement about some basic facts.[4] Flynn, the boyfriend who moved out when I brought William home, died in January, 2020; a few weeks after the night when friends and family members gathered in Bloomington to celebrate his life and share the grief of his loss (he'd recently retired from research and teaching, then moved to Germany to join his partner, Susanne, only to die of an apparent heart attack), I thought "at least he didn't have to see the devastation caused by widespread denial of the dangers posed by COVID-19."

Now, faced with the odds of my own likely demise, I've revisited this question that had become a longstanding mental experiment: Is it better to die before such tragic events than live through them? No, I conclude: it seems indisputably better to have the chance to face seemingly unbearable loss alongside those we love. This, too, is related to a sense of agency: Anything can happen. We have only so much control over events themselves, but we can usually control how we respond.

---

[4] Of course I am aware that many consider the very idea of "facts" to be passé. I'm not using the word in an absolute sense, but to denote a fundamental ability to agree on shared observations based on rigorous evidence.

THE CATTLE DOG AND THE PIGS

Most of us spend years learning to do things that are good for us and those around us; this has traditionally been considered a defining feature of growing up. We learn to speak, read, use the bathroom, tie our shoes, insert tampons and apply contact lenses, in spite of the sometimes-exasperating difficulty involved in mastering any of these operations. We get ourselves out of bed before dawn to prepare for work or school. We show up because it's our job, because we have responsibilities to others as well as ourselves, because it's the right thing to do – whether or not we may feel like going to work on a given day. We learn to pace ourselves by forming a view of the big picture and appreciating that step by step, our contributions have the potential to bring at least some of our vision to life, whether we're painting an interminable expanse of wall, riding a bicycle across the country or wiping summertime sweat from our eyes while scribing cabinets to fit walls and floors. We run, walk, swim and lift weights to keep ourselves in shape. We voluntarily take ourselves to clinics and cringe while a nurse sticks a needle in our arm so that we can be immune to one contagious disease or another. We have pap smears, prostate checks, colonoscopies and mammograms. We focus on the long view, the end result, and ideally learn to enjoy many of the steps along the way.

All of this work entails adjusting our motivation and desires. I wish I could spend this balmy, sun-struck Saturday weeding the flower beds in our garden, but if I'm ever to complete this book, I have to keep writing in the office. Do I literally *have* to write in the office? Of course not; I could put it off and indulge myself in garden time. But I want to finish this book and be alive to see it published. Working in the office today increases the likelihood that I will reach that goal, so I will forgo a day of pleasure in favor of something I want even more (if not quite so viscerally, as I admire the egg yolk-yellow ragwort blooms through the window and watch new elm and maple leaves dance in the breeze).[5]

Nothing about this ranking of desires is new; most of us just don't think about it that often. In some cases, it really is integral to the process

---

[5] Charles Taylor calls this "second-order desire" and elaborates with vivid examples in "Human Agency and Language: Philosophical Papers, Vol. 1."

of growing up. At 12, I set aside my desire to stay safely on the ground in favor of my wish to overcome my fear of heights and climbed what was reputed to be the tallest pine in Sussex. While riding my bike through the rain on my way to and from Farmstead Furniture before I learned to drive, I had to remind myself that I wanted to work at that place, in particular, because I could learn a lot while supporting myself and finding challenge in new materials and techniques; otherwise it would have been all too easy to feel overwhelmed by a desire to end my soggy discomfort and look for a job closer to home. So instead of dwelling on my misery, I focused my attention on the drama of the glowering sky.

When Jonas was 15, he made every provision he could think of to ensure that his experiment on the fringes of human consciousness would end with him safe: To the best of his ability, he thought through the possible scenarios and planned for them – padding the rope at his neck, setting the rope as close as possible to the door's edge so it would slip off when he fainted to his right, keeping his feet on the carpeted floor. Narrating his observations through the experiment, he acknowledged the possibility of dying; he reported that he was going to have to will himself to overcome his deeply ingrained aversion to taking risks and relax so that the blood flow through his neck would be blocked enough to make him faint, drop to the floor and regain consciousness – in his words, "Once you're gone, you're back. It never happened." The thinking is not that different from the first time you fly across an ocean or switch on a 5-horsepower shaper with huge knives that roar like a 747 revving its engines prior to takeoff. (A shaper is a spindle moulder in the U.K.) Never mind launching yourself into space on a shuttle. All of these are arguably insane. Risks are everywhere. But the greatest risk factor for dying is simply being born.[6]

It's easy to dismiss Jonas and others who have unintentionally caused

---

[6] In the aftermath of Jonas's death we heard all about the teenage brain and the arguable inability of those under the age of 25 to think risky behaviors fully through. I'm not convinced by these claims, especially after seeing so many people far older than 25 engaging in extremely risky behavior, even as they rationalize it. I am guilty of this myself.

Irresistible. Jane Goodman's cat, Jemma, in the flour bin from her original kitchen cabinets.

their own death as stupid, careless or unthinking, without making the effort to understand their behavior. This is the way of least resistance and little effort. But life is so much richer, so much more engaging and worthy of our human capacities, if we make the effort to understand.

Most of us also learn to take pleasure in things that initially repelled us: the bitterness of coffee, whiskey's sting, the soreness of hard-worked muscles. We cultivate habits, a fascinating idea when you consider that, etymologically speaking, our habits, once developed, instead *have us*; they direct many of our actions and even our sense of what feels good or normal. Derived from the past participle of the Latin verb "to have," a habit is by definition so ingrained that it becomes a constituent of who we are – and not always in a good way.

***

"Nothing that you have or have not done has caused this," the oncologist told me at our first meeting last November. His statement came as a relief; I had been brought up with the idea that we are each responsible for our health. To a significant degree, I'm convinced we are; does anyone honestly believe that they will support their physical (or mental) health on a steady diet of refined cereals, sugary sodas and deep-fried food with the occasional addition of one of "America's favorite vegetables" – ketchup or French fries – to their plate? Bodies require nutrients beyond mere calories to form new cells of all kinds, as well as keep bodily functions running and fight off disease. On the other hand, I had no say in being born with pyloric stenosis, a severely constricted pyloric valve that, without surgery, would have resulted in malnourishment and possibly starvation.

The conviction that a wholesome diet and a lifestyle designed to optimize nutrition and health (with or without the addition of such potentially cancer-preventing supplements as certain mushrooms and green tea) will keep you from developing all manner of life-threatening conditions is naïve in a world suffused with ever-new toxins. And the corollary notion that any malady, from a cold to cancer, is the direct result of individual behavior breaks down in cases of heritable conditions such as muscular dystrophy and spina bifida.[7]

---

[7] You can certainly point out that would-be parents who proceed to have children even when they know that those children will likely (or certainly) be born with such conditions have, as individuals, in effect said yes to these conditions. But in most cases they are not choosing the condition as such; rather, they may be acting out of the principle of Double Effect articulated by Thomas Aquinas – choosing to allow a

We all know someone who has broken the rules and outlived people who stuck to a wholesome or even downright ascetic diet. Our 94-year-old neighbor is one example: a lifelong cigarette smoker who has lived on a diet of refined carbohydrates, a few vegetables and meat (organic? grass-fed? pshaw), he's in full command of his faculties and lives alone with his dog in a house he built with his now-late brothers – a place he keeps neat as a pin, with an acre of yard he mows every week and a patch of zinnias that passing drivers slow down to admire each summer. And then there are those who do everything right – a diet of unprocessed whole food, much of it organic; no smoking or alcohol; regular exercise, yoga and meditation – only to die in their 30s of cancer that was diagnosed too late.

Many infer from this paradox and other evidence (much of it based on economic, rather than ecological studies) that organic farming is no better than the dominant agribusiness model reliant on pesticides and herbicides, feedlots, prophylactic antibiotics, synthetic fertilizers and genetically modified crops. What too few seem willing to recognize is that as much as we go on and on about our rights, preferences and abilities as individuals, we exist in systems – ecological, social and economic, among other types. Everything – energy and matter – is constantly recycled, transformed into something new. Nothing goes away, whether household trash or nuclear waste; we just stop seeing it after it's buried in the ground. But the landfills grow, and their liners will eventually break down. The oil spills wreak havoc with habitat and the health of successive generations (sea creatures, shore birds, people, dogs who play at the beach). The per- and polyfluoroalkyl substances (known as PFAS) found in nonstick pan coatings, waterproof fabrics, packaging materials and many personal care products collect in the blood of even the most remote indigenous peoples and non-human animals, where they can lead to immune system disruption and the development of cancers, among other serious problems.

There are genuine common goods, principal among them clean air and potable water, which are beyond the capacity of any individual to

pregnancy to reach full term because they believe that is the right thing to do, and accepting that a child with spina bifida, or even stillborn, is God's creation.

Kitchen designer Johnny Grey with Richard, November 2020. "He came with us on a detour to Northumberland," wrote Johnny's wife, Becca, in a note accompanying the image. The other family dogs – Margot, a dachshund, and their young Labrador, Ken – went home from the Highlands with the couple's grown children, but as Becca explained, "Richard gets special treatment since his back surgery in 2018 which makes him too weak to fend for himself" – for example, on stairs. "Incidentally," she added, "he does a funny thing with his lip, bunching it up a bit on one of the long canine teeth as you can see in the photo. He also 'sings' to the music Johnny plays. We don't know if he loves the music or hates it, as he competes with the notes." (Photo: Becca Grey.)

protect, even as we must each play a part in protecting them. At some level, we are all responsible for one another. Concern for the health of the systems that support life as we know it, rather than this or that individual's health, is the best reason to use water judiciously and do what we can to avoid polluting the supply; to reconsider the value of organic farming that builds up the soil instead of depleting it, then attempting to make up for that with synthetic fertilizers; and treat our fellow animals as sentient beings worthy of respect, instead of as mere means to ends.

***

My relief at the oncologist's statement that nothing I had or hadn't done had caused me to develop cancer was short-lived. Sure, he's the one with a medical degree and a career devoted to saving lives, but when he proceeded to tell me that nothing I ate or drank would make any difference to the development of my tumor, I was ready to move on to the next topic in our discussion. It's just silly to suggest that a diet that leaves the body under-nourished (if overfed in terms of glucose and basic calories) is OK. I already knew that some things made me feel worse; I'd all but stopped drinking alcohol before my diagnosis, after noticing that my first sip of a drink was followed shortly after by a new, sharp pain in my back. And the stronger a patient feels, the greater are the odds that treatment will be successful (however you define success – and the sheer ability to feel well during chemotherapy is one such definition; luck, too, plays a part).

Given that my maternal grandmother had died of pancreatic cancer, there was some concern it might run in our family. The hospital where I had my first biopsies encourages patients to have their tissue sample examined for genetic mutations, partly to build up data for research, but also in case those mutations are in line with available clinical gene therapy trials. My tissue sample revealed three mutations, none of them inherited – good news for the rest of Esse's descendants. I knew from general reading that mutations can be caused by all kinds of factors, among them stress, prolonged physical damage and exposure to

Cat yoga. Wally is one of the three cats who visit the Lost Art Press workshop from the upstairs living quarters. "Somehow," writes Chris Schwarz, "he has decided that he should get treats when he turns his head over like an owl. And, of course, he does." (Photo: Megan Fitzpatrick.)

carcinogens, whether in food, water or our environment. I had been aware of likely carcinogens I encountered in my work. Beginning in my late teens I stripped old furniture with methylene chloride, often spattering it on my hands and never wearing more respiratory gear than a paper mask designed for far larger particles than the molecules from the stripper that burned my nose. I had also handled and sawn treated wood (the kind that was treated with chemicals more toxic than those used today) without gloves or a mask and brushed commercial wood preservatives on countless building timbers that were destined to live outside. At shops where I worked in England, we sprayed catalyzed and nitrocellulose lacquer, usually with no more protection than a paper mask (which is to say, with no protection at all). At one place where I worked, wearing even a paper mask to spray finishes was viewed as evidence that you were a sissy. (It was the '80s, and I was working in a rural workshop with a culture that scoffed at many recommendations concerned with health and safety.) I have used solvent-based brush-on finishes for decades, never wearing a respirator when I was brushing or wiping the finish.[8]

Living in London and other English cities from the early '70s through the mid-'80s, I was not only exposed to gobs of airborne lead from petrol (gasoline, in the States) and in the dust that gathered on horizontal surfaces such as window sills; the water we drank from the taps in old houses was plumbed through lead pipes. Our oven mitts in London were made with asbestos inserts; raised to be thrifty and use things until they wore out, we continued to use those mitts to pull quiches and trays of oatmeal cookies out of the oven even after their fabric covering was worn through to the heatproof fibers. Most contemporary Americans would be shocked to learn that the dangers of both lead and asbestos were not even on the radar screen of the safety police well into the 20th century's middle years; lead-based paint was only banned in the late 1970s. A little research turns up old ads for lead-lined fruit storage bins on farms; the Dutch Boy paint company

---

[8] I am grateful to Joe Prytula for bringing to my attention the potential risk of gene mutations caused by exposure to organic chemical solvents and methylene chloride.

published "A Paint Book for Boys and Girls" titled "The Dutch Boy's Lead Party" featuring cartoon-like drawings of cheery characters including a shoe sole, a light bulb and a "tin" soldier (made from lead). Other ads celebrated flameproof asbestos curtains, heat-proof pads for your dining table and asbestos "snowflakes" to sprinkle on your family's Christmas tree, an excellent way to ensure that potentially deadly particles became airborne. While helping my mother and stepfather rework old houses, I had breathed in decades' worth of coal dust and dust from lead paint, and undoubtedly scraped up more than my lifetime recommended quota of asbestos from taking out mid-century resilient floor tiles with a spud bar, then sanding away the adhesive that had held them in place.[9] Before I was aware of the dangers of glyphosate to amphibians and other species, including ours, I used it to kill weeds that were hard to dig.[10]

Our childhood diet featured a variety of tasty carcinogens, among other less-than-wholesome ingredients: preservatives, artificial food dyes and flavorings such as the chloroform in the Victory V lozenges I bought at the Forest Row sweet shop, never mind residues of carcinogenic herbicides and pesticides. Before the hippies arrived, one of our favorite snacks was bologna fried in a worn Teflon pan – as if nitrites alone weren't bad enough. In recent years we've learned that there is no escape from microplastics, which we have effectively distributed through the air, land and water across the entire planet.

And then there was my diet as an adult. Sure, I'd stopped eating meat, which many people equate with being a health nut; for protein I relied on yogurt, eggs, cheese and plant sources such as nuts and

---

[9] I am aware that asbestos is primarily implicated in respiratory diseases such as mesothelioma and lead has a less direct connection with cancers of any kind. My point is not to indict these substances in my own development of cancer, but to note that despite the efforts of public agencies to minimize health risks by controlling how we use and dispose of various substances (in some cases by simply banning them), we are surrounded, inside and out, by toxins. The dangers posed by plastics, which have proliferated over the past 80 to 90 years, are only just beginning to be understood.

[10] https://www.centerforfoodsafety.org/files/glyphosate-faq_64013.pdf

THE CATTLE DOG AND THE PIGS

"Hmm. What are you eating? I'm trying to figure out whether I want some."—Tony, to Mark.

beans. Thanks to my parents' interest in nutrition, I had read plenty of books about this or that healthy diet. But I really loved carbohydrates – bread, pasta, cake, pudding, potato chips, chocolate. Many plant sources of protein such as legumes are also high in carbs. More important to me than building health was limiting my intake of calories so I wouldn't get fat (or ideally, would be thin; in my 20s, no words were sweeter to my ears than expressions of concern that my weight was dangerously low). Our grandfather was always lamenting that no man would want us if we weren't thin. "Would you look at that," he'd say, shaking his head in disappointment as he watched me dive into a pool in a bikini when I maxed out around 160 pounds after my first broken heart. Grandma Stepha didn't hesitate to tell Maggie, who was 15 or 16 at the time, that she was "stout"; she urged her to emulate my supposedly admirable thinness. I cringed inside on hearing these words, aware that the suitably "feminine" look of non-threatening fragility that our grandmother valued so highly was the product of my dangerous flirtation with anorexia. Controlling my weight was more important to me than my health. Being thin was an achievement – evidence of self-control in the face of temptation. Even then, I knew my self-control was misdirected, but as long as I felt basically OK and was able to work, I carried right on.

The first alcoholic beverage I recall drinking was just before my 12th birthday, in 1971. We had recently arrived in England with my grandma when we stopped at a pub in the countryside for a ploughman's lunch. This was a proper ploughman's lunch, not some pretentious platter of canned giardiniera with a round of goat cheese, a few sprigs of arugula and a scattering of cracked-pepper crackers glorified by the title "charcuterie platter" in one of today's so-called gastro-pubs. No. I'm talking about an unapologetic hunk of crusty bread served with a thick wedge of sharp cheddar and a dollop of pickle on the side.[11] We were sitting outdoors on a patio, with birds singing

---

[11] The legal drinking age in England was 18. Traditional English "pickle" such as Branston is a piquant treacle-based relish (molasses, in the States) made from swede (rutabaga), onions and other ingredients.

THE CATTLE DOG AND THE PIGS

Betsi's late dog Izzie in one of the sinks in a bathroom vanity I built for her house. Betsi adopted Izzie from a Scottie rescue group after someone reportedly found her in a southern Indiana sewer. (Photo: Spectrum Creative Group.)

from a gnarled apple tree and bees buzzing 'round clover blossoms in the lawn. I said I'd like a glass of apple cider to go with my lunch, and Esse or Mom placed the order.

I felt more and more relaxed as lunch went on. Whatever bad mood had possessed me due to boredom or hunger in the car gave way to a carefree state of contemplation. It was only after I'd finished the small glass of cider that one of our parental figures put two and two together: The word Americans use to denote apple juice is the same as that used in England for a fermented, alcoholic version.

There would be no more cider for me until I reached the legal drinking age of 18. Sure, my mother let us have a small glass of Liebfraumilch for Christmas dinner and such, but that was just for special occasions. The absence of alcohol was no hardship, as I had no interest in drinking. I didn't even really like the taste, but I wanted to cultivate an appreciation of alcohol because people associated it with sophistication and a good time.

When Patrick and I lived in Congreve House, a monolithic brick building in a publicly subsidized "estate" in Newington Green – at the time, a dirty, impoverished corner of London (which explains how we were able to afford to live there) – we'd go to the pub across the cracked asphalt yard on a Friday night. Sometimes I had cider, but I often just drank tonic water. We nibbled on a bag of KP peanuts and talked about our respective work weeks while Debbie Harry or Chrissie Hynde belted out songs from an amplified cassette player. Alcohol would have been superfluous to me at that point; I was already intoxicated by the contact high, crammed into a confined space with so many jovial folks (not to mention the cigarette smoke that floated in the air and had stained the Lincrusta walls and ceilings yellow-brown).

Back then, I was the kind of drinker who answered life insurance questionnaires with a tick in the box under "less than one drink per week." The first beer I remember drinking was at a pub in Friday Bridge when I was 20 or 21. It was a Friday night, and I was out with my mother and stepfather. I drank a 12-ounce bottle of Pilsner lager and nearly fell off my stool at the bar; I remember my stepfather cracking some joke about me being a lightweight. It wasn't until a decade later,

Merryweather Berman, who lives with David Berman of Trustworth Studios, is elegance personified – unless he's having one of the rambunctious manic spells that reduce him to a less-refined dog more in line with his origins in Indiana. (Merry typically stands next to David at the bathroom sink and waits for David to brush his teeth.)

Christine Matheu, architect, with her late dog, Ginger, who was loyal and independent and always had her own agenda. (Photo: Spectrum Creative Group.)

when I injured my back pushing the monstrous hard maple armoire up the stairs while paying more attention to our clients' wallpaper than my own safety that I can ever recall really *wanting* a drink. I found that red wine eased the pain, at least for a few hours. When one glass stopped doing the trick, I had another.

Gradually, drinking became a habit. When I bought my bungalow in town, I'd take a glass of wine outside in the evening to drink over a couple of hours while I worked in the garden. Beer and wine were still all I drank; anything else was too expensive, so why even try it? After Flynn moved out, William and Teddy weren't the only ones keeping me company; I also had the local community radio station, WFHB. I'd listen to "Hora Latina," "Crawfish Fiesta" or "Scenes from the Northern Lights" and drink a couple of beers as I spent winter evenings stripping wallpaper or patching plaster. Who needed a party?

With beer, I had my own work party, between the house, the dog, the cat, my tools and the radio.

I never got falling-down drunk or woke up with my head stuck in a dog's bowl on the kitchen floor, as one of my former partners told me he had in high school. I was functional and, on the whole, responsible. Still, I had my moments. The night after I heard about Bill's sudden death on his motorbike, I had beer for dinner and screamed my outrage in the shower. On another occasion I was out with a boyfriend at a swanky bar on a Friday night. It was during the brief interlude in my 30s when I loved to get dressed up in tight clothes and high heels and walk downtown. (My 30s were my personal adolescence, 15-plus years behind schedule; I'd regressed to primary school at the age of 12 in a subconscious but predictable effort to experience the part of childhood I spent as a proto-adult.) Sitting on a barstool, I was recovering from a bout of hysterical laughter when I suddenly became aware that one of the pads I'd stuck down my front to transform my work bra into a push-up had fallen out onto the floor. *Shit!* I thought. *I must really be drunk.* I'd had three glasses of wine. I felt suitably chastened.

After Jonas died, we switched to stronger stuff. Mark's generous pour of bourbon that night was followed by many more over subsequent weeks and months. Two-and-a-half years later, when we moved to what had been my house, it was summer. Mark and I wrapped up each sauna-like workday with at least one trip from his house to mine, carrying furniture and boxes of books, clothes, dishware and pottery down the hill to our trucks, then unloading it all at the other end. We kept a bottle of vodka in the freezer, ready to make a dry martini once the night's moving was done. Covered in sweat and dirt from the day's work, and then the move, we'd sit down in the living room and enjoy the creeping relief as the cold alcohol went straight into our veins. It became the antidote to whatever ailed us. I could get through almost anything if there was a drink at the end of the day.

I was aware of the recommendation against women drinking more than one unit of alcohol a day. I drank two, and sometimes three. And then there were those special occasions – weddings, visits from old friends – when I had more. I never missed work or had any other kind of problem due to alcohol consumption. I knew that alcohol was a risk factor in some kinds of cancer, especially of the breast, colon and liver. I had never heard any warning about the pancreas. It was only after reading about the function of the pancreas, which had taken a distant back seat to more glamorous parts of the body in high-school biology – the brain, the kidneys, the sexual organs – that I made the connection between injury to the pancreas by chronic inflammation due to a diet high in carbohydrates, which are metabolized to sugar. Of course – the pancreas is the organ responsible for producing insulin, among other hormones and digestive enzymes. For what it's worth, I might not have acted any differently had the warnings about risks from alcohol mentioned the pancreas, considering that I also value my breasts, colon and liver. Still, at this point I haven't had a drink in months. The oncologist and surgeon have told me it's fine to have a glass of wine, but my body has decided that alcohol needs to be reserved for a rare treat.

There's something weirdly comforting in believing that between my exposure to the ubiquitous toxins of my youth, followed by a career in the building trades, a high-carbohydrate diet focused on thinness instead of health, and my reliance on alcohol as a crutch to see me through hard times (and celebrate good ones), my own behavior played a part in my development of cancer. This seemingly perverse sense of comfort is inextricably bound up with agency.

***

I'm often struck by how happy I am when working alone. It's not just because I am by nature a loner; it's because there's no one else to blame when things go wrong. And something always goes wrong; as my first cabinetmaking boss, Raymond, used to say, "it's all problems." Cut the legs for two commissioned chairs too short? That's really annoying, but put those legs aside and get on with the business of replacing them. Make the doors for a cabinet an inch too long? Kick yourself if you must, then rework them to the correct length. Have to spend the weekend finishing up a job to meet the Monday deadline? Suck it up, make some coffee and get to it. I am no less responsible for the problems and

THE CATTLE DOG AND THE PIGS

headaches than I am for the successes. No one else gave me the incorrect dimensions; no one else made the mistakes; no one made me spend an hour on the phone with a family member or a friend who needed to talk when I should have been working. Because I'm self-employed and work alone, I'm responsible for what happens to me much of the time. I find that liberating; something about it feels integrated. Cause and effect come together in ways I have to resolve. That's a creative process, whatever the outcome. I have been fully engaged in making my own life, and on the whole, notwithstanding my protracted experiences with depression, it's been a blast – especially since my late 40s.

I remember leaning against the brick wall outside the pub in Newington Green one winter night when I was 19 and trying to decide whether to continue my studies at Cambridge. I was struck by the sense that I could choose between two roads. In the first, my life would be in black and white. I would transcend the silliness of so many lives I saw around me and on the television – the petty jealousies, the concern with fashion, the ambitions, the passion, the general *Sturm und Drang*. What a waste of time. In the second, I would allow myself to live a life in which I cared about more than just toeing some safe, esoteric/monastic line. I wanted to feel, even if it meant I could be hurt. On the whole, I wanted to be and do good, but not at the complete expense of experiencing what it is to screw up. I chose a life in color.

Despite our national ethos of individualism and belief in our power to shape our circumstances, we have a relatively limited say in what actually happens to us. Some years ago a doctoral student of one of my close academic friends was flying to India with her boyfriend when their plane was hit by a missile and exploded in the air. A couple of years back, a friend managed to hit her car brakes in time to avoid being crushed by an oak tree that fell without warning across the road. I was lucky to survive my icy car crash in Vermont unscathed when I might just as well have been seriously injured or died. At boarding school, one of the girls in our dorm had been born with hands growing almost directly from her shoulders, due to her mother's use of thalidomide to control pregnancy-related nausea. Any one of us could rattle off a long list of cruel, unfair, unlikely and tragic events. And how many more responsible, law-abiding Black men such as 2nd Lt. Caron Nazario and Ahmaud Arbery will be harassed or even killed for nothing more than the color of their skin?

But we do have a say in how we respond. The response begins with how we perceive and interpret what is taking (or has taken) place. Interpretation is an integral part of perception; making sense of hard stuff in ways that enable us to carry on is no less creative an act than whatever we end up doing by way of response. When I heard that Karen Vaughan, whose positive outlook, strength of character and encouraging words have helped me so much, had died on April 30, I was heartbroken; she was in her early 50s and just last summer had married her high school sweetheart after raising a family in an earlier marriage. After chemo became ineffective at controlling the progress of her metastases, I developed a new perspective on chemo's less-desirable side effects: I am *lucky* to be able to continue with my own treatment.

Now I am living for her, as well as for myself and others.

While injury, illness and death may be no less scary or disturbing when viewed this way, we can reclaim a sense of agency that a heartbreaking loss or terrifying diagnosis can all too easily squelch, reducing us to suffering as we focus only on what has happened *to* us. We go on endlessly about the joys of making but too rarely acknowledge that making something constructive out of challenging circumstances is every bit as creative as baking a loaf of sourdough bread, building a canoe or assembling a kumiko panel.

Bibliography

Alexander, Christopher, Sara Ishikawa and Murray Silverstein, *A Pattern Language: Towns, Buildings, Construction* (New York: Oxford University Press, 1977).

Berger, Peter L. and Thomas Luckmann, *The Social Construction of Reality: A Treatise in the Sociology of Knowledge* (New York: Doubleday, 1966).

Berry, Wendell, *What Are People For?* (New York: North Point Press, 1990).

Carruthers, Annette, with Mary Greensted and Barley Roscoe, *Ernest Gimson: Arts & Crafts Designer and Architect* (New Haven, CT: Yale University Press, 2019).

Churchill, Winston S., *A History of the English-Speaking Peoples* (London: Cassell and Company, Ltd., 1958).

Durrell, Gerald, *My Family and Other Animals* (London: Macmillan Collector's Library, 2016).

Frank, Arthur, *At the Will of the Body: Reflections on Illness* (Boston: Houghton Mifflin, 1991).

Fuller, Alexandra, *Cocktail Hour Under the Tree of Forgetfulness* (New York: Penguin, 2011).

Fuller, Alexandra, *Let's Not Go to the Dogs Tonight: An African Childhood* (New York: Random House Trade Paperbacks, 2001).

Fuller, Alexandra, *Leaving Before the Rains Come* (New York: Penguin Books, 2015).

Grandin, Temple and Catherine Johnson, *Animals in Translation: Using the Mysteries of Autism to Decode Animal Behavior* (New York: Simon & Schuster, 2005).

Gubar, Susan, *Memoir of a Debulked Woman: Enduring Ovarian Cancer* (New York: W.W. Norton, 2012).

Herriot, James, *All Creatures Great and Small* (New York: St. Martin's Press, 1972).

Hillenbrand, Laura, *Seabiscuit: An American Legend* (New York: Ballantine-Random House, 2001).

Hiller, Nancy, *English Arts & Crafts Furniture: Projects & Techniques for the Modern Maker* (Cincinnati: Popular Woodworking Books, 2018).

Hiller, Nancy, *Making Things Work: Tales From a Cabinetmaker's Life* (Covington, KY: Lost Art Press, 2019).

Kerasote, Ted, *Merle's Door: Lessons from a Freethinking Dog* (San Diego: Houghton Mifflin Harcourt, 2008).

Kingsolver, Barbara, *Animal, Vegetable, Miracle: A Year of Food Life* (New York: HarperCollins, 2007).

Knott, Sarah, *Mother is a Verb: An Unconventional History* (New York: Sarah Crichton Books, an imprint of Farrar, Straus and Giroux, 2019).

Lakoff, George and Mark Johnson, *Metaphors We Live By* (Chicago: University of Chicago Press, 1980).

McLelland, Jane, *How to Starve Cancer* (London: Agenor Publishing, 2018).

Montgomery, Sy, *How to be a Good Creature: A Memoir in Thirteen Animals* (Boston: Houghton Mifflin Harcourt, 2018).

Noah, Trevor, *Born a Crime: Stories from a South African Childhood* (New York: Spiegel & Grau, an imprint of Random House, 2019).

Pollan, Michael, *The Omnivore's Dilemma: A Natural History of Four Meals* (New York: Penguin, 2006).

Powers, Richard, *The Overstory* (New York: W.W. Norton, 2018).

Rodgers, Diana RD, and Robb Wolf, *Sacred Cow: The Case for (Better) Meat* (Dallas: Benbella Books, 2020).

Sandweiss, Lee Ann, *Lock Ness! And Other Tales of Nessie the Scottie* (St. Petersburg, FL: Booklocker.com, 2019).

Scarry, Elaine, *The Body in Pain: The Making and Unmaking of the World* (New York: Oxford University Press, 1985).

Susanka, Sarah, *The Not So Big House: A Blueprint for the Way We Really Live* (Newtown, CT: Taunton Press, 1998).

Taylor, Charles, *Human Agency and Language: Philosophical Papers, Vol. 1* (Cambridge, UK: Cambridge University Press, 1985).

Taylor, Charles, *The Ethics of Authenticity* (Cambridge, MA: Harvard University Press, 1991).

Wampler, Fred, with illustrations by Maryrose Wampler, *Trees of Indiana* (Bloomington, IN: Indiana University Press, 2000).

Alison Zook and Susan, a rescue she has adopted. (Courtesy photo.)

Support The Ranch Cat Rescue

The publisher and author have agreed to donate 10 percent of net profits from the sale of "Shop Tails" to The Ranch Cat Rescue of Bloomington, Indiana, an organization founded and operated by Alison Zook to save the lives of cats and kittens.

theranchcatrescue.org/about